DATE DUE

FEB 05			

AN
AMERICAN FAMILY

JON AND MICHAEL GALLUCCIO

WITH DAVID GROFF

ST. MARTIN'S PRESS ❧ NEW YORK

AN
AMERICAN FAMILY

This is a true story. In a few cases, names have been changed to protect the privacy of those involved.

AN AMERICAN FAMILY. Copyright © 2001 by Jon Galluccio, Michael Galluccio, and David Groff. All rights reserved. Printed in the United States of America. No part of this book may be used or reproduced in any manner whatsoever without written permission except in the case of brief quotations embodied in critical articles or reviews. For information, address St. Martin's Press, 175 Fifth Avenue, New York, N.Y. 10010.

www.stmartins.com

Library of Congress Cataloging-in-Publication Data

Galluccio, Jon.
    An American family / Jon and Michael Galluccio with David Groff.—1st ed.
        p.   cm.
    ISBN 0-312-26123-3
    1. Gay adoption—United States.   I. Galluccio, Michael.   II. Groff,
David.   III. Title.

HV875.72.U6   G35   2001
362.73'4'08664—dc21   00-045764

First Edition: February 2001

10   9   8   7   6   5   4   3   2   1

To those who think they can't

CONTENTS

ACKNOWLEDGMENTS

So many people have helped us build our family and create this book.

We owe great gratitude to the caring medical professionals who have helped our children thrive, especially the staff of the O'Neill Center and all the doctors and nurses who committed their care and love to Adam and Madison. We thank everyone who supported our family through sunny times and dark ones: Michael Adams, Tanya Boyle, Lenora Lapidus, the late Michael Losee, Loretta McCormick, our friends Tim and Kevin, the Honorable Sybil Moses, the Lesbian and Gay Rights Project of the American Civil Liberties Union, the New Jersey Civil Liberties Union, and Lambda Families of New Jersey—as well as the coworkers, parents and children, media people, and clergy across the world whose concern and good cheer have sustained us. We are grateful to our priests, the Reverend Ellen Barrett, the Reverend Kevin Coffey, the Reverend Canon Elizabeth Kaeton, the Reverend Canon Linda Strohmier, and to our brave bishop, the Right Reverend John S. Spong, along with all the parishioners of the Episcopal Church of the Atonement in Fairlawn, New Jersey.

Many other people contributed a great deal to the making of *An American Family*. Our agent, Todd Shuster, was as enthusiastic and persistent about this project as he has been around his own fathering. Michael Denneny, our pioneering editor at St. Martin's, has been a wise advisor and vigorous advocate. Assistant editor Christina Prestia has been a steady resource. Clay Williams gave essential support and love to our co-author, David Groff.

Most of all, we are grateful to our families, to whom we grow closer every day, and to God, who promises never to give us more than we can handle.

AN
AMERICAN FAMILY

ONE

FOSTER SON

Michael Galluccio

It was the second day of winter, 1995, and the city snow had melted and refrozen into a jagged crust, the kind of snow that crunches under your feet. Just after dawn, Jon and I were driving carefully through the streets of a run-down neighborhood in Paterson, New Jersey—only eight miles from our own suburban Maywood, but a different world. We were on our way to meet our son for the first time.

The social worker had given us excellent directions—even in the excitement of the previous afternoon's phone call—and we made our way through Paterson's back streets until we found Hine Street, an offshoot of the main avenue. The neighborhood looked unkempt; the sidewalks had buckled, paint was chipping off the houses, fences were rusted, and the trees seemed to sag beneath the weight of more than the winter ice. Even the few Christmas decorations seemed gray. No one was out this early in the morning, as our Grand Am slid silently down the street on fresh snow that coated the frozen tire ruts.

The O'Neill Center was a typical city row house—three floors, plenty of windows, small front porch. Painted a rusty red, it sat tall and unadorned at the end of the street next to a steel-shuttered pharmacy. Once some family's home, it now housed babies who basically had no families. While they were still in the womb, their mothers had habitually swallowed, injected, snorted, or smoked just about every substance known to damage a developing fetus: alcohol, marijuana, nicotine, crack, cocaine, and heroin. Their children had literally become drug addicts in the womb. They were all also HIV-positive.

Most of the children living at the O'Neill Center had been abandoned to the state at birth, and New Jersey would be the only parent some of these children would ever know. Their fathers and mothers didn't want them, were too ill or drugged to handle them, or were themselves dying or dead. And because these "medically fragile" children were sick, drug addicted, and might die in two months or two years, few families wanted to adopt them. Some of the kids would spend their entire lives being handled by people wearing disposable latex gloves who had already held hundreds of babies just like them. For the somewhat more fortunate children, the O'Neill Center would be the first stop in an odyssey of foster homes, some of them good, some bad, some perniciously indifferent. Every now and then, a healthy and lucky child would be adopted into a permanent family.

"We're way too early," Jon said, cracking his knuckles inside his gloves. He drew his overcoat closer. Having been his partner for thirteen years, I could tell when he was tense, even though he tried to hide it beneath a determined efficiency. He was working to stay calm, but excitement and anxiety showed clearly in his usually impish blue eyes. He looked up at the silent house. "Nobody's awake yet. You can't even hear a baby crying."

"What should we do? Should we go in?" I asked.

"It's not time yet. Jean was very specific." He paused, looked at me, then back at the house. "We've waited this long. I guess we can wait a little longer."

We had been anticipating this day for months, and yesterday the call had finally come. I was at the back of the house working in my office—the paneled, shag-rugged space we planned to remake into a family room. In the midst of a conversation with one of my company's most important clients, I heard the house phone ringing and Jon answering it. After a moment, my office door burst open. Jon was standing there with a look of utter happiness on his face. "It's Jean," he blurted out. "She says she has a Christmas present for us."

Jean was the placement specialist for children with special needs at the Division of Youth and Family Services (DYFS). "Kim," I said into the phone, "I have to go. I think I just became a father."

I stood up and rushed into the kitchen, where Jon was already back on the phone with Jean. We moved to the living room and sat together on the couch and I watched as Jon took notes:

Boy . . . Blond . . . Brown eyes . . . 3 months old . . . Preemie . . . Hep C . . . Hole in heart . . . HIV+ . . . TB+ . . . RSV . . . Severe drug withdrawal/crack . . . Apgar 8/9 . . . Birth name . . .

"Jean." Jon's forehead wrinkled and his eyebrows connected at the center with the look I knew meant confusion. "A black baby with blond hair? What did the drugs do to this kid?"

Jean must have suppressed an urge to laugh. "Oh, no," she told Jon in her usual warm, level, matter-of-fact way, "he's white."

Since there were so many minority children in the system, we had been certain we would become an interracial family. That is what we had prepared for, but this baby was the son of a thin, red-haired, twenty-six-year-old woman in nearby Paterson. She was an intravenous drug user who had already given up four children to institutional care. The father was unknown.

I watched as Jon scrawled FOSTER ONLY. We looked into each other's eyes and I could feel my chest tighten. This child could only be temporary in our lives. Not only would we have a medically fragile baby to care for, but as foster parents we would risk having to return a child we had opened our hearts to and wanted to adopt. I realized we were just starting down a long road.

"When can we see him?" I asked. Jon relayed the question to Jean, and then I saw his face drop. "Not until after Christmas," he told me.

"No, tomorrow," I insisted. "Honey, beg her." He did. Jean said she would need to make a few calls and get back to us. As it turned out, she had to ask some favors, but she had gotten us a visit—and now here we were, just fifteen hours later, still an agonizing sixty minutes from meeting our son.

We drove around the block a few times and finally parked right in front, waiting for the O'Neill Center to stir to life. Jean had told us not to come until 8 A.M. at the earliest. We'd both lain awake most of the night, thinking about what might happen today, how our lives and the life of one baby might start to change. We had no choice but to arrive early; there was no way we could just sit home and wait.

"What do you think he'll look like?" Jon asked me.

"I guess he'll look like a baby, won't he? A sick baby?"

"Yeah . . . but what exactly does a sick baby look like?"

I had no real idea. When I thought of babies, I thought of my nieces and nephews, round, little bundles of Italian-American health. This child would not be like that. With all our basic training, did we know enough to care for him? *Would this baby even live?* Had we let our desire to be parents get us in over our heads? They say God does not give us more than we can handle, but right then I had my doubts.

We sat there looking at each other, then out through the windshield. The car heater droned on. God, we were so early. Finally, as the winter light brightened, I convinced Jon that we could at least go and wait on the front porch. We looked at each other, took deep breaths, and got out of the car.

The cat litter and ice remnants on the old wooden porch cracked so loudly under our feet that I was afraid we would wake everyone up—and I kind of hoped we would. I peered in the window next to the door, but the inside was illuminated only by the early-morning light. To one side was a hallway and a door. Right in front of the door was a steep staircase leading up to another door and what looked like another hallway. The upstairs door caught my eye—light was coming from underneath it. I stepped back and shrugged to Jon. We just stood there staring at each other, our breath smoking in the icy early-morning air.

From behind I heard the crackle of footsteps. We turned to see someone standing with one foot on the bottom step and a hand on the rail. A woman—big, middle-aged, with sharp blue eyes and strawberry-blond hair—looked up at us from under the hood of her tan parka. In the first measured seconds, she looked sturdy and stern. I wondered what she thought as she encountered the two of us, Jon shivering almost motionlessly in his brown overcoat and me pacing about him on the porch, running my hand nervously through my hair. She smiled and her face blossomed. "Oh, I know who you are," she said. "Couldn't wait, could you?"

Her name was Joanne Harraka. She was the head nurse at the O'Neill Center, for all practical purposes the mother the O'Neill children didn't have. Her job was to oversee the love, care, discipline, and comfort given to children she knew she would, in one way or another, lose. She had come to work on her day off, two days before Christmas, to introduce us to our baby.

"You boys must be cold. Come on in."

The hallway we entered was clean but worn, with an infant's car seat and a folded stroller propped in one corner and a stack of boxes filled with used clothing. The air held a combination of several smells—old house, medicine, baby formula, a touch of diaper, and sickness. Joanne indicated we should follow her up the stairs. But she paused at the bottom, and we all looked at each other. "You ready?" She gave us a wry smile.

"Well, here we go," Jon breathed. He put his arm out to let me go first.

"Thanks, Dad," I said. His face lit up.

The steps groaned under our combined weight. I had never been so nervous in my life. During those fifteen seconds, dozens of past scenes flickered through my head: the two of us sitting in parenting classes, taking pages of notes; my last cigarette, on the day we'd decided that the parent of a sick child should not smoke; my mother crying with fear and worry when we'd told her we intended to adopt a baby; my father's look of resignation; the puzzled and aghast looks on the faces of friends; the two of us practicing CPR so we could take on a "special needs" child; and the evening just last week when we'd painted clouds on the sky-blue walls of the room we had just turned into a nursery.

When Joanne opened the door, it was almost like the scene from *The Wizard of Oz* where Dorothy leaves her house and everything goes from black and white to color. Fluorescent light poured out into the hallway. The door opened into a large "all-purpose" room. I barely noticed the white linoleum floors, the white walls, the mismatched furniture, or the television trumpeting the overture of *The Lion King*. All I saw was one small baby, directly across the room from me, sitting in a loud, windup baby swing.

I had no doubt he was my son. He was tiny, too tiny for a child three months old. He looked well below the fifteen pounds you would expect for a child his age. He was wearing a red sweatshirt and a blanket over his lap. And he was so bald you could see the veins in his head. The skin of his face was pale and pinkish, shading into gray, which made me wonder if the hole in his heart—common among pree- mies—was affecting his circulation. His eyes were open almost un- naturally wide and had huge dark circles around them. His lips were pursed into a tight knot. As I walked toward him, his hands clutched frantically in front of him as if he were trying to grasp something only he could discern. He looked like an old man in a nursing home—an old man desperate for his next fix.

The baby was staring right at me. For what seemed like hours all I beheld was the sight of this child and the click-click, click-click, click- click of the baby swing. I stared at the baby and in an instant I fell deeply in love for the second time in my life. There would be nothing I would not do for him. My son. He was sick, and he might be dying, and he was beautiful.

Then the world came back in a huge rush. The noise in the room was deafening. Five children, infants and toddlers, were cooing and crying from their cribs and baby chairs. The TV was blaring Disney tunes, and I realized that other adults were at work here—caregivers finishing up their night duty, holding two of the babies and deftly forcing medicine down their throats. I saw another child arching pain- fully in his rocker as he tried to watch the television. He was two, maybe three years old. One of his arms was constricted. The circles around his eyes showed clearly even through his dark brown skin. HIV had done a job on him.

He looked at me and gave me the easy smile that comes with the innocence of childhood. Then he rolled his eyes in pain and struggled to focus again on the television. He did not look as if he would last too much longer. My eyes returned to my baby and I prayed silently: *Please don't let that be you.*

I had not even taken off my coat yet—but here we are, meeting our new son.

Finally Joanne asked, "Would you like to meet the baby?" We immediately went to the swing and bent down. The baby looked back and forth between us, curious, vague.

"Go ahead—you go first," Jon said to me. I had not even taken off my coat yet but I unstrapped the baby and carefully lifted him into my arms. I had never held an infant this small. I could feel the heat from his body in my hands, smell baby lotion on his skin. His breathing was ragged. I cradled him and looked into his face. His little eyes trembled and darted from place to place. They actually shook. This was the pain and panic of drug withdrawal. One arm shot out from his side and he grabbed for one hand with the other. He clumsily guided the thumb of his left hand into his mouth. His breathing sounded almost like grunting while he feverishly sucked his thumb, as if it held a drug he needed more than breathing.

"Look at him," Jon said as I put the baby in his arms. I watched the same feelings of magic and terror wash over Jon.

"Would you like to give him his bottle?" Joanne asked.

"We'd like that very much," Jon said.

Joanne led us into a small room that housed three cribs. It wasn't a nursery with puffy clouds painted on the walls, but more like a hospital room from the fifties, which is probably when its furnishings had begun their institutional life. The cribs were lined up along the white walls, next to a rocking chair, and between them stood a menacing-looking examining table made of white-enameled metal, chipped in places. On the table sat a black metal baby scale. The only splash of color was a single black, white, and red mobile dangling over one infant's crib.

Joanne handed me the bottle, and sitting in the rocking chair, I fed the baby. Jon was getting over a cold and we had decided it was safer for the baby if Jon kept a little distance. I could feel the baby's throat working against my wrist as he furiously swallowed the formula. It seemed as if he'd never encountered food before. Joanne said he weighed only eleven pounds, and he had to use huge amounts of fuel to support his precarious lungs and his liver. Three months after his birth, his organs had to work overtime to filter out the deadly toxins that still raged in his system.

"So, you boys are adopting him, right?"

Our eyes shot up to meet Joanne's gaze. Was this a trick question? Yesterday on the phone, and all the while we'd been seeking to take a baby into our home, Jean, the DYFS placement specialist, had drummed into our heads that at best we'd be getting a foster child. Adoption was such a distant possibility that we barely allowed ourselves to think about it. Like many couples before us, we had decided to take the risk of being foster parents first, even if we didn't get to have that child permanently as our own. Now Joanne was making it sound as though our parenting this baby for good was a given.

"Yes," Jon said sharply, "we intend to adopt him."

"Are you going to keep his name, or are you going to change it?" Joanne asked.

Here was another question that we thought spoke more to our dreams than reality. Before surrendering him to the state, this infant's mother had given the baby a name. Jon and I had discussed for a long time what name we would like our son to have. I looked at Jon, who nodded slightly, and I spoke up. "We have a name for him. Adam."

"Adam stands for *Adolph, Dorothy, Donato,* and *Ann Mary,*" Jon added. "Michael's father and mother, my late father, and my mother."

Joanne gave us a big smile. "Adam is a beautiful name. You know, we'd better get the staff to start using it." Before we could react, she stuck her head into the other room called out to the other nurses in a loud voice. "Ladies, from now on, this boy's name is Adam. Got it?"

I looked down, stunned, at the child who lay against my chest. Had we actually just been able to name this baby? That was a breathtaking notion.

"When can we take him home?" Jon asked.

"Whoa, whoa, whoa." Joanne held up her hand and let out a belly laugh. "You have no *idea* how long a road you've got ahead of you. First we have to teach you everything you need to know about Adam—food stuff, how to bathe him, how to change an infectious diaper, all that. Then you have to get past Dr. Hutcheons—she's the medical director for all these kids—and convince her that you can care for Adam on your own, even for a single day visit. You've never had a baby of your own before, either of you?"

We shook our heads no.

"No? Well, boys, you've got a lot to learn. We're going to take this nice and slow and make sure you know what you're doing before you have to face Dr. Hutcheons. She's not too keen on handing out her children to just anybody. You'll have to spend some time with Adam, get more of his medical history, learn to give him his medication. Ever squirt medication down a baby's throat? It's easier doing it to a *cat.*"

"Can we start now?" Jon was never the kind to be shy about asking for what he wanted.

"You *are* eager, aren't you. It would be best to wait a day or two, I think," Joanne said.

"Can we come back tomorrow to see him?"

"Christmas Eve?" Joanne frowned, thinking.

"We have presents for him," I said, putting Adam on my shoulder as I began patting his back.

Father and son, at the O'Neill Center.

"Well, I won't be here until the day after Christmas, but I'll let them know that you'll be visiting. How about Christmas Day? You can wish Adam a merry Christmas." She smiled at us. "Then the next day we'll start your orientation to little Adam here."

At that moment Adam let out an adult-sized burp of satisfaction, huge and healthy and ordinary, against my shoulder.

Joanne looked at him and then at us. "That was one phenomenal burp. I think you boys are going to be just fine."

On Christmas morning, Jon and I got up early so that we could be at the O'Neill Center when Adam woke up. I had a Santa Claus hat on and Jon carried a teddy bear, a gift from my parents. My mother and father were still uncomfortable with the whole idea of their son adopting a child, but they were trying to be supportive. They'd provided their prospective new grandchild with a stuffed animal bigger than he was.

When Adam opened his eyes, he smiled at us. I decided he was glad to see the two guys who had bounced him on their knees just forty-eight hours earlier. He held out his arms, and I lifted him out of his crib, all eleven pounds of him. He didn't hesitate or hold back from me, and within a minute he was happily nestled against my shoulder, drooling down my back. "Merry Christmas, Son," Jon said as he rubbed Adam along his disturbingly protrusive spine. Adam was bleating, coo-ing, making sounds like a regular baby. But with the other kids crying and the fluorescent lighting and the linoleum, this Christmas morning felt like something out of a modern *Christmas Carol,* complete with half a dozen Tiny Tims.

We fed Adam, then sat with him on the couch to play. He seemed to be connecting with us, gripping our fingers, squirming happily when we moved his arms and legs. He went for his thumb again like a drunk aching for a bottle, and that scared us both. I could tell Jon was ex-amining him carefully to see how he reacted to us and to stimulation in general.

"He seems like he's basically a pretty good baby," I said.

"Yeah, well, is he a good baby, or is it the phenobarbital?" Jon mut-tered. It was a serious question. Both Jean and Joanne had already told us about the medication being used to ease Adam's withdrawal from his prenatal infusion of hard drugs. It was possible that right now this baby was just high and floating; so far, we had no way to figure out his natural disposition. It would take several more months and a com-plete detox before we would feel any confidence that we knew the personality of our baby. We did everything we could to keep him en-gaged: we sang to him, made silly noises, laughed, and hugged him hard so that he'd get more familiar with the warmth of another body.

Of course, before long Adam spit up on my sweater. (For some reason, I have always been the one he spits up on.) I was standing across the room cleaning myself off when I heard an odd sound. I glanced over at Jon. He and the baby were "talking." "Gitty—gitty—gitty—gitty—goo," Jon would say, and Adam would respond with some strange sort of chatter; and then they would giggle together as if they had just shared a delicious secret. For a long time, I stood back and watched as the two of them "spoke" to each other, cooing and laughing in the private language of parent and infant. Any question I might have

Daddy and his boy, at the O'Neill Center.

had about Jon's ability to be a parent, or our decision that he would be the "stay-at-home" dad, was answered in that moment. Jon had taken a fitful shadow of an infant and brought him to life in no time. A wave of love and gratitude swept over me.

"Next Christmas he's at our house," Jon told me. I nodded. Within a year, if we could satisfy the state, and if Adam lived, he would be our son. As we left, Jon began to cry. He would cry every time we left until the day we brought Adam home for good.

The first thing the following morning we went back to the O'Neill House to work—learning how to care for a baby we desperately wanted to take home. Amid the roar of the other children playing and being cared for by the nurse's aides, Joanne took us into the bathroom, an all-white, L-shaped room with one small window, also painted white, at the far end. I noticed an oversize porcelain tub that looked as if it had stood there for at least a hundred years. A separate wall-mounted, metal bathing sink, hovering just below a large industrial-style mirror, was far more hospital-like than the old tub. Below the sink sat a light blue wastebasket marked BIOLOGICAL HAZARD, and affixed beside the basin was a large metal, cylindrical pump that sprayed an oily, pink disinfectant that stung our skin upon contact. After we washed our hands, Joanne instructed us on what she was doing as she bathed Adam in the infant sink. "You wash him with Dove soap—he's too sensitive for anything else. All right, boys, now you take over." She stood back, appraising our technique. "Don't be too cautious with him. These kids aren't breakable, even the sick ones. You just grab him and hold him like a football."

Fortunately, Adam loved the bath. Unlike Joanne, who had worn white latex gloves, Jon and I washed Adam with our bare hands. We had decided we would not keep a layer of latex between us and our baby, except when we were dealing with bodily fluids and had no choice. It seemed important to make sure he felt warmth.

When Jon told his mother about our decision, she had looked at him startled—less by the risk we were taking than by the fact that a parent would even have to consider whether to wear gloves while bathing a child. She too had adopted a child: Jon himself. She and her husband had become his adoptive parents when he was only eleven days old.

Jon's mother and all of us had needed a lot of time and effort to get used to the implications of parenting a foster child. The consequences had hit home the day six months before when Jon and I had sat on our living room couch and filled out the four-page questionnaire the state Division of Youth and Family Services handed out to prospective foster parents. Some of the questions had to do with our income, our home life, education, and child-care plans, our psychological preparedness, and our motivations to be parents. We could answer those questions with confidence. The state did not challenge us at all about our fitness as a gay couple to be parents. Other questions were more daunting. Would we accept a boy or girl, an African-American or Latino child, one whose health was robust or one who was "medically fragile"? Would we take a child if he had cerebral palsy? Would we take a child if his mother had been diagnosed with syphilis? With herpes? Hepatitis? HIV? What if the father had been diagnosed with any of these maladies? What if the parents had lived on the streets, been unmarried, worked as prostitutes, or served time in prison? Would we accept a foster child with one schizophrenic parent? With two?

We were happy to accept what the social workers called a special-needs child. Our only limitation was that we wanted to parent a child who had a reasonable chance of growing up to live independently. Now, as we held Adam in our arms, the reality of a medically fragile child was truly brought home to us.

"We haven't yet given Adam his meds," Joanne said. "We decided to hold off until you got here so that you two could learn to do it. Here's his med chart." She handed us a thick clipboard with a grid on it where she and other nurses had scrawled the thrice-daily medical regimen Adam had to follow. From birth to six weeks old he was on AZT, the antiviral drug that has been shown to keep HIV from taking hold in the bodies of antibody-positive fetuses and newborns. The virus might have been thwarted, but only time would tell. He was still on a prophylactic dose of Bactrim, a drug that suppresses HIV-related pneumonia. He was also on Proventil, a drug that would treat the meconium aspiration syndrome in his lungs which had been detected at his birth and which had been complicated by an RSV (respiratory syncytial virus) infection only a month later. The drug had to be inhaled as a mist via a noisy, nasty-looking machine called a nebulizer. Maybe most vital to Adam's immediate well-being was the phenobarbital, which reduced the physical symptoms of his drug withdrawal. Without it, Adam would still suffer from tremors and seizures as the cocaine, heroin, and other drugs drained from his body.

So many drugs for such a little boy. Jon sat Adam down in a bouncy chair in front of The Lion King as Joanne prepared the needleless syringes that would shoot the drugs into Adam's mouth. You can't exactly hand a three-month-old baby a handful of pills and ask him to swallow them. This meant holding Adam still and getting his mouth open—and that entailed a fierce struggle to keep Adam's thumb out of his mouth. Holding Adam's mouth open, Jon would slowly release the syringe of phenobarbital against the side of Adam's lower jaw. The Bactrim was as pink and viscous as Pepto-Bismol, and when I gave it to him, Adam spat most of it out. That happens, Joanne told us.

Next Joanne introduced us to the nebulizer, a machine that looked like a small portable air conditioner, only noisier. She briefed us on the controls and the various cords and attachments. Then she said we had the option of holding the mask over Adam's face or just getting his mouth and nose directly into the mist, which was almost as effective a way of providing him the dose he needed. I decided to test out the contraption and held the mask to my face and inhaled the medicine. It tasted salty, and the mask made me feel as if I couldn't breathe. We decided immediately not to use the mask. The last thing this kid needed was one more scary, unnecessary, and even mildly invasive procedure. Then Joanne told us that the medicine was absorbed best when Adam was crying, as he would be taking deeper breaths. With a quick jounce of his chair she startled him into tears, and soon he was inhaling his Proventil. I secretly resolved that Jon and I would try never to make Adam cry—we'd use the nebulizer on him during his normal baby-crying.

Already we were overwhelmed. There was so much to remember. Would we know how to do all this when we got home? "You gotta know what to do in a crisis. You know how to rescue him if he's choking?" Joanne asked. We did, and we knew CPR too. "You know how to protect yourselves from his fluids?" Joanne showed us all her cleanup precautions and held up the container of bleach she used to clean the table area after she changed Adam's diapers. "You gotta keep everything in the house dry," she said, "and I mean *very* dry. Bacteria can live in a puddle for ten hours, and that's the last thing you need around a sick kid, right?" I felt as though we were back in the third grade with our teacher rehearsing the steps for a fire drill.

She looked us square in the eye. "With all this medicine to administer, plus diapers and the sleep patterns of a three-month-old—you realize you're going to be up every two hours doing something for Adam, right?"

"What will it take before Dr. Hutcheons lets us take him home overnight?" Jon asked.

Joanne sighed. "Lots of practice. In the meantime, I suggest you guys stock up on sleep."

———

Dr. Nancy Hutcheons was not only the pediatrician in charge of all the children in the O'Neill Center, but was also supervisor of the care of all HIV-positive children who had either been born in or treated at Paterson's St. Joseph's Medical Center. The staff at the O'Neill Center spoke of her in such hushed tones that we were already awed just by the idea of her. They also made it clear that she was not releasing one of their children to anyone—especially, we suspected, two men—until she was quite satisfied that we knew what we were doing. By the end of our orientation session with Joanne, Jon and I had developed a healthy fear of the woman who would or would not give us permission to take Adam to that nursery we'd painted with clouds the week before.

Three hours after we'd tried to memorize all of Adam's medications—and after we'd seen *The Lion King* for the second time that day—Joanne bundled up the baby and sent one of her aides up the street with the three of us to the O'Neill clinic. Sooner than we expected, we would have our first meeting with the revered Dr. Hutcheons. We might get to take Adam home for a couple hours on a day visit, if we were lucky and showed we could provide him basic care.

The clinic was yet another converted row house, this one a brown-shingled structure standing forlorn at the top of Hine Street between a parking area for the hospital and a vacant lot. The parlor floor had been converted into a makeshift lobby complete with a play kitchen, a shopping cart, various children's toys, and a three-foot Christmas tree on a little table. Stacked on the radiator next to the Christmas tree were a pile of HIV update newsletters. They looked a bit like a Christmas gift, but of course they weren't. It seemed wrong that children even had to be in the same room with information on HIV. And then the reality struck home that these kids were exposed to HIV itself. My son was one of those children. It hit me all over again that Adam was HIV-positive, extremely ill, and might very well die.

Across from us, waiting, was an older African-American man with three children gathered around him. One child, a girl about five, sat restless and bored in her seat, while a boy a little younger was playing furiously, trying, it seemed, to handle all the toys at once. A little girl about three lay listless against the older man's chest. Her skin was less black than gray, her hair was made up of frayed grayish threads, and her eyes were as dull as pewter. Probably the old man was their grandfather. He met my eyes and looked at me steadily, as if he could say a lot of things to me, if only he could bear to. I was left to imagine what woe had brought his family here today.

We were summoned up a narrow flight of stairs. Jon held Adam as we made our way up. "I'm afraid I'm gonna drop him and ruin the whole thing," he muttered. "Then she'll never let us take him home."

"You want me to take him?" I asked.

"Nope. I just feel like we're meeting the Wizard of Oz."

Upstairs we were escorted into a small examining room, about as inviting as a police interrogation chamber and featuring yet another baby scale and a large red plastic container with yellow and black signs on every side identifying it as an infectious-waste container.

BIOHAZARD WARNING, it read. AIDS lived there, I thought.

Dr. Nancy Hutcheons was normal-sized, professional looking, bespectacled, not at all grand. Somehow I had expected a superwoman, a passionate expert, a pediatric AIDS pioneer. Instead, with her severe wool skirt and her graying and efficiently bobbed hair, she looked like a more waspish version of Joanne—yet another worker in the trenches. But if her presence was not intimidating, her demeanor was. She flicked half a smile at us, sat down on a stool alongside the examining table, and began listing facts.

"This baby"—she glanced quickly at Adam, blissed out on Jon's lap—"was born premature. Approximately thirty-one or thirty-two weeks. Five pounds three ounces. He went straight into intensive care from the delivery room, onto a ventilator. You know what meconium aspiration syndrome is?" She looked up from her file and raised her eyebrows at us. "His lungs were filled with blackish, bile-type fluid from the womb, and he couldn't breathe on his own. They may be damaged."

"Joanne had us administer the Proventil to him on the nebulizer," Jon piped up.

Dr. Hutcheons paused and looked at him. "They had also detected a cardiac arrhythmia at birth, as well as a hole in his left ventricle," she went on, as if she were briefing a first-year medical student. "The hole may heal. We don't know yet. After birth his coloring remained good. Shortly after birth he went into drug withdrawal. Blood tests revealed the following substances in his system." She consulted her file. "Heroin, methadone, marijuana, cocaine, alcohol, and nicotine. He had tremors immediately and within twenty-four hours he was having his first seizures. At that point he was given phenobarbital."

"Two cc's," I said. "Joanne just showed us how to administer it."

Dr. Hutcheons's eyes met mine, then dropped to her chart. "His liver enzymes continue to be way out of range, and so are his triglycerides. We don't know why. It's possible that is just genetic, not something he picked up in the womb. He might have liver damage for life, even if the HIV antibodies disappear."

"What's his CD4 count?" Jon asked.

With that question Dr. Hutcheons's entire manner changed. She looked from Jon to me and back again. "You gentlemen have done your homework."

Clearly she knew that we had some information about AIDS in general and Adam's health in particular. It was as if the air in the room had gotten warmer. Now that she knew we spoke the same language, Dr. Hutcheons grew comfortable talking about Adam's prognosis, which actually was not all bad. The PCR (polymerase chain reaction) tests recently performed on him had indicated that while the HIV antibodies were still present, the actual AIDS virus had not yet taken hold in his bloodstream. His CD4 immune-system cell count ranged from 400 to 800—not stable, but never in the danger zone. Of course, as she reminded us, the tests were not reliable, especially in a child as young and small as Adam. There were no guarantees that Adam would stymie HIV. And there certainly were no assurances that he had not been permanently traumatized by his mother's drug use. Even if Adam lived, a thousand possible challenges were on the road ahead: attention deficit disorder, learning disabilities, emotional or mental problems, fetal alcohol syndrome.

"He scored eight and nine on his Apgar tests," Jon said. "Doesn't that bode well for him, in the long run, after he detoxes?" The Apgar test given to newborns determines neurological function and mental acuity. Ten, we knew, was the top score.

"Possibly," Dr. Hutcheons said, eyeing us thoughtfully. She looked down at Adam, asleep on Jon's shoulder as if it were the most comfortable nest in the world. Then she looked us square in the eye. "I don't see any reason why you men can't take this child home on an overnight visit."

An overnight! We'd barely hoped she'd let us take Adam out on a day visit, and here we were winning the right to wake up with our foster son every two hours! I looked at Jon and together we suppressed a shout of joy and victory. We had passed the first test that would help ensure that our Maywood house became Adam's permanent address.

"Well, that's settled." Dr. Hutcheons closed Adam's folder. "Now we've got some blood work to do on this baby. Routine stuff." She called for a nurse. A big, bustling, black-haired woman charged in, glanced at us for a millisecond, and without a word grabbed Adam right out of Jon's arms. Her face looked somewhat bloated, and she reeked of cigarette smoke. "Blood work," Dr. Hutcheons said to the nurse on her way out. "Standard array."

"Hmm," the nurse said, cracking her gum. She scratched at her hair and then looked Adam over, probing him like a watermelon. "I don't see a vein in the arm. We might have to take blood from the head."

Jon blanched. "The head!" I exclaimed.

"Undress him, please," the nurse commanded. "Let's weigh him."

By now Adam was awake and alarmed. The nurse hefted him onto the scale as if he were a pot roast: "Eleven pounds, nine ounces. Still a little thing." She stretched out his right arm, squeezed it.

"Will you have to take from the head?" Jon asked, his voice small.

"Nah. But you'll have to help us with the papoose."

With that she produced from behind the examining table what looked like an ironing board, a brownish red, foam-covered plank, about three feet long, with gray Velcro straps dangling ominously from it. As soon as the nurse laid Adam into this device, he began crying convulsively, and by the time she had strapped down his legs, arms, and torso, his screams were reverberating off the walls. His face turned purple, a vein on the left side of his neck stood at attention, and tears were streaming down his face into his mouth and down the stalk of his neck. Adam was stretched out as if he were being crucified. I was stunned; I could barely bear to watch.

"What are you *doing?*" Jon shouted over the baby's cries.

The nurse looked at him and shrugged. "Got to take blood." She snapped on latex gloves, wrapped a rubber tube around Adam's right biceps, tapped it hard to raise a vein, and jammed a needle into it. I couldn't even hear Jon's loud protests against the blast of Adam's screams. I watched as the blood ran out of my son's body into a long, flexible tube that led to a plastic vial. My knees were shaking and I suddenly had to leave the room. I was queasy at the sight of blood, but more than that, I was unnerved by Adam's shrieks and that I could do nothing to help him.

I went out into the hall, where Adam's crying was slightly less loud, and tried to calm my breathing. Then suddenly I heard the nurse swear, and Jon yell something, and Adam's sobbing escalate, and I dashed back in. Adam was stretched out in the papoose, his face a red fist. The nurse was bent over Adam's right arm.

"What happened?"

Jon looked up at me, his face chalky and streaked with sweat. "He was fighting so hard his arm got loose. He bent the needle in his arm. Just bent it."

I wanted to stop this now, I wanted to push the nurse away and grab my child out of this torture device, but I knew I couldn't. As Jon stroked Adam's head and spoke in soft, strained tones, I steeled myself as I watched the nurse jab in a fresh needle and, slowly, drain not one but six vials of this baby's blood.

And I knew: This was not a normal child who was getting a vaccination in his thigh. Ahead of us lay lots of crying.

"Congratulations," Joanne told us as soon as we made it back to the O'Neill residence center. Adam lay ashen in Jon's arms. Jon's face matched Adam's. "Let's get him ready so you can take him home."

As Joanne gathered together Adam's light blue sleep suit and other small collection of clothing, and a shelf-ful of various-sized vitamin and medication bottles, I gazed at the other children in the day room. One, an olive-skinned girl with short, curly brown hair, probably about a year old, was strapped in a baby swing, watching *The Lion King* for what must have been the hundredth time. Another infant was buckled into a gray, metallic mechanical chair, wakeful and fussing. Sitting on a little child-sized chair painted pale blue was the three-year-old we had come to know slightly over the last three days, the one I had encountered just moments after seeing Adam for the first time.

The other child in the room was Adam's roommate. His name was Abdulla, and he was a little over a year old. He had spent his life here so far, with occasional visits from his father, who played with him and then, looking unhappy and helpless, left him at the end of the day. Doolley, we called the boy. Doolley was watching me pack, and to me his big brown eyes looked full of things he wasn't old enough to say. He saw us preparing to take home the child we had given a new name. Doolley was too sick to take home, and he had a father of sorts. Moments later, when Joanne handed the bundled and wrapped Adam into my arms and wished us luck and told us we could call at any hour if we had a problem, my joy was tempered by what Doolley's eyes had told us. He knew what we knew: *We were taking home just one child.*

The next morning, I was upstairs with Adam when the doorbell rang at our stuccoed, two-story house on Lincoln Avenue in Maywood. Jon answered the front door. I could hear my parents' voices in the living room. I was pretty sure I could hear my grandmother too. I finished changing Adam's diaper and quickly buttoned the snaps of his blue-and-white fleece jumpsuit, complete with the little yellow football stitched on the chest. We had purposely dressed him in blue. It matched the sky blue of his bedroom walls, and the color—not to mention the yellow football—added to the ordinary-boy aura I aimed to create. I wanted him to look as adorable as possible when my family met him for the first time. Maybe the nice clothes and Dr. Spock surroundings would minimize how sick he appeared. I didn't want the first look he got from his grandparents to be one of pity. I wanted it to be a look of joy.

During the thirteen years we had been together, Jon and I had had a complicated relationship with our parents, especially mine. When we had met as fraternity brothers in college, we had both been taken by surprise by the bond we developed. Adolph and Dorothy Galluccio had been surprised too, but far less pleased. The two are every-Sunday members of Blessed Sacrament, a large Roman Catholic church in Paterson, where Dorothy sings in the choir and Adolph serves as a frequent lay reader. Both of them perceive themselves as "good Catholics," and when they found out about our relationship, they pretty much told me that I was going to hell. Jon and I retreated for several years to Los Angeles. Once we came back, my family had gotten into the habit of accepting us, even if they tried to ignore that we weren't just good pals but a real, permanent couple.

Tall, well-built, with graying dark hair, intense cobalt eyes, and a strong nose and chin that cry out "Italian," my father, Adolph, is a hearty and tolerant man. But he keeps his true feelings—especially his sadness or disappointment—masked behind a bravado and sociability. If we wanted to know his true opinion of us, we had to interpret it from his signs and portents. For example, when he greeted Jon with a slap on the back at one Christmas dinner, let out a throaty guffaw, and referred to us as "you men," we knew we'd advanced one step further along the path to acceptance.

Our announcement that we wanted to adopt a child had snarled the genial but sometimes glacial progress we had made to become part of the family constellation. Jon and I were going to deliver on the promise every Italian-American son makes to his family—providing grandchildren—but that didn't mean my parents had to be happy about it. The previous summer, we had baby-sat for friends of ours, a gay white couple raising two African-American children. They were going away for the weekend, and we wanted to give ourselves a sense of what it would be like to supervise kids. That Sunday, we had brought the boys to my parents' house. It was a nice, ordinary suburban weekend; the kids swam in the pool, and we had a barbecue Sunday evening in my parents' sprawling backyard. We ate lasagna, spaghetti with homemade meatballs, and sausages and peppers my father grilled as though it were part of his genetic programming. The kids and Jon guzzled lemonade while my father and I washed down the Italian seasonings with an Amstel Light. The next week, my parents got an anonymous letter in the mail: "Too bad your son's a fag. Now they're bringing the blackies around."

That incident had left my parents understandably rattled, although both of them were too tough to shrink back because of a threat. Several months later, I had a long talk with my family alone, over dinner one night in my parents' big formal dining room. When I told them that Jon and I were thinking of adopting, my mother removed her gaze from the chandelier above the table, glanced at my younger sister, and then burst into tears. My father, looking stony, got up from the tall mahogany chair at the head of the table and said, "You need to know that I don't approve of this." His face was serious and sincere beneath his shock of salt-and-pepper hair as he walked into the kitchen, staring down at the floor the entire way.

"Dad, I understand," I called after him. "But you need to understand that I'm not asking for approval. I just thought you needed to know."

I couldn't raise a child surrounded by shame, I told them. My parents would have to look upon my children and not have their warmest feelings stymied by embarrassment. It would have to be that way if they were to be included in my kids' upbringing.

"They'll never let you do it," my mother had said, still crying. "You'll want it so badly and you'll never have it. You're just setting yourself up for heartache."

So far, our experience at the O'Neill Center was proving my mother wrong, and over the last several months their curiosity about our progress in the foster-parenting system had grown. Still, the anticipation of introducing our son to my parents made our first encounter with Dr. Hutcheons feel like lunch with Florence Nightingale.

As I sat next to Adam's crib, I could hear my parents talking, coming up the stairs from our living room, as Jon prepped them on Adam's

Adam meets his grandparents. Grandma Grace, Michael holding Adam, Grandma (Dorothy), and Little Poppy (Adolph).

sleep skills and feeding habits. "Be adorable," I whispered to Adam. The words seemed to penetrate that tender, blue-veined skull of his as he scrutinized me thoughtfully.

I bent over the crib, picked him up, and held him in my arms as my mother entered the room. Her face crinkled into a smile. She stretched her arms toward Adam. Grandma Grace, her mother, my grandmother, stood behind her, short and round and maternal, grinning, angling to get a bead on the new baby. Jon appeared next to them, nervously rubbing his hands together, looking as if he thought he should make formal introductions.

My mother hugged me and the baby in the same embrace. "Oh, he's beautiful." She took him from me and held him up in the air. If the state allowed it, and if her heart was open, Adam would be her seventh grandchild.

Last in the room was my father. I watched his face carefully as his big blue eyes flicked to the baby, then to me, then back to the baby again. He was smiling, but the expression seemed to arise more from social obligation than pleasure. He stayed back a few steps and let events unfold within the room.

Mom hugged the baby and held him tightly. "Adolph, come see Adam," she coaxed.

Dad moved forward and took Adam from my mother. He held the baby up in front of him and looked him in the face. The man of fifty-seven and the child just three months old stared at each other, man to man, for a long, long moment. Adolph gazed at Adam. Adam gazed gravely back. I watched as my father's eyes began to glisten and then thicken with tears. When he blinked, the tears ran down his face and he held Adam tightly to him. Grandfather, grandson.

I looked past my parents and caught Jon's eye. His eyes were also glittering with tears, and he smiled back.

TWO

PART OF THE FAMILY

Jon Galluccio

Three days after the New Year began, on a cold and beautiful winter morning, Michael and I brought Adam home to stay. This time when we pulled up in front of the house with Adam, we knew he wasn't going back the next morning—he was ours, as a foster placement, a baby we hoped would survive and thrive to be our adopted son for good.

Adam sat snugly in the Grand Am's backseat, strapped into an elaborate combination car seat/infant seat/high chair/toddler table that was supposed to adapt to new uses as Adam grew but, as we would find out, couldn't withstand the damage a kid inflicted on it. He was wearing a blue-and-white-dotted snowsuit that the O'Neill Center had provided us, along with a lot of other clothing, some of it new and nice, some of it items outgrown by prosperous infants in the suburbs and then donated to O'Neill's homeless babies.

Michael and I had packed the rest of the backseat and the trunk with twenty brown grocery bags from the O'Neill Center—all containing baby essentials, some of them required for all babies, such as diapers, and other things only necessary for "medically fragile" infants such as Adam. The nebulizer for his Proventil treatments, which Joanne had trained us to use over Christmas, was only a little bigger than a toaster oven and fit in one bag, but it had more attachments than the most elaborate vacuum cleaner I'd ever seen, from extra hoses to that face mask we'd resolved never to use. The O'Neill caregivers had given us packets of saline solution for the nebulizer, and an entire box of disposable rubber gloves even though we didn't want to use them either, feeding bottles, disposable diaper-changing pads, three bottles each of bubble-gum-colored Bactrim and phenobarbital, which looked like cough syrup, and four boxes of needleless syringes.

With help from our friends and parents, the two of us had tried to obtain everything else Adam would need, from diapers to bibs. In some cases it was hard for us to find baby stuff that men would feel comfortable using on their kid. When we had tried to buy a diaper bag, every one we saw had flowers on it, as if only moms ever changed diapers. We ended up getting a denim diaper bag that wasn't exactly high style but was butch enough for me to carry without feeling like a female impersonator. As the man slated to be the stay-at-home dad, I was dealing with no longer having a salary, and in a society where men are required to go to work and make money, I was feeling emasculated. I was already sensitive when people called me Mr. Mom, which is why the choice of a diaper bag was so important. *Miss Thing* was fine, but *Mr. Mom*—that was a whole other story. Go figure.

Once we got into the house, the first thing I did was hand Adam to Michael and leave the two of them alone. It was hard for me to do this, but I had a reason: within twenty-four hours, Michael would be flying off to a consumer electronics show in Las Vegas. He'd arranged with Mike Losee, his boss at Nokia Mobile Phones, where Michael was sales manager for the Northeast region, to take whatever time he needed to settle in with his new son. But this trip was unavoidable, and it had unfortunately coincided with our first chance to take Adam home.

I could tell by Michael's face that it was killing him to know he'd have to part from his new son the next day. This was never our plan. I wasn't too happy about it either. In fact, even though I'd known about this trip for months and Michael had already arranged to cut it short, I was still resentful that the biggest event in our lives so far had to be interrupted for Michael to entertain clients with Las Vegas dancing girls.

But there was stuff to get done, now that Adam's presence was real. I unpacked the three sets of crib sheets we had bought that week and tried out each one on the crib we'd bought several weeks before. It had little stars carved into the wooden frame that I had glued rhinestones onto, so Adam could gaze up not just at the blue clouds of his bedroom walls but at stars as well. I set up his medications in a cabinet in the kitchen and cleared a space in the refrigerator for the Bactrim and any other medicines he'd need in the future. I decided where we'd plug in the nebulizer at night, and I put diapers and diaper pails not just at the nursery changing table but downstairs in the living room and every other place we would have to make a change. Every few minutes I'd come into the living room to see Michael snuggling with Adam, who was nestled against his chest inside his robe, and I felt an insurmountable love for this father and son—my family.

That evening we ate pot roast and noodles that my mother, Ann Mary, and her husband, Herb, had brought over, then bathed Adam—who cooed in his bassinet as if he'd lived in our house for the whole three months of his life. When Adam started crying for no particular reason at 7:30 P.M., I ran upstairs, unplugged the nebulizer, grabbed the saline and the machine, ran downstairs to set it up, and administered his treatment as he lay within Michael's robe.

Adam's breathing was still disturbing to hear. It was so raspy that he sounded like a child blowing bubbles in his glass of milk with a straw. Joanne had cautioned us to keep our eyes on him. When his breathing became excessively labored, we had to examine him to see if we could see the skin of his abdomen sucking into his ribs. If that happened, we would know he was in respiratory distress and we'd need to take quick action. A session on the nebulizer was supposed to ease the attack, but there was no guarantee. If we didn't see quick results, we would need to get him to the emergency room. There would always be the chance that he would go unconscious or stop breathing altogether. Our CPR and resuscitative breathing skills would need to be expert.

Needless to say, bedtime was frightening. What if he was to have an attack in the night? What if we did not hear him? This fragile infant could die without our ever hearing it. Adam slept well that first night, but we didn't. His nursery was next to our bedroom, and both of us lay awake with the doors open with the baby monitor next to our bed, his ragged breathing staticky in our ears.

"Are you sleeping?" I whispered to Michael.

"No, I'm listening," he whispered back.

"Me too." We lay there quietly for a while. Then all we heard was silence. Michael and I looked at each other in the dark. Was he sleeping more deeply or had he stopped breathing? Our panic rose. Michael jumped out of bed and ran into the other room, then came back in. "He's asleep. He's fine."

An hour or so later as I lay there, the monitor went quiet again. This time I got out of bed to check on him. But Adam was sound asleep, his breaths so even we couldn't hear them from a room away. This was going to take some getting used to, I told myself as I felt my way back to bed.

On Saturday morning, Michael stayed holding Adam until the last possible moment before he had to go to catch his plane at Newark Airport. Waiting this long was unusual for him; he's a neurotic traveler who would be happy to arrive at the airport a day before his scheduled flight. Both of us were worried about Adam because he'd woken with a fierce rash on his face. I left a message with Joanne at the O'Neill Center about that, but otherwise he seemed fine. And he was certainly a lot more rested than we were.

It was a long and painful good-bye. "I'm calling you every hour on the hour," Michael said. "You'll do great. You're a great dad. Remember, you can call me anytime, and don't be afraid to ask for help from me, from anybody. I'm home in three days—Monday night. I love you so much."

Watching Michael drive away in his old, taped-together Nissan Stanza, with Adam in my arms exhaling visibly in the cold air, I felt my first real stab of fear. Was I going to be able to handle all this child care by myself? I felt terribly isolated, in charge of a sick baby who was helplessly reliant on no one but me. I'd just have to handle it, I told myself. But even though I was irked that Michael had to leave, I was also secretly delighted I had Adam all to myself. I was all alone with my brand-new son. When we'd visited Adam at the O'Neill Center, Michael and I would have to negotiate who would get to pick him up first, who would get to feed him, change him, sing him to sleep. We'd practically tugged off his arms in our eagerness to care for him. At O'Neill, I'd already seen how he recognized us more and more, getting more animated, eating better. I wanted to witness more of that. Now, at least for me, there would be no more scarcity—just baby abundance.

The first day was great. Adam slept, ate, took his medicine on schedule, and inhaled from his nebulizer without complaining. When he was awake, I couldn't keep myself from hugging him to me. Even after I rocked him to sleep in my arms for his nap—I was testing out different lullabies, standing up with him in the living room like a lounge singer— I held him a few minutes longer before putting him in his big white wicker basket which our neighbors Mike and Maria had given us. I cleaned the house and made bottles for Adam's next meal as he slept, surrounded by the baby swing, another basket of diapers, wipes, toys, and his nebulizer. The baby had taken over. So much for our fabulous, well-appointed, tchotchke-filled, aubergine living room.

As I examined him sleeping in his basket, I noticed one thing freaky about Adam: when he slept, his eyes didn't close all the way. Alarmed, I closed his lids for him with my fingertips, but they popped back open. So I called Joanne at the O'Neill Center in a little bit of panic, to ask why his eyes wouldn't close. "Adam's just being Adam," Joanne told me. Later, as I observed him, I noticed that even when he was sleeping, if Adam saw me, he would smile. Nothing has ever been as heart-warming to me as watching Adam break into a grin while he slept simply because one of us entered his line of vision. Because he is sleeping when he smiles, we know that the recognition and love that triggers that response comes from deep within.

When Joanne heard that I'd not gotten much sleep the first night because I was listening to Adam breathe, she sighed. "Is the nursery next to your bedroom?"

"Yes."

"Do you sleep with the doors open?"

"Yes."

"And is your bed next to the wall his crib is on?"

"Yes."

"And you have a monitor on?"

"Yes, ma'am."

"Turn the monitor off and get some sleep." In the unlikely event that Adam stopped breathing, we wouldn't hear it anyway, she explained. And our room was so close to his that if he was in distress, we'd hear it without the monitor. I felt a little relieved, but it would take me another two days before I could turn off the monitor.

Our dogs Topaz and Winston reacted strongly to the new creature in the house. Topaz, a reddish blond Welsh-corgi mutt with a weight issue, seemed almost maternal in the way she paid so much attention to Adam. When Adam cried, Topaz would cry too. But Winston, a black Pomeranian, was jealous of the baby. He had been the little boy of our family, and I could tell he felt replaced in our affections. He fought for my attention when I picked up Adam or talked to him, and he cried to be held all the time. Before long, he was urinating and defecating on the floor. What was worse was when I caught him nibbling on Adam's fingers and toes. Right away I learned I had to keep a close eye on Winston and keep him apart from Adam at all times. If the dog kept this up, he'd have to go.

Not too many of our friends or family called that first day I was alone with Adam. I think they wanted to give father and son time alone, but I found I hated the isolation. I wanted to share the joy of Adam with them, but I also wanted their support. They had all been calling us every day to ask when we were bringing Adam home, but now that he was here, everyone was gone, including Michael. I decided I would take him to church with me the next morning, for some company and some spiritual sustenance for both of us. Although he was still sick and the drug withdrawal clearly made his behavior less predictable than that of the average baby, I felt the need for him to be in the house of God. Over the last years, my growing urge to be a father had made me change my life in some pretty drastic and hard-won ways; it had also spurred my spirituality. At the start of our life together, I wanted Adam to have a dose of faith.

I was also motivated by some archaic notion that if I took Adam to church, he would be seen by God. I'd been raised Catholic, and like so many gay men, I'd fallen away from a church that wouldn't accept me. Over the last two years, however, as Michael and I prepared to be fathers, we found ourselves opening up to a spirituality that we were still defining. In fact, one of our references for the foster parent program at the state Division of Youth and Family Services had come from the Reverend Gladys H. (Punky) Dennis, an Episcopal priest who was then working in nearby Haworth. She had been a good friend of Kevin and Tim's, a couple we knew well who were adopting the two boys Michael and I had baby-sat for a weekend more than a year before, up at Adolph and Dorothy's house in Wyckoff. Punky agreed to be a reference with the understanding that we meet with her for counseling regularly, to talk about what it meant socially, psychologically, and spiritually to parent a child. That was something we were relieved and happy to do. From the beginning, we'd been led to explore our spirituality further by our urge to give any child we'd adopt a firm religious foundation. We had joined what seemed to be an openhearted congregation at Christ Episcopal Church in Hackensack. That Sunday, I wanted the priest there to bless Adam.

My Mom and Herb had agreed to go to church with me in the morning. I was afraid of going by myself with him—would I be able to manage a baby and all this new equipment, this car seat, his bottles, diapers, and the denim diaper bag? That required practice I hadn't yet had. And besides, I thought to myself, the weather didn't look good.

Beneath cold skies we drove in two cars to church, a little Adam caravan, and the congregation greeted us sweetly. The music, the liturgy, and the glances from the other congregants soon warmed me. Adam was alert and attentive all through the service, as if he were already studying for exams at seminary. I figured that the outside world was just so much more interesting to him than the O'Neill Center had been that he couldn't help but be intrigued, even by a grown-up church service.

I brought Adam up with me for Communion, and while I swallowed the wafer, the priest laid his hand on Adam's head and murmured, "God Almighty bless you, Father, Son, and Holy Spirit." Those words meant a lot to me. In case God had missed Adam over at the O'Neill Center, He'd have to notice him here.

An infant was being baptized that day at church, and the priest invited all the children up to join the family for the ceremony at the baptismal font. My mom poked me in the side and whispered, "Take him up! This is so exciting!" I thought about it for a moment, and then I handed Adam to Herb. My stepfather looked at me, a little shocked, as Adam gurgled into his wide neck. Herb Allen had been a background figure in my life, marrying my mother when I was already a young adult living with Michael in California; he'd actually called me up in Los Angeles to ask my permission to wed Ann Mary. The two of us had never had a chance to get close. But now he was beaming as he hefted Adam higher against his shoulder and trundled down the aisle, a big man holding a tiny baby, to join the other children and their parents.

At coffee hour everyone came up to congratulate us. "He's beautiful," said one grand old Episcopal lady, patting his little blue-plaid blanket, which had been mine as a baby. "Good luck with him!" No one remarked on the dark circles under Adam's eyes or the blue veins they saw ribboning his skull when I took off the little blue knitted cap that my mom had made for him. Adam greeted everybody with a toothless smile and plenty of seductive eye contact. "God bless you," said Bill Brooks, a member of the church vestry and the straight father of a boy and a girl, who had been especially friendly to us when we joined the parish. "Michael's in Las Vegas? Too bad, what with that snowstorm ready to hit."

Snowstorm? Yes, it was going to snow, everyone said. I hadn't exactly been glued to the Weather Channel over the last four days, so the weather was news to me.

We packed up Adam, and Herb and Ann Mary helped me get the

car seat into the Grand Am, which with its tight corners was already proving itself not too family friendly. I was really new at this and not too deft with the car seat yet, so I was glad for their help. I hugged my parents good-bye, got in, and turned on the heater and the radio: a weather advisory. They weren't predicting a snowstorm. They were predicting a *blizzard*. And it was going to hit us any second.

In the three miles and four stoplights it took me to get back to Maywood, the snow started coming down, thick enough to dust the roads. The snow might fall hard enough to down power lines, the radio said, and cause whole towns to lose water or power. Be prepared with candles, water, flashlights, and extra batteries. People could be snowbound in their homes. *Oh, God—Adam's nebulizer,* I thought. It relied on electricity. And what if something goes wrong with him and I can't get him to the emergency room? *How can this be happening?* I asked myself.

By the time I got home I was in a complete and utter panic. Everything seemed awful, primed to go wrong as soon as the blizzard really hit. I put Adam down for his nap in the basket in the living room and began shaking. I didn't think to call Michael—he was too far away to do anything for me here and now. Instead, the first thing I did was call my twelve-step sponsor, one of the people who had supported me when I'd stopped drinking a year and a half before. "Bill, I need help," I said, and soon I was sputtering into the phone. My breath was going short with sobs. The blizzard was coming and Michael wasn't here and what if Adam got sick or couldn't get his nebulizer treatment—are his lungs going to fill up with fluid? And what if the lights went out and I couldn't find my baby in the dark? I wasn't worried that my terror would spur me to take an alcoholic drink—I just knew I had to figure out how to use the tools of the program that I had worked so hard to develop over the last eighteen months of sobriety and make sure that nothing happened to Adam.

My sponsor, whose name happens to be Bill W., started talking me down. "Nothing bad's happened yet, Jon. Do you have candles in the house? And a flashlight and batteries?"

"Yes, but what if I have to light the candles and get Adam at the same time, and he's crying—"

"Jon, look down at your feet. That's where you are, *right now*. You're projecting doom and gloom, the absolute worst. Fears are not facts. You can do all you can, and then you can trust in your higher power to see you through."

"But Bill, this is a *blizzard!*"

"Remember, Jon, it's one day at a time. And if that's too much, take it one step or one minute at a time. You're in no danger. Now, what about the neighbors? Can you ask for help?"

The notion of asking anyone for help was new to me then. I'd grown up with the idea that seeking help showed weakness, not strength. But since moving to Maywood ten months before, Michael and I had grown close to several of our neighbors, especially Mike and Maria, who had been remarkably supportive of the gay couple next door who wanted to adopt a child. They had volunteered to be references. Mike had helped Michael haul stones and plants to build his rock garden last fall; Maria had started giving me her old copies of *Good Housekeeping*, with all the coupons already clipped out. I composed myself, blew my nose, thanked Bill W., hung up the phone, turned down the doom on the Weather Channel, and called Mike and Maria. But the moment I heard Mike's voice on the phone, I burst into tears again.

"My God, what's happened—is Adam okay?" Mike asked. I'm sure he was ready to call the fire department or the EMS or maybe even the psych ward at Hackensack University Medical Center.

"I'm just scared—what if the lights go out and I can't get Adam and . . ." I went through my whole litany of awfulizing. "My friend told me to call you and ask if you could help out." (Somehow, asking for assistance seemed okay only if I could say somebody else had put me up to it.)

I worried Mike might laugh, but he didn't. He promised that if the lights or phone went out, he'd come over immediately, that he'd help light the candles and locate Adam, and that we would damn well get to the emergency room if we needed to. "You got nothing to worry about, buddy," Mike said, and I almost believed him. Maybe I could white-knuckle my way through this, with other people's help and a lot of praying. I wouldn't be alone.

I might have people around me to help, but I wouldn't have Michael.

He was off in sunny Las Vegas, entertaining clients, eating steak dinners and watching Siegfried and Roy. Needless to say, visualizing this picture did not make me happy. Once I got myself together, watched Adam doze obliviously in his basket, and took a long, hard look at the snow coming down like white linen sheets, I called my husband. He didn't answer his cell phone. He wasn't in his room. I paged him on his beeper.

He called me immediately. "What's up, honey? Everything okay?"

"No!" I managed to get the story out, about the impending catastrophe of the blizzard and how we could lose power and that would put Adam at risk, and even though Mike and Maria had promised to help out, "you have to come home, *right now!"*

"Honey—"

"This is an emergency! I need you. Your son needs you!"

"Jon, if the snow's so bad, I'm not sure I can—"

"You don't believe me? Here, I'll turn up the Weather Channel." I pushed the volume to high, enough to wake up Adam, so that Michael couldn't miss the piercing beep-beep of the weather advisory. "Can you hear how bad it is?"

I rambled on about how it was scary and that I needed help. "I can't do this by myself! It's too soon! This isn't fair!"

"Jon, I'll do what I can. Let me talk to Mike Losee." Mike was the one who'd insisted Michael go to Las Vegas, so he wasn't my favorite person at that moment. "We're taking a client to a dinner and a show tonight, so—"

"This isn't fair to me. Get back here!"

Before Michael could say anything else, I hung up. I had things to do and a sick baby to care for.

Michael called back an hour or two later, which seemed like twenty-four hours to me. I'd been busy putting candles everywhere, digging out flashlight batteries, making ice for Adam's Bactrim, which had to stay cold, and filling every container we had with fresh water. Adam was awake now, and I was holding him. Outside, the snow had already buried the sidewalks and the road.

"Listen, Jon, I talked to Mike, and I told him it was gonna snow back in New Jersey—"

"I didn't say it was *going* to snow. I said we already have a blizzard here!" I let out a stream of swear words to accentuate my point. The Weather Channel was still beep-beeping in the background. Here I was holding Adam at the same time I was yelling and swearing at Michael, which wasn't something I'd ever planned to do—and all in the first two days of having a baby in the house. "You don't get it—if you don't put yourself on a plane right now, you're not going to get here at all!"

"Okay, okay—I get it!" Michael yelled back. "I called the airline, and it's going to be tough, because the show doesn't get over until eleven o'clock."

"The *show!* You have to go to the *show?*" Adam and I were about to be snowbound and Michael was going to a Vegas show. What was wrong with all these people and with my husband that they didn't understand what was going on? I'd been in sales jobs, and I knew about schmoozing clients, but was sitting next to a client watching tigers jump through hoops really going to accomplish anything for Nokia? "I can't believe this is happening!" I really lost it at this point, and I was letting Michael know exactly how alone and betrayed I felt.

There was silence on the other end of the phone. Then I realized Michael was crying. "I'm doing the best that I can. I'm trying to make everybody happy."

For a fleeting moment I felt what he was feeling. But then I looked out the window. "I don't care about making everybody happy. You need to make me happy. Get home." I hung up on him.

He called back an hour later. "I've got my seat on the plane. Everything's fine. I called the airport and I think I can make it."

"Don't bother. If you're leaving eleven o'clock Las Vegas time, which is two A.M. our time, there's not going to be an airport open. The snow's too heavy. You're not coming home." Looking out the window, I could see that the blizzard had smothered the shrubbery—there was no way a plane would land in this. By this point I was resigned to it.

I worked like a robot, getting bottles of formula ready for Adam where I knew I could find them if the lights went out. I called my

mother and Herb, who promised they'd make their way over if we had
to go to the emergency room. My mother was a nurse and would be
able to help monitor Adam's symptoms by phone if necessary. I called
the O'Neill Center and was reassured that he would be fine if he
missed a treatment in case of a blackout. Yes, but what if we had to
get him to the emergency room? Nancy Begin, one of the O'Neill
nurses, calmed me down, telling me that I'd done such a good job in
training that I could handle whatever the snowstorm sent my way.

"What about this rash on his face?" I asked. "I think it's going away
a little. Am I supposed to be worried about that?" In all our foster-
parent training in CPR, diaper-changing, and infant-rescue breathing,
nobody had ever educated me about facial rashes.

"You know what I think that is?" Nancy said. "I think it might be
from your beard. Or Michael's? Were you guys holding his face close
to yours?"

Of course. Michael had spent his whole last day hugging Adam,
face-to-face. Our little baby had beard burn. Poor Michael. I felt a stab
of sympathy.

Later that night, Michael called for the third time, in tears, telling
me that another flight had been canceled and that he'd make it home
the next day. He had spent the night prowling his hotel room on the
phone, yelling at his secretary, travel agent, and all the airlines, trying
to get any flight out. He'd book a flight and then it would get canceled,
and he was being pushed from flight to flight. "I'm trying everything, I
really am."

Lying in bed in a quiet house, I felt much more understanding as I
heard the frustration in his voice. "Keep trying, honey. I know you're
trying."

"Are Mike and Maria helping out? Did you call my mom and dad?"

"I did fine today, Michael."

"Everything went okay?"

"Yes, it did. I miss you so much," I said.

"I know. I'm trying."

"I know you are. I love you."

"I love you."

I was starting to believe I'd make it until Monday. But what if the power went out while I slept? I stared at the digital alarm clock, thinking that if we lost electricity, I'd know because the clock would go dark. On the other hand, how would I know if I was sleeping? That thought kept me awake for another hour or two.

I woke up early to find Adam snug in his crib and the snow falling so hard that I couldn't even determine where the Grand Am was. Michael called again. Every flight he had booked was canceled. Newark Airport was closed. This time, faced with an indefinite time all alone, I wasn't so nice to him. "If you'd only come home when I told you to!" I yelled, warming a bottle for Adam. "Instead you had to go to that damn show!" He apologized. He would keep trying.

I started focusing on the snow. I love snow—a blizzard, theoretically, should have thrilled me. I went to the window and showed Adam the snow—his first. He blinked and looked bewildered at all the brightness outside, and I tried to explain to him what all this white stuff was. On the Weather Channel, there was much less talk about electricity going off, and at least we had daylight for a while. I started making the most of my time with Adam. Lying on the living-room carpet together, then dancing to *Judy Garland Live at Carnegie Hall,* Adam and I continued to expand our repertoire of sounds, coos, and gurgles. His smiles seemed to come more easily to him than they had the week before at the O'Neill Center.

I read him *The Cat in the Hat Comes Back,* a snow story. He listened to the pitch of my voice intently and grabbed at my fingers as they traced the book's illustrations. I made up little songs and sang to him— about the snow, about Adam, about Father (the name we had all chosen for Michael), and Daddy (me). I sang "Lavender's Blue," a song my mother used to sing to me when I was growing up. But the song we liked best was "Rock-a-bye Baby," so I sang that again and again, holding him tight in my arms. He liked the bough-breaking part, his little blue face laughing when I swung him toward the ground and up again.

He was surprisingly strong. He could sit up and hold himself up standing. Gripping my fingers, he even tried to walk—and all this at three months old! I was amazed he could do that at such a young age. This was behavior unlike that of any other kid I'd ever heard of. With his broad chest and his defined arms and legs, he had an oddly muscular physique. He looked like a tiny Popeye, which struck me as puzzling, strange, and possibly a good thing. Being a Bionic Baby seemed like a good portent for his health.

That week, I got to know his cries. I realized how new parents could pick their baby's sounds out of a crowd, because Adam had a cry that belonged to him alone. Each sound had a pitch change that I came to recognize and define. All his cries had meanings. Hunger was a long little whine. Per my education from the O'Neill Center, I was keeping him on a strict food schedule, a bottle every three hours, to counterbalance the "chaotic womb" syndrome he'd suffered prenatally from the drugs circulating into his body. If he was hurting from drug withdrawal when his phenobarbital was wearing off, his cry would be rapid, achy, a series of loud gasps in breathless succession. The attention cry was the loudest of all, the "Hey, I'm here—where are you?" cry that would turn into a smile as soon as I entered the room.

Once the snow stopped on Tuesday, Michael's parents, Adolph and Dorothy, phoned to check in, alerted by Michael that I could have used some help. "Well, I'm sure you're fine," Dorothy said, rather dismissively I thought, and more to reassure herself than to comfort me— as if we were distant neighbors, not relatives. I wasn't happy about this.

I could sense in her words what I'd seen in her in the decade and a half I'd been in a relationship with her son—her lingering uncertainty about how to treat Michael and me. Now we had put a baby into the mix, and more than ever she didn't know how to react to me or to my new child—there was no rule book for this kind of relationship. Dorothy would certainly have acted differently if her daughter Terri were alone with a child in a blizzard. But when it came to me, a man she wasn't related to by marriage—a man rearing a baby she wasn't yet sure was her own—I felt her trepidation about what to do. Did two men need her help? Was this baby truly her grandson? After all, he was a foster child—would we even be able to keep him? Even with her initially positive reaction to seeing Adam that morning when we'd brought him home from O'Neill for an overnight visit, I was still sensing that when it came to this grandson, Dorothy was holding her grandmotherly instincts in check. She'd wait and see what was going on, once the blizzard of unfamiliarity cleared.

Michael was constantly calling even as the snowstorm abated, giving me the latest on how he might be home in twelve hours or tomorrow or Thursday at the latest. "I'm trying the best that I can. If they can get me close enough—Charlotte, maybe—I can rent a car and drive." He paused, waiting for me to say something. "What's Adam doing now?"

"He's smiling. I'm trying to bathe him," I said, the phone crooked between neck and shoulder. I could tell my voice was a little short.

"God, I want to be there."

"Well, Michael, I want you here too." Strange as it is to say, by this time his calls were more of an interruption than a support, because I was so caught up with Adam. I didn't want to be bothered by the details; I just wanted Michael home. Even as I felt distanced from his trials, I could hear the frustration and sadness in his voice. He knew he was missing something, and now he needed me more than I needed him.

I felt bad venting my annoyance when I could hear the snowplows lumbering down the street, but I was realizing that the conflict we had had over the snowstorm was to be expected. Being new parents, I knew, wasn't all about cooing and rocking and the joy of a baby's smile. It was also about the responsibilities of having a kid, the division of labor, the reality of resentments and frustrations as well as joy. The snowstorm may have brought all those feelings to the surface, but the feelings were real, and they happened to every new set of parents. We'd keep having to deal with them once the snow melted.

"I miss you so much," Michael said. "You're a great dad, you know." He was bending over backward to make me feel good. "Adam's so lucky to have you. I knew you'd do a great job."

"You know what, Michael? Adam *is* lucky to have me."

Tuesday was the first day people were allowed to drive. My mother came over with Herb and my eight-year-old godson, Danny. Only one lane was plowed on the street, and the cops wouldn't let them park in front of the house until Mom explained that a medically fragile child was inside. Herb and Danny dug a path from the street to the house and then dug out the four-and-a-half-foot snowdrift in front of the door so that I could open it for the first time in three days. Herb's a big guy, and when he shoveled, his face got bright red, which gave me a new worry, that my stepfather was going to keel over while doing me a big favor. So much snow was in the driveway that I had to take on faith that a car was buried in there. Together we shoveled out the Pontiac. Our neighbors Rick and Debbie from across the street had called during the blizzard to make sure we were okay, and I could see the look of relief on their faces when they saw Adam squinting at the brilliant snow.

The next morning, Wednesday, Michael made it home to Maywood. I heard the crunch of snow under his Nissan tires in the driveway and went to the window, with Adam in my arms. "There's Father," I said to Adam. "Remember him?"

Michael looked like hell—unshaven, clothes rumpled and askew, and his hair amazingly messy, which for Michael is a rare thing. I took Adam into my arms and opened the front door, the dogs barking all around us. Michael put down his suit bag and the three of us hugged and kissed. His body felt familiar and unfamiliar. We both began crying. It was like being reunited after a war. Then I handed him his son.

"Hiya, Son," Michael said, rubbing his unshaven cheek against Adam's milky face.

Adam gave his father a big, cheery smile.

Once the roads were cleared, we settled into a real life with our son, the three of us a real family. And we fell into a real routine. Once the two of us got Adam up and about, Michael would go to his back office and work, making sales calls and then ducking out of the house to go meet clients all over the state—and sometimes all over the region as well, which meant more air travel and more time when Adam and I were alone. Most evenings, Michael would take over care of Adam and I would get a little break to attend a twelve-step meeting, watch television, or just collapse into a chair. Together we would put Adam to

Adam spends some quality time with his great-grandparents Grandma Grace and Papa Nooch.

bed, singing him "Rock-a-bye Baby" and Michael's childhood favorite, "La La Lu," from a cheap, 1960s version of *Peter Pan*.

As the snows melted, just about everyone in our lives decided to give baby showers for Adam. It was kind of a daunting prospect for Michael and me, but a good one as well, introducing Adam—not to mention the idea of our alternative family—into the larger community of our different families and friends. It also was our first big encounter with the strong opinions of mothers about how to bring up children.

Ann Mary threw a shower for us, complete with all our women relatives and a few of their husbands at the house I grew up in, a little, stone-front colonial half a mile from our current home in Maywood. Ever since I'd first came out to her, my mother had always been one to revel in the drama of having a gay son. At every family gathering, she would hurl the two of us out of the closet at relatives and strangers alike. At the shower, as we greeted our relatives and met her coworkers, Ann Mary introduced us by saying, "This is my son Jon Holden, and his husband, Michael, and their new son, Adam." Her tone dared any-one to cross her. A few people may have gulped a little at how in-your-face she was, but they smiled and shook our hands and exclaimed over Adam.

Adam was eating more, and in the three weeks since we'd brought him home he'd already gone from eleven to thirteen pounds. He re-mained amazingly strong. He could do sit-ups on his own, and he went wild in his jumper seat, bounding up and down among the guests like Mick Jagger. Michael grabbed him and rolled around with him, and Adam laughed and laughed. "Michael, you're being too rough on him," Ann Mary said. Adam's laughs drowned her out, but before long, amid all the gifts of clothes, stuffed animals, and enough hand-knitted caps for an entire baseball team, the mothers all started quizzing us about Adam's weight, how he was sleeping, and what he was eating. Mothers, of course, know best and tend to treat men, gay or straight, as ignorant and unintuitive parents. I'd seen that just the week before: Adam and I were in a grocery store and a woman came up to us, peered into Adam's baby carriage, and pulled his thumb right out his mouth. I read that woman for filth. Forget the old wives' tales—Adam's thumb be-longed in his mouth. His thumb was his methadone.

One woman asked Michael if our family got stares or comments when we went out in public. After all, the tableau of two men with an infant seems to be something more familiar from sitcoms than shop-ping malls. "Everybody's been pretty great," Michael told her. "Some-times we get asked if it's mommy's day off. And we just say that there is no mommy—Adam has two dads." Usually, Michael said, the person asking looked shocked and puzzled and then broke into a smile.

"He's eating cereal? At four months he shouldn't be eating cereal," said Bernice, one of my mother's friends, who'd given Adam a cute blue outfit that reeked of cigarette smoke. "Mother's milk only at that age." Then she looked at us as if realizing for the first time that we were men. "Or formula."

"The nutritionist we consulted at the O'Neill Center, the place we got Adam from, said it was okay to have barley, a little, once a day," Michael said brightly. He scooped up Adam and balanced him on the palm of his hand. Delighted, Adam squirmed around as if he were doing the breast stroke.

Ann Mary looked dismayed. "How do you feed him? I mean, in what position?"

"Upright, with his head against my heart." I grabbed a bottle, took Adam from Michael's palm, and demonstrated my technique.

"Where did you get that bottle? It doesn't have a collapsible nipple. With a collapsible nipple he'll get less air and have less gas."

"The bottle's from the O'Neill Center." They were cheaper than the ones that most middle-class parents would buy, but they worked just fine, and Adam didn't have any problem with them, so I saw no need to change them.

"He doesn't have a lot of gas?" someone else asked. "Especially with all that barley?"

"No," Michael said firmly. "He doesn't."

This provoked a cacophony of conversation among the shower-givers about gas levels in four-month-olds and what we should do about them.

"That's it!" I announced. "I've had it." I put down the bottle and handed Adam to Michael. "Would everyone here who is certified by the State of New Jersey to care for a child please raise your hand."

My mom's living room went silent. Michael and I raised our hands. The others looked at each other with mixed looks of shock, acknowledgment, and some amusement. Nobody else raised a hand. After that, we had a lovely shower.

To their credit, none of our relatives expressed any fear or prejudice about Adam being HIV-positive. As a nurse, Ann Mary had a pretty good sense of the issues around Adam's health. She knew that he might well not have the actual human immunodeficiency virus, only the antibodies to it, which his body would discard. She'd worked as a nurse in public schools for the last twenty years, bandaging cut knees and swabbing sore throats, and she was accustomed to the precautions any sensible person would take in dealing with potentially infectious bodily fluids. I think her no-nonsense attitude made it easier for the rest of our relatives to confront Adam's uncertain health.

Nearly thirty-three years earlier, Ann Mary had done what Michael and I aimed to do: she had taken a baby out of a group home to raise as her own. She and her husband, Donato Dell'Olio, had brought me home from a Catholic Charities home for newborns when I was less than two weeks old. I had grown up knowing next to nothing about my birth mother, and as Michael and I were preparing to be foster parents, I'd grown more and more curious about the woman who had given me up at birth. My mom understood my interest, even if it made her a little nervous. She was struck that we already knew a few details about Diane, the woman in Paterson who had handed her newborn over to the O'Neill Center. Whereas my mother-in-law quite under-standably said, "I could kill her for what she did to that little baby," my mother and I had our own private reasons for feeling some sympathy toward a difficult woman with a difficult life.

As I was growing up, my mom had always taught me that my birth mother, whoever she was, had given me up for adoption because she loved me. She must have known that she couldn't handle me, but she wanted what was best for her child. That is a lesson that Michael and I intend to teach Adam. Although she had done drugs and put her son at terrible risk, Diane, I believed, was not a bad person. She was an addict; she had a disease. She couldn't help it that she used drugs; she couldn't surmount the disease of addiction. But she could ensure the welfare of her son by giving him up to the state, and sad as it was, it looked as if that was what she was doing.

I might rail against Diane's actions, but I would try not to judge her character. I understood Diane because of my own addictions. Ever since I'd joined a twelve-step program to deal with my drinking, I'd met people who had used drugs or kept drinking during pregnancy, and I'd developed what I hope is some humility about the issues all of us face. When Michael and I applied to be foster parents and DYFS asked if either of us had any substance-abuse problems, I said no, based on their criteria; I was dealing with my problems. When one of my references told DYFS she was proud of me for not drinking, DYFS raised an eyebrow, but they too seemed satisfied that I'd come to terms with my problem in a way that showed I would be a responsible parent.

The gay men in my twelve-step "home group" gave Adam a surprise shower in the well-decorated Manhattan high-rise of a close friend of mine from the program. Except for Nancy LaMott's CD *You Must Have Been a Beautiful Baby,* nearly all the gifts were from Nordstrom's and Neiman's and bore designer labels. "Really?" one man exclaimed. "Ralph Lauren makes baby clothes?"

"Oh, please, honey," another guy retorted. "If they'd let him, Ralph Lauren would put his name on *Depends.*"

As it happened, none of the clothes fit Adam. He'd not be able to wear most of them for more than a year. Most gay men, we found out, didn't have much familiarity with the dimensions of a four-month-old, but their hearts were in the right place. They were all fascinated by Adam, passing him around gingerly as if he were a curious, unfamiliar object, like a football or large leg of lamb. As I handed him my son to hold, one friend said to me, "I really admire what you're doing. It's going to be a real healing thing—you'll see."

My in-laws Adolph and Dorothy Galluccio threw a shower for us on Super Bowl Sunday. It took as much effort to plan as a family wedding and as much strategizing as a military exercise. Dorothy was worried about who should be invited and who shouldn't. Having a shower for Adam meant bringing him into the family and explaining to relatives and friends their son's relationship to me and to our sick but happy foster son. Everyone in the Galluccio clan knew Michael was gay, and some of them had known me longer than they knew their own spouses, but this event would make it official—a coming out not just for Adam, and not just for our fatherhood, but for Michael's and my nearly fourteen years of being together. Thanks to Adam, the Galluccios would be physically, publicly acknowledging our relationship for the first time.

We had gone through a lot, the Galluccios and us. Michael and I had left college to move to California in 1983, to escape our families and establish a life together on our own. By the time we moved back to New Jersey, we were all growing closer. Having Adam brought us further together, although I could sense in Michael's parents—and my own—some reluctance to embrace Adam as one of the family. It wasn't just because we were gay fathers, nor was it because Adam was a foster

One of our *many* baby showers. We got so much.

child, not an adopted one. I realized with some shock that all our families were keeping their emotions in check because at any moment the state could place Adam back with his birth mother. Or Adam could die.

Dorothy and Adolph may not have believed that we were headed to hell, as they had wondered about Michael when he came out to them, but others in the family did. Angela, Adolph's older sister, had become a born-again Christian years before. A childlike woman who had once been Michael's favorite aunt, she lived with Otto, Michael's grandfather—Granddaddy, everyone called him—and looked after him. A woman of fierce religious beliefs, Angela was known for preaching to family and friends and for handing out antiabortion pamphlets featuring pictures of aborted fetuses whenever she had a captive audience—including at one family wake. I knew that she violently disapproved of us.

Angela had made her censure crystal clear the previous spring, at Michael's sister's wedding reception. Angela had come up to me to chat and make conversation and asked me what work I would be doing, because she knew that I'd left my job at AT&T Wireless some months before. "I'm actually going to be staying at home," I told her. "Michael and I have moved to Maywood because we want to adopt a foster child. The baby's going to need full-time care, so—"

Aunt Angela stared at me with a mixture of horror, pity, and contempt, let out a ferocious breathy groan, turned on her heel, and stalked off. Somehow I didn't think that in her nightly prayers she'd be asking her God to preserve our little two-father family.

Two of Angela's sons are as fundamentalist as she is. One son, Ralph, sold front doors for houses. We'd chatted with him at weddings and had at one point even considered buying a new door from him, as Adolph and Dorothy had. Angela's son Bob Enyart had been an Operation Rescue radical antiabortion activist who ended up in Denver, where he now broadcast a cable show, *Bob Enyart Live,* that showed up in various markets around the country. Bob would hold forth about political and religious topics from the horrors of abortion to the worth of the death penalty and how today's Christians were nicer to the wicked than God is. A few months earlier, after a family funeral, I'd sat across from him, at an old pizza hall in Paterson where all the Galluccio cousins had hung out when they were kids. He was perfectly amiable to us, but I was suspicious that his mother would be reporting back to him on our efforts to become parents and that we might become fodder for his religious-right screeds on cable.

In the drama around who would come to the shower, Dorothy had made it clear that Angela and her sons deeply disapproved of our parenting Adam. Did they have to be invited to the shower? They were family, after all, Adolph argued. They should be invited, and they were.

So it was with a churning stomach that I drove the Grand Am ten miles up the road to Wyckoff to the Galluccios on the Sunday morning of the day the Steelers played the Cowboys. "They're going to treat me like the mother," I muttered to Michael, who was leaning over into the backseat to wipe drool off Adam's face. "Promise me you won't leave me alone and go off and watch the game."

"Don't worry. It'll be fun."

"We'll see. And if Aunt Angela says something about Adam—"

"I'll handle Aunt Angela," Michael told me.

Dorothy met us at the door, the sounds of the pregame show bellowing from the living room behind her. I peered over her shoulder to see about a dozen men, most of them fifty or over, sprawled in the living room eating snacks and drinking vodka tonics and manhattans in front of a big-screen television next to the fireplace, Michael's father's portrait over the mantel, which was adorned with family photos dating back to the 1800s, featuring all the current Galluccio families except Michael's and mine; I wasn't included. Present were all Adolph's friends, the lawyers, judges, and businesspeople who helped run Bergen and Passaic Counties. Adolph waved at us. "See you at halftime, right!"

"Right, Dad!" Michael called out as Dorothy and Michael's sisters, Terri and Karen, hustled us to the family room, on the other side of the house, where more than a dozen women—from Dorothy's mother, Grace, to various aunts, along with many of Adolph and Dorothy's longtime friends—swarmed to Adam and cooed over him, exclaiming how great he looked, helping us undo Adam's blue-dotted snowsuit, and then taking him from us to pass around the room—a kind of domestic laying on of hands. Adam loved the attention. More than most babies I've known, he's always been comfortable in the hands of women, even females who are strangers to him, I think because all of his early caregivers were women. I believe he'll have a special love for black women also, since so many of the nurses who have loved him were African-American.

Gifts were everywhere, arrayed across one entire end of the family room on two big chairs, and a table groaned with vegetables, Swedish meatballs, franks and beans, baked lasagna, cheeses, and antipasto. I looked around. Angela hadn't shown up. I sat back and relaxed.

When I started to unwrap the first gift, I looked over at Dorothy and saw the questioning expression on her face. Tradition declares that at a baby shower the ribbons and bows from the gift wrappings are fashioned into a bonnet for the mother to wear. Dorothy's hands played at the bow as she glanced up at me. I met her gaze and smiled.

"Hey, Dot, don't even think about it," Michael said.

"Oh. That's fine. Okay." Dorothy smiled back and I could tell that she was relaxing.

The gifts were wonderful: a playpen, a set of Winnie-the-Pooh pajamas, a stroller. From the other end of the house came sounds of thumping, cheering, and good-natured argument between Steelers fans and Cowboys partisans. Sometimes, as a commercial blared, one of the men would wander down and glance in on us on his way to the kitchen for a refill. We just smiled up at them happily.

Then came halftime—I could tell by the bands trumpeting on the television and the absence of cheers and groans. Then I heard the thump of many male feet in the hall. Adolph, Dorothy's father "Papa Nooch," and a whole group of strangers, all men of accomplishment and strong opinions, trouped into the room. "You guys doing okay over here?" Adolph asked. "You like your gifts?" He looked down at Adam, sleeping in his basket.

"Dad, they're great. Thanks."

My father then gently picked up Adam and turned to the other men. "Come meet my new grandson, Adam. Not bad, huh?"

THREE

THE EDUCATION OF TWO DADDIES

Michael Galluccio

"Please don't hang up on me!" Jon pleaded. I watched his urgent face as he paced the kitchen, wrapping the phone cord around himself. "I have a five-month-old foster child. He's HIV-indeterminate, he has cardiac arrhythmia, he was born drug-addicted, he's tested positive for tuberculosis and hepatitis C, he's classified as medically fragile—and we need a good pediatrician."

Jon paused for a minute as the receptionist on the other end said something, and then he plunged ahead. "We've been taking him to the clinic but we really need someone who can deal—"

Jon stopped pacing. I'd heard these calls before and knew what the receptionist was asking him.

"Yes. We have Medicaid. He's a Medicaid baby. But we really need—" He stopped. "But if you could just see him, you'd understand—"

Jon's face hardened as the receptionist said something. "Well, you're not as sorry as I am." He put down the phone hard and I could see that he was about to explode in frustration. "I can't believe I can't get our son medical help! He's been through so much already, and I thought doctors were supposed to cure the sick! All they care about is their miserable payments!"

Adam was jumping in the doorway in his bouncer, laughing, as if Jon's tirade were first-class entertainment. I got up and put my arm around Jon. "Don't worry, honey. We'll find somebody, I promise." But I knew my consolation was all bravado. Would any doctor be willing to take on our son?

Adam was a foster child and thus did not qualify as a dependent for my insurance at Nokia. All he had was Medicaid, which, as a child declared medically fragile, would cover him until he turned eighteen. Being on Medicaid was making it almost impossible for us to find him the good private pediatrician he needed. When Jon would get a receptionist on the phone, one of the first questions was always: "What kind of insurance do you have?" When the receptionists got their answer, they would turn us away. Some doctor's offices were friendly, but one receptionist actually hung up the phone right in Jon's ear. Medicaid seemed to be an insurmountable obstacle for most private pediatricians. The government program for people in medical need apparently caused too much paperwork and didn't reimburse enough.

We continued to take Adam to the children and youth clinic in Paterson where the "state's kids" and the uninsured went for their checkups. The clinic was a typical public building set in a not-so-nice area of the city; across the crowded parking lot was a halfway house for intravenous drug users. It was nerve-racking to haul the baby carrier through that lot as the struggling addicts watched from the opposite stoop. The clinic's waiting room, a pale institutional green and lined with vinyl chairs, was a dreary place that the staff tried to make look cheerful with pictures of kids, some children's art, and a ton of construction-paper cutouts. It was always filled with wan and coughing kids of all languages and colors, their parents, and their grandparents. As we sat there waiting our turn, people would look at us with a curious smile, trying to figure out who was who in our little group. A sort of camaraderie existed among all of us who had to rely on the basic care we received here. Medicaid meant that most of these people would get minimal treatment in the most crowded and unkind conditions. For those kids not as fortunate as Adam, institutional Medicaid was all they would ever have, and it kept them desperate.

We wanted Adam's doctor to be someone we could trust and know, preferably one with an office in a safer neighborhood where Jon and Adam wouldn't risk their lives getting our baby a checkup. Dr. Hutcheons of the O'Neill Center had recommended that to ensure the care he needed we should get our own doctor for Adam.

At Ann Mary's suggestion, Jon had called his own childhood pediatrician, for whom his mother had worked years before. Dr. Burke had treated Jon for over a dozen years through all his childhood illnesses, and as a boy Jon had felt secure and comfortable with him. "Oh, it's Medicaid?" asked the nurse when Jon called. "We won't be taking that."

"But Dr. Burke was my pediatrician growing up," Jon hurried to say. "And my mother, Ann Mary Holden, used to be his nurse. If I could just talk to him for a minute, I'm sure—"

"I'm sorry. We don't take Medicaid babies."

That upset everyone in the family, especially Ann Mary, who wrote Burke an angry letter, and I grew even more resolved to hurry up getting Adam adopted. Then my insurance at work would cover him, with Medicaid as a backup. (No company I've ever worked for has provided spousal benefits for domestic partners. Jon has been covered, minimally, by Blue Cross/Blue Shield of New Jersey.) Besides the security of having Adam permanently, adopting him would mean we could get him his own doctor on my insurance.

At the point of exasperation, Jon reached Dr. Douglas Fenkart, the head pediatrician at Bergen West Pediatrics, in Wyckoff, just blocks from where I grew up. Jon explained our predicament to the receptionist, how sick and wonderful Adam was, and how we had to rely on Medicaid. When she hesitated, he started to cry on the phone. "You don't understand, we have a very sick baby and no one will see him. He needs good care. He's got all these things that need fixing!"

"Hold on." The receptionist paused. Jon waited. "Let me go talk to Dr. Fenkart."

Jon held his breath. After two minutes or two hours, the receptionist came back. "Okay, we'll take him."

"You will? You will?" Jon burst out in groveling exuberance. It was as if Adam had gotten into Harvard.

Although his office was not accepting any new Medicaid patients, Dr. Fenkart would make an exception. His office, in a medical arts building surrounded by young trees and a carpet of manicured grass, was a parent's dream come true, right down to the *Sesame Street* characters painted on the waiting-room wall, a child's slide built into the floor, and the kindly old lady receptionist behind the sliding-glass window. I was just glad that the place smelled clean. Dr. Fenkart was young, tall and lanky, studious, intelligent, and expertly caring and comforting. He was versed in the most up-to-date treatments for HIV, which was a big relief, and he immediately dove into exploring Adam's medical problems, suggesting we needed specialists to do a total workup on Adam's liver, heart, and blood. He immediately agreed with Dr. Hutcheons's referral of us to Babies Hospital, at the Columbia Presbyterian Medical Center in New York City. "You've got a great child on your hands," he said, bouncing Adam on his knee like a lean, efficient Santa Claus. "But he's got some less obvious but severe conditions we have to deal with. His liver is a problem. It's enlarged. It belongs inside a four-year-old. His heartbeat is off—I can still hear the arrhythmia. And his blood—well, I've never seen triglycerides that high in a child this young. We've got our work cut out for us."

To make sure I could go with Jon on most of Adam's numerous doctor's appointments—which could number as many as three a week, from heart tests to HIV testing to standard baby follow-ups—I had to juggle my work schedule constantly. I would race home from meeting the buyer at Bell Atlantic, say, load the family in the car, and then shoot back out for business as soon as we were done. Luckily my job allowed for some flexibility. I could easily make up a few lost daytime hours by working evenings or weekends.

My biggest problem was that I had to travel a lot. My territory stretched from Maine to Washington, D.C., as far west as Pittsburgh, and I had to make occasional forays to places like Florida and San Diego—not to mention my infamous trip to Las Vegas when Jon and

Adam were snowbound back in New Jersey. I spent at least a quarter of every week somewhere other than home, getting up at 4 A.M. to drive to Newark Airport in the dark, my little wheel-behind suitcase stuffed with clothes, toiletries, and samples, to head to Boston or Syracuse for a day crammed with meetings. I did all I could in one day—no leisurely golf games or Siegfried and Roy shows with clients, just meeting on top of meeting, followed by the most efficient client-schmooze that American business has ever seen. At night I sat in my hotel room missing Adam and Jon, knowing how much care Adam required and feeling guilty that Jon had to manage it alone.

Mike Losee, my boss at Nokia, was about as vehemently heterosexual as a man could be—opinionated to the point of obnoxiousness, sardonic, with a wisecrack for every occasion. I'd heard rumors about how cruel this short, stocky, sarcastic guy could be about anything gay, so when we began to work together, I was wary of what I expected might develop into a classic case of homophobia on the job. But the more I worked alongside him, the more I saw how decent he was beneath his cocky attitude. Still, even though I knew how fairly he had treated me, I'd never actually discussed with him my relationship with Jon, much less told him that we were planning to adopt a foster child.

One night in March 1995, when Jon and I were putting together our application to DYFS to be foster parents, Mike and I ended up trapped in a Rochester hotel restaurant during a snowstorm. He was my age and fairly sophisticated, and in spite of being a wise guy he'd proved himself to be pretty human, so I figured he could handle the whole story. Over a Michelob I told him about our plans to adopt a child.

Mike listened to me without once cracking a joke, which in itself was a strange phenomenon. When I was finished, he gazed down over his beer, then looked up, his hard, bald head glowing a little in the light, and actual tears in his eyes. "I guess it would help if they knew how good and responsible an employee you are, wouldn't it?"

I was surprised. "It sure would."

His blue eyes gazed at me intently. Then he snapped back to himself. "So you want me to write a recommendation for you or not?"

I smiled. "Really? That would be great!"

Mike looked down into his drink. "Well, then. It's done."

Once Adam came into our family, Mike would constantly check on his progress and tried to give me as much leeway as he could. Everyone at Nokia knew my situation. At first, when word got around that I was going to have a child, a couple people pulled me aside and said, "Wait, I heard you were adopting. I thought you were gay." They didn't have much of an answer when I asked them why I couldn't be a gay man and be a father too.

It had been a long time since I'd kept silent about my sexuality, and Jon and I were both determined that we would not hide or downplay the truth that we were a longtime gay couple preparing to adopt a foster child. Over the last dozen years, we had both worked hard to surmount the feelings of shame about being gay that society, the church, and the family hand every gay person to wear like a lead apron. Similarly, we were determined to be forthright and proud about parenting a child—not only for the sake of our own self-esteem, but because we didn't ever want our children to feel that they had to hide who their parents were out of shame. As a result, I felt I had no choice but to come out of the closet about being a gay man parenting a child.

Just as we'd seen in the awkward, uncertain behavior of our parents and their friends at Adam's baby showers, a lot of people at Nokia didn't know how to react to an HIV-positive child being cared for by two gay men. If I talked about it, people would let their curiosity run rampant. But not many would initiate the conversation. A few who did came out to me as gay or lesbian; afterward, some of those people were careful to keep a distance from me and not be outed by association.

For most people, I was an oddity. In a fairly progressive corporate environment where it was still a new thing for a person to be open about his or her homosexuality, nobody could even conceive "politically correct" terms to use about a gay man adopting a child. Even though I viewed our parenthood as a private matter, I had to realize that Jon and I were exploring unmapped territory in our society.

A lot of our life as new parents revolved not around standard baby care but Adam's health. Although being covered in regurgitated formula or sprayed by the occasional surprise diaper-time fountain took some getting used to, these minor trials paled in comparison to making silly sounds with our son, reading Dr. Seuss, and tripping over the assortment of infant paraphernalia that littered our once-pristine house.

For all its ordinariness, our parenthood was overshadowed by a necessary seriousness. Even while we played, read, bounced, and laughed, we always knew we had a profoundly ill baby on our hands. We examined every move Adam made—from his ability to use his thumb as a pincer to his crawling. When he started to gain weight regularly, we were completely relieved. We knew that if a baby doesn't begin to thrive early on, it is a sign that the HIV has taken hold. We were determined not to have that happen. I would take heart when Jon or I would wake him for his bottle, and still half-asleep, he would suck it dry. And as he gained weight, he began to take on the healthy pink color of a young infant.

Dr. Hutcheons and Joanne had said to us from the start that Adam would need a great deal of structure in his life to ground his behavior and counteract the physiological effects of the chaotic womb he'd endured. Before we started to plan for Adam's arrival, Jon and I had led an extremely spontaneous life, dropping everything to do whatever we wanted, such as weekends in the Hamptons or a quick trip to Eighty-Eight's cabaret in Greenwich Village. All we'd had to be responsible to were Winston and Topaz, the dogs. Now, we went out of our way to keep Adam on the same waking/sleeping/eating schedule he'd been on for the first three months of his life at the O'Neill Center. He got up at seven o'clock for the rude awakening of a nebulizer treatment; then Jon would bring him into my office to sit him on my lap while Jon made coffee for us and breakfast for the baby. Adam napped at precisely ten and two o'clock every day, for two hours each, and ate his meals at exactly the same time, while getting his Bactrim twice a day, once in the morning and once at dinnertime.

Jon began putting the Bactrim into a Ziploc bag with ice, which liberated us to take Adam out of the house for longer periods. We'd decided that we wanted Adam to be a child who would see the world— the more things he could see, feel, and experience, the harder he would fight for his life. But we were determined we wouldn't let our expeditions interfere with his well-being. "Oh, do you really have to leave?"

my mother would cry at 7:45 P.M. as we threw our napkins down during a Galluccio family dinner to bundle Adam up and take him home. "Can't you just stay for my famous coffee?" (My mother is notorious for her horrible coffee.) But we would hightail it out of there in time to get Adam home for his final nebulizer treatment and into his crib by eight-thirty. It wasn't until May that we decided to join some other couples to go to a Broadway show—but even though everything was set and we had an experienced baby-sitter coming in, we decided we didn't feel we could go across the Hudson and be that far from Adam. Manhattan seemed very distant to us right then, even though it was only ten miles away.

Four times daily Adam needed an orally administered dose of phenobarbital. He fought us at first, every time, pulling his head side to side until he got those first few drops of the thick, red liquid. Then he would suck furiously, almost as if he knew it would stop the pain. He would lie there cradled in my arms or Jon's, wrapped in his yellow cotton blanket, and look up at us as we emptied the contents of the syringe into his mouth. His eyes shook, almost vibrated, as he examined our faces. He had such a serious look in his eyes. When the plastic tube was empty, we would withdraw it from his mouth slowly. It exited with a *pop* as he tried to suction any drops left behind. Within a few seconds his thumb would shoot back into his mouth and he would devour it. Then his eyes would roll back in their sockets, and he looked for all the world like a junkie who had just gotten a fix. We hated having to give this medicine to our son, but we had no choice. We hated that he needed it so badly.

Adam was supposed to receive the phenobarbital for several months at least, but almost from the start we asked Dr. Hutcheons if we could accelerate the weaning. She agreed we could try, as long as we watched to make sure that Adam didn't develop excessive irritability or tremors, which could lead to injuries. Dr. Hutcheons supervised us. Given how much Adam seemed to be thriving otherwise, we wanted to be as aggressive as possible in getting him off the phenobarbital. We didn't want to cause him extra withdrawal pains, but it didn't seem healthy for him—or for us, for that matter: seeing our son get high in front of our eyes was creepy.

Right about the time of the Super Bowl shower, we began decreasing Adam's dosage. Every week he was supposed to have a smaller amount of the phenobarbital; we cut it every couple of days. We'd monitor him, see how he took to it, and if he seemed okay, then we would decrease it again by another millimeter. Week after week we inched along. Adam got less shaky; he didn't suck his thumb as frantically; he was more alert and present. At the end of six weeks Adam was drug free. His shaking had stopped; the wild look in his eyes was all but gone. Our son was a recovering drug addict.

Now, after half a year of life, Adam was truly waking up for the first time, having gone from the womb to phenobarbital to reacting to the world without a screen. He had to be alert, with no recourse to the stupor or euphoria he'd felt early on. For example, for the first time in his life he was getting stuck with needles and feeling the pain in a way he hadn't before. He was more skittish, getting connected with reality for the first time, head-on.

Even after Adam was weaned off the phenobarbital, his behavior seemed to show residual effects of the crack, cocaine, and marijuana he'd been born with. Every night when I came home from my meetings, as Jon handed off baby-care duties to me, Adam would greet me smiling and babbling. After we'd all eaten dinner together, I would take Adam into our living room to read to him or to play with his hanging *Sesame Street* toys. Sometimes I'd do a little photo session; Adam loved posing for the camera. But then at about seven-thirty every night, Adam underwent a personality change and turned into an infant werewolf.

As we sat together on the couch, with Adam facing me, propped against my bent knees, he would start to squirm, grunt, and whine, almost as if he were in pain. He became violent, thrashing and screaming, his face purple with inexplicable anger. As I tried in vain to calm him down, he continued to scream, twist in my arms, and claw at my face with his fingernails. Sometimes he drew blood. Such a small baby with so much rage. I worried that he was mad at me, this unfamiliar being who wasn't home enough. My mother tried to console me. "All babies have a crabby time of day," she told me. "You did, when you were that little." That made me feel better, but it was clear that my baby's crabby time was pretty severe.

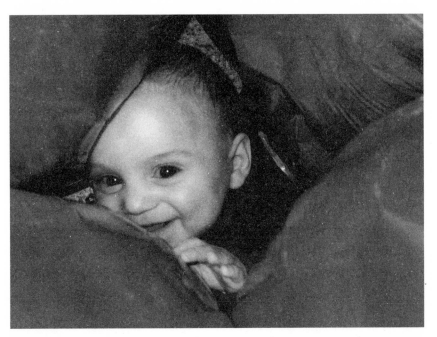

Our boy *loved* to get his picture taken. He was thriving more and more every day.

Adam wasn't just crying; he was acting out. Dr. Hutcheons suggested that his rages were a bad habit left over from his early craving for an evening fix of phenobarbital and that it would dissipate over time. Even when the periods of his anger lessened a little, we also had to wonder if the drugs had wrought some basic psychic damage on him. With all he required all day long, getting him to bed at night felt like winning a war. I felt drained and scared by the inexplicable fury my little son held inside him.

Bedtime was frightening not just due to Adam's behavior but because his breathing was still so ragged. I was feeling all over again much of what Jon had felt those scary nights during the snowstorm. What if our baby had a lung attack in the night? What if we didn't hear him? What if we lost him to SIDS—sudden infant death syndrome? This fragile infant could die without our ever hearing it. Sleep did not come easily. Because I woke up so early for work, Jon agreed to be the one to get up at three o'clock to give Adam his dose of Proventil. Often I lay awake listening to my baby cry as the

After Adam's crabby time, we nearly fell asleep out of pure exhaustion.

machine loudly buzzed. The process took about ten minutes. Jon would rock Adam back to sleep in the rocker I'd bought Jon for Christmas. (The chair was unfinished wood. I thought I would finish it for him. I still haven't. Who knew a baby would take up so much time?) Eventually Jon would come back to bed and collapse into light slumber beside me.

Dr. Fenkart in Wyckoff had done blood work showing that Adam's liver enzyme count was elevated and that his triglycerides still remained sky-high, just as Dr. Hutcheons had told us back at the O'Neill Center. High levels for an adult would have been around 150; Adam's were topping 1,000. Adam's heart wasn't beating correctly either. The hole in his heart might heal on its own or might require surgery. Jon especially was unnerved by the possibility that Adam might have to have major heart surgery; at age ten and again at age twelve, Jon had watched first his father and then his stepfather die of heart attacks.

Luckily, our first trip to Babies Hospital occurred on a day when I could arrange my work hours to go along. I got up at 4 A.M. so I could finish my office work before Jon and I packed up Adam into the Grand Am and drove across the George Washington Bridge. This late-winter day with the promise of thaw in the air made us feel hopeful after such a long winter of intensive baby-parenting.

Even the name Babies Hospital struck me as sad. Babies shouldn't have an entire hospital devoted to their care—babies should be bouncing, happy little bundles of diapers and joy that don't need enough medical attention to have a hospital named after them. Looking up at the huge facade of the hospital, with its massive and intimidating gray brick, I realized that this place wasn't about an emergency room visit for a toddler who had fallen down and hit his head. Inside those walls were sick kids, and in spite of all the medical care our baby had already undergone, I didn't want to think of Adam as a sick child.

We announced ourselves at the rather shabby front desk and were directed down a long, echoing corridor to wait. We sat at what seemed to be old school desks in a room void of any decoration except for a lone print of flowers. My uncertainty and anxiety mounted. We were still very new fathers, and I had no idea how we might be treated, and this place seemed to have a catchall quality that didn't inspire confidence.

After we completed some insurance forms the nurses directed us down the hall so that Adam could give blood. No more of that papoose, which had so terrified Adam—and us—back at the O'Neill Center. Adam just sat back and thought of something else—apple sauce, dry diapers, the lullabies Jon and I sang him, whatever it is that passes through a baby's mind—while the Babies Hospital nurses took blood.

Our kid was a trouper with needles. He'd had hundreds stuck into him by now, and he'd given gallons of blood in his short life. From our first days with Adam, it's always saddened me that my son has been so good with anything intravenous. Needle punctures should have happened so seldom that they still scared him. But I admired his bravery. I wished I had some of it myself. Ever since I was a little kid, whenever

I see a needle, I just keel over, and the sight of my own blood makes me sick. From the first day at the O'Neill Center with Dr. Hutcheons, seeing Adam give blood has only made it worse.

At last we were handed the vial of Adam's blood and directed upstairs. Getting off the elevator, we entered what looked more like a hotel lobby than a hospital reception area, compared to downstairs—and especially compared to the clinic in Paterson. It felt like a television version of a hospital—with paneling, glass walls, a reception desk with a marble top—and I half-expected to see Chad Everett striding down the halls. I felt incredibly hopeful. Okay, I told myself, we're out of the clinic mentality now—no more stressed-out doctors doing triage on the battleground. Everyone was nice to us, and not one nurse blinked an eye when we explained that we were both fathers to this foster child. We'd wondered at what point our joint fatherhood would start to become an issue, but these medical professionals were just that.

As we waited for the doctors, the staff fawned over Adam. He lay there smiling and laughing, his raccoon eyes glowing, as he practically wrestled with the nurses tickling him. "He looks healthier, doesn't he?" I said to Jon, and Jon nodded. Adam's eyes, though still shaded by dark skin, didn't shake anymore, and his skin had lost most of its original sallowness. His only drugs now were the antipneumonia Bactrim and the Proventil for his lungs, damaged by the meconium aspiration syndrome he had experienced at birth, and RSV, an infection that had landed him in the intensive care unit of St. Joseph's Medical Center in Paterson just weeks before we met him. Chubbier, happier, weaned off drugs, our son could almost pass for healthy. But what about his heart and liver and the HIV that might still lurk in his bloodstream? What would these fancy doctors tell us about what was really going on inside him? Was his good health only skin deep?

A man sporting a sophisticated-looking stethoscope strode out to us and said, "Robert Stark. I'm this boy's cardiologist." With his salt-and-pepper hair and rumpled manner, he resembled Steven Spielberg in a lab coat. He shook hands firmly with both of us and peered over to look Adam in the eye. "He looks like one happy, healthy baby, doesn't he?"

I glanced at Jon and could tell he was feeling what I was—relief that we were now in the hands of a specialist who looked like a walking medical degree, his subspecialty a serious but generous bedside manner. We followed Dr. Stark to an examining room, with Adam in his carrier drooling amiably.

"Dr. Hutcheons told me all about you," Dr. Stark said as he propped Adam on the examining table. "You've really come a long way with this child, haven't you?" Dr. Stark propped the vial of Adam's blood against his computer screen while he talked to us about what he'd be checking for. I kept staring at that blood, my stomach churning. As I watched, the blood began to settle in the test tube, the plasma separating and rising to the top, as if the blood were oil-and-vinegar salad dressing. This was normal for blood, I knew—but then I saw, rising into clear plasma, chunky white pieces of what had to be fat. Was Adam's blood so fatty that the fat could actually congeal, the way it does in chicken broth? I glanced over at Jon, who was also staring at the test tube. I knew he was thinking what I was thinking.

Dr. Stark had lifted Adam out of his carrier and was playing with him. He followed our gaze to the vial and raised his eyebrows. Adam's blood was not doing what an infant's blood should.

Adam gave a little cry and spit up on the doctor's white coat. Now Dr. Stark had the entire Adam experience.

Dr. Stark sent us off to put Adam through an echocardiogram. When we'd called to make the appointment, the radiologists had told us that if the baby was moving around or crying, then they would have to strap him down and sedate him to do the procedure. Nothing in that prospect thrilled us, especially since we were trying not to overload Adam's liver with more drugs. Fortunately, Adam slept through the entire thing, one more little trauma averted. I watched as the electrodes were taped to his pale little chest, and I felt choked up to the point just before tears come.

The tests showed that he still had a hole in his heart between his left and right ventricles, down in the lower half of the organ. "This could go a couple of ways," said a kindly woman radiologist. "In an infant, often the hole closes up on its own. But sometimes we have to go in and close up the hole surgically."

"What do we do?" I asked.

"Is there anything we should watch for?" Jon asked.

"You just have to wait," the radiologist said simply.

Next we went to visit the hepatologist, Dr. Janice Collins, who was middle-aged, blond, and serenely professional, a lot like Dr. Hutcheons. She warmed up as soon as she saw Adam squealing at the monkeys and flamingos painted on the walls of a waiting room that was blessedly empty. In her institutionally overheated office, Dr. Collins palpated his liver, confirmed it was enlarged, said she didn't know why, and told us she wanted to do more bloodwork. One more needle went into my son's arm.

The heart, the blood, and the liver. As with the HIV, we could do nothing about these but wait.

A week or so later, we were back at Babies Hospital to find out from Dr. Collins that Adam's liver enzymes were still off the charts. "It could be the result of the phenobarbital he was taking, it could be from the drugs his liver has had to process. I'm sorry, but we just don't know." Her face showed concern and sympathy for our obvious distress.

"Well, what do we do about this?" Jon asked. "What does this mean? Is there some way we can tell what happens next?"

"We wait."

Again. We wait. From there we more or less staggered to Dr. Stark's office to get the latest news on Adam's triglycerides. Once more we crammed ourselves in a doctor's small office, with Adam sleeping in his carrier, keeping his spit-up to himself.

Dr. Stark looked solemn and said, "Dr. Fenkart was right to be concerned. Adam has familial hypertriglyceridemia number four. His triglycerides in his blood are permanently elevated. Where an adult would have high triglycerides with a count of one hundred ninety, Adam's count is eleven hundred. This is unbelievably high, in fact. It's very rare in infants—usually you see it in older people who've eaten steak all their lives. And it's very serious. Unchecked, it could cause severe pancreatitis, kidney damage, liver damage, diabetes. Any number of maladies can arise from it."

Looking at Dr. Stark hard, Jon hefted Adam into his lap. "Is this reversible, like the drug addiction? Is it a result of the drugs in the womb?"

"No," Dr. Stark said. "It's familial—that means it's probably genetic. And it's treatable through medication. And through diet."

Jon and I both perked up at that. "Diet?" I asked. "Is there any way to do this through diet alone? We really want to keep him off as many drugs as possible."

"I've already arranged for you to talk to someone." Dr. Stark reached for the phone and pressed a few buttons. "Send Dr. Couch in, would you?" He looked back at us. "Dr. Couch is going to make this work for you. She's a nutritionist—up on all the new stuff." He smiled, introduced us to Dr. Couch, and left.

Sarah Couch, Ph.D., was a perky young woman, focused and enthusiastic, like an extremely competent sorority girl. She was up on Adam's case and seemed to be new at what she was doing. And since we were new too, that relaxed us. Before she did anything, she took Adam from Jon's arms and made his acquaintance, something we had found that a lot of doctors didn't do. Then she sat down and leaned intently forward toward the two of us, seated across from her in our green vinyl office chairs. "I'm glad you want to do this through diet. But let me tell you, both of you and Adam have a challenge ahead of you."

"Is it okay he's on fatty milk, fatty formula?" Jon asked.

"That's fine," Dr. Couch said. "He needs a high-fat diet to thrive in his first months. But he's already moving to solid food, right?" We nodded. Adam was on Pregestimil, an expensive brand of formula we had to drive back to Paterson to obtain and pay for with Adam's Women, Infants, and Children (WIC) assistance coupons. But he was already devouring baby food such as chicken-and-stars and strained carrots and potatoes.

"In the long term, as Adam's organs grow to adult size, he's going to have severe triglyceride issues. And to treat Adam successfully without resorting to medication, he will have to be on a low-fat diet. *Very* low-fat. Ten percent fat, no more. Five percent saturated fat. That is very, very hard to do on a consistent basis." She looked seriously from one of us to the other. "He's not going to be a normal kid who can have peanut butter and jelly. He won't be able to have ice cream or eat at McDonald's."

She stared me in the eye. "What he's really going to need is to be a vegetarian. And if you start him off eating only vegetable-based foods, you'll have a much better shot at maintaining his health through diet."

Slowly we nodded our understanding, accepting what she had to say, resigning ourselves to it. Poor Adam, I thought. On top of everything else, he's going to have to be a vegetarian. "Michael, do you think we can do that?" Jon asked.

"It makes sense," I said. "We really want to do this without medication. And if we start now, he won't have a taste for Big Macs."

Dr. Couch sat up straight and put her hands on top of the date book she had carried in with her. "You really, truly understand the importance of his being a vegetarian, right, if he wants to live a long and healthy life?"

"Yes, we get it," I said, a little puzzled.

Dr. Couch looked straight at us. She spoke hesitantly, as if she didn't quite know how to go on. "And you know, the only way Adam can be a successful vegetarian is if he can emulate his parents."

It didn't hit us at first what she meant. Jon and I looked at each other, confused, and then at Dr. Couch, who had a small smile on her face.

"So what are you saying?" Jon asked. "We have to be vegetarians too?"

Dr. Couch nodded and kept looking at us.

Beef. Meat. Chicken. The only things we knew how to cook. We were two men, we were meat-eaters. All Jon knew how to cook was meat—he made the best Yankee pot roast ever, along with sauerbraten, meat loaf, filet mignon wrapped in bacon . . . Not to mention my mother and father's Italian specialties—veal Parmesan, roast beef, steaks in the summer on the grill . . .

Jon let out a mock wail like a little kid.

I looked at him. We didn't even have to nod to each other.

"Well, if we have to do this for Adam, we'll have to do this," I said. "We'll become vegetarians."

Dr. Couch went on to coach us on how to make the change—which was to do it gradually, in stages. It wouldn't be healthy for us physically or psychologically to give up meat the next day. We thanked her, packed up, put Adam in his carrier, went out through the marble lobby, and drove, in complete disbelief, straight to McDonald's for bacon double-cheeseburgers.

Two more tests went by and Adam's liver remained enlarged. By now it was April and Adam was seven months old, and we were as familiar with Babies Hospital as we were with the IGA grocery store in Maywood. On another visit to the hepatologist, Dr. Collins palpated Adam's liver—it was smaller, which puzzled and pleased her—then handed him back to me and sat back in her chair to study the latest test results on Adam's enzyme levels. A grim look passed across her face. "Those numbers are very bad," she said. "The only other thing we can do now is to perform a biopsy."

A biopsy. "Why a biopsy?" Jon demanded, his voice quavering a little. "What would that tell us?"

"We take a long, hollow needle and push it through an incision in his abdomen to remove a sample of his liver. Then we study the sample, in the hope that we'll know what's wrong."

I felt physically sick at the whole scenario. I knew it was painful. "The best-case scenario would be that we could then put him on medication," Dr. Collins said. "But there are other things we might have to consider. If the biopsy tells us his liver is damaged, he won't be able to keep it."

"He won't be able to keep it?" I repeated. "What does that mean?" Even as I asked I knew what she meant.

Dr. Collins looked at us evenly. "We might have to perform a liver transplant on Adam."

A wave of panic swept over me. I looked down at Adam. He was still sucking his thumb, looking up at me, a baby happy to be here, trusting that we would take care of him.

I looked over into Jon's eyes. After fourteen years we could communicate without words. I knew he was about to cry because I knew I was about to cry. How much more did Adam have to take?

"We'll take blood for one more enzyme test as part of the prebiopsy series and see what happens," Dr. Collins suggested gently. She could see what we were going through. "But I do feel you need to know about the possible prognosis here."

What would a liver transplant mean? What would it do to Adam's still infantile and HIV-compromised immune system? Where would the liver come from? That meant some child had to die first, didn't it? Could he live a normal life with an organ transplant? As Jon shot questions at Dr. Collins, I looked down at Adam in my arms. You don't even know, kid, what you might have to go through next. I'm so sorry.

God, I wished I could go through it for him. With news like this, all your selfishness drops away, I guess. Your sense of self-preservation disappears in favor of love. From biopsy to transplantation, I would gladly have taken the pain and risk instead of having Adam do it. He had already fought so hard. He trusted us so much.

As we waited for news about Adam's liver, we took charge of the parts of Adam's health that didn't require we just wait and see. That meant keeping him on his schedule, giving him his medicine, loving him a whole lot, and introducing him to the joys of vegetarian life.

"You know, Adam won't be able to eat his own birthday cake," Jon said as we drove back across the George Washington Bridge to Maywood after our first meeting with Dr. Couch.

"Yup," I agreed glumly. "Wait. Isn't there a way to make him a no-fat birthday cake? We could do that, couldn't we? I mean, there's fat-free Entenmann's. We could learn to make a birthday cake for him. That's doable."

It was doable. Jon spent four hours in the grocery store one afternoon comparing labels for saturated fat levels on the foods that we all would be eating. I set myself to intensive study to put together a nutrition program for us, worrying whether we'd all receive the protein our bodies required, even though Dr. Couch declared that, yes, if we ate beans and maybe sprinkled just a little protein and vitamin powder on top of our oatmeal, we'd all be fine, including a growing child like Adam.

We set June 23 as the day we would give up meat, June 23 being a significant date for us since that was the day two years earlier when Jon had given up drinking. On June 23 one year before, in anticipation of having a baby in the house, we'd given up smoking. In the meantime, we ate more meat than ever, while Adam began eating organic vegetarian baby food. We let him have some chicken-and-stars at first, but then we began to wean him off the chicken in favor of summer squash and sweet potato and potato and spinach, which he ate with gusto. And on June 23, 1996, we joined Adam: no more red meat. We resolved that the two of us would keep eating ever-diminishing amounts of poultry and seafood for another year.

"There's nothing you can eat in my house!" my mother complained. She and my father understood why we had to do this, but our refusal to eat meat clearly puzzled and inconvenienced them. We went to my parents' house, and amid my grandfather Carmine's sausage and peppers, or meatballs, or Dad's grilled steaks, or Mom's lamb chops or lasagna dripping in oil and cheese, we could eat nothing but the watermelon. Sometimes both Jon's parents and mine tried to seduce us back with the pleasures of red meat. "A little wouldn't hurt, would it?" as my grandmother Grace always says. And sometimes Jon and I would tangle with friends and relatives who tempted Adam with a spoonful of ice cream or a piece of cupcake. "Can't he have just a little? The poor thing . . ."

In some ways, becoming vegetarian made us more peculiar to our parents than being gay or having children. The Adam revolution now truly hit home. He was transforming not just our lives but our dinner plates.

A week after she'd taken more blood to test Adam's prebiopsy liver-enzyme levels, Dr. Collins called us at home. Jon picked up the phone, and when he heard Dr. Collins's voice, I could tell by his face he was expecting the worst. I grabbed the phone in the office and hurried into the kitchen to join Jon and Adam, our Superbaby who was vigorously trying to pull himself to his feet by holding on to the table leg.

"I don't know how to tell you this," Dr. Collins began, sounding bewildered. I tensed, expecting the worst—surgery the next day. "His liver is fine. The last test shows that his enzymes have dropped to a normal range. I'm baffled. I don't know why it's shrunk or why the enzymes went down. It's good news I can't explain."

The good news felt like a miracle to me. I looked at Jon and went to hug him, both of us still on the phone. Adam was rolling around our feet, and we scooped him up into our arms and cried.

He still had a hole in his heart, and he still had HIV antibodies. But we had struggled to get him off drugs and we had succeeded. His body seemed not just sturdy but blessed. When Adam looked up at Jon and me, questioning us with his clear eyes, we told him the angels were watching.

FOUR

NOT OUR SON

Jon Galluccio

We were not the only gay men in Maywood raising an HIV-positive child. Kevin and Tim, a couple we had been introduced to by my mother, had taken in an eight-year-old African-American child, Lee, who was symptomatic with AIDS. Kevin had adopted him as a single parent. At the same time, Tim had adopted a boy named Kyle. In 1992 and 1993, they had fought the school system to get them enrolled, and my mother had vocally supported them in town and grieved with them when their son Lee had grown ill and died. He was thirteen years old. Kevin, who was working on becoming a licensed psychotherapist, had counseled the two of us as a couple. Early on, he had helped us challenge our preconception that Michael and I couldn't be parents because we were gay, and because gay men didn't do such things as have children in their lives. He helped us see ourselves, for the first time, as first-class citizens.

When Kevin and Tim brought home Corey as a foster son, we started hanging out even more with the family, accompanying them to the Jersey shore, baby-sitting, and visiting Michael's parents with them—an experience that several of Adolph's neighbors apparently didn't appreciate, if their racist anonymous note was any indication. Now that we had become foster parents to Adam, we had less time to spend together, but both fathers still provided us with a lot of sensible advice and solidarity.

That April, Kevin went to court to be named Kyle's second parent, and both Kevin and Tim were to be named joint adoptive parents of Corey. The judicial action appeared to be pro forma. Tim and Kevin scheduled a party early Friday evening to celebrate. But as their friends gathered in their house ready to celebrate the legal recognition of a complete family, Kevin and Tim returned home, shaken: a rightist judge had seen two men in his courtroom asking to coparent a child and promptly demanded that DYFS do yet another "home study" to approve the second-parent adoption, which was neither standard practice nor necessary. Corey's adoption was postponed.

Instead of a jubilant party to commemorate two kids being adopted into a family, this family celebration turned out to be sad. As we stood in Tim and Kevin's tiny beige dining room surrounded by framed photographs of the kids that the state was not easily allowing these men to adopt, a short, middle-aged woman in white slacks and big costume earrings came up to us and helped herself to a segment of the six-foot Italian hero that ran the length of the dining-room table. Ham and salami were no longer in our diets, thanks to Adam's triglycerides, so we weren't eating.

When I heard her voice, I knew who she was—Yvette, the social worker who had been our first contact in the New Jersey foster care system back when Michael and I were still living in New York City and making our initial preparations to become foster parents. As Adam hung in his Snugli on my chest, we chatted for a few minutes about the New Jersey foster care system and Adam's still-fragile health. Then, as I was thinking about how good that Italian hero must taste, Yvette remarked, "I just hope you get to keep your baby."

I looked at her hard. Adam was making cooing sounds in my left ear. "What do you mean?"

"You know, the couple that adopted Sean, Adam's big brother? They're looking for a second child. Well, the state is always interested in keeping families together. They stand a good chance of getting Adam if they're interested." She shrugged, matter-of-fact, as if what she was saying were as obvious as sunrise and injustice.

I was stunned. I looked at Michael, whose face had gone white.

It had never really occurred to me that we could lose Adam to another adoptive family. I knew we could lose him forever to illness and death, or even to a responsible member of his biological family. This news cut so deep, on so many levels, that I couldn't even speak. The tiny dining room kept getting smaller and smaller. I handed Adam to Michael and went outside and stood in a corner of the yard, staring at the trees and trying to remember to breathe.

Yvette was acting like a social worker—I knew that, although she had no business dropping such a bomb in the middle of a social occasion, without authorization. She was operating with a social-services mentality, assuming that some foster parents don't bond with their children. For a lot of them, sheltering kids is a business, and if one foster child doesn't work out, they just bring another one home. But Yvette was at a party where that very day two foster parents had been traumatized by not receiving the rights of parentage they'd worked so hard to achieve, and she'd seen how much we connected with Adam, if she'd paid any attention. The more I thought about this, the more upset, indignant, and worried I got.

I had to cut out of the party fast before I caused a scene. Michael and I packed Adam into his car seat and drove the few blocks home. As soon as we entered the house, we began pacing. What were we going to do about this? I held Adam hard and couldn't let go of him, but it was difficult to look him in the eye, as if the state could come in and commandeer him right then. It was Friday night, and I couldn't even call Audrey Malick, our placement supervisor or "family finder," the woman who the year before had trained us, led our classes in child care—from discipline to diapering to transitioning from foster to adoptive parenting—and even fingerprinted us. But I didn't really want to call her anyway.

Once we had put Adam to bed, the more Michael and I talked about it that evening in our living room, pacing and sitting Indian-style on the couch, the more agitated I got. I'd lost not one but two fathers in my lifetime, and somehow this time around I felt as if I had become Adam, who might lose his father. Michael, as usual, didn't speak his feelings as fast as I did, but I could tell by the way he held my hand and listened and comforted me that he was rattled too.

Over the weekend we tried to assess this issue rationally; after all, it was only a dippy and irresponsible social worker who'd sparked our anxiety, and who knew if it was based in fact? But then Adam would cry or laugh and the prospect of losing him would stab me once again. From what the O'Neill Center had told us, we knew that Adam had siblings who were spread out among other families. One brother was with a couple called the Saxons, who lived a few miles east of us. I didn't think reuniting Adam with a sibling he'd never met was justification for taking him from the home he was happy in—or for denying us the right to parent an infant we loved. Would the state prefer to put him with heterosexual parents instead of a gay couple? Was that what was going on? We'd had no indication of any prejudice from DYFS so far, but who knew what went on in their bureaucratic heads?

We were his parents, I was his daddy—that was it. By the end of the weekend we had resolved that if DYFS tried to place Adam with another family, we'd fight them the whole way. We wouldn't lose Adam; we couldn't. We went so far as to talk over the idea of leaving the country with Adam if we had to. Michael had a former coworker at Nokia who now lived in London, and he thought she would shelter us in her flat until we figured where we could go and live safely with our son. On Sunday when I relayed the entire story to my mother, trying to be cool about our situation and to hide our panic, she rose to the occasion majestically. "No one is going to take Adam from us!" she declared, the monarch rallying the troops. When I told her there was a chance we might run off and not leave a forwarding address, she begged me to promise I'd tell her where we'd gone. "They'd have to kill me to get it out of me," she announced. "I wouldn't even tell Herb." I agreed, but even in my anxiety I reminded her she was being as premature as we were; we hadn't even packed yet.

Monday morning came, and I couldn't bring myself to dial the number for Audrey Malick. I just didn't want to hear. On Tuesday, I felt the same way. Nudged along by Michael, I finally called on Wednesday morning. "Audrey, I have to talk to you about something," I said, spilling out the words. "We are so upset. I understand that the Saxons—Sean's parents?—are interested in adopting Adam."

"Huh?" Audrey said. "Where did you hear that?"

"Yvette. We were at this party and—"

Audrey interrupted me. "No, they are most definitely *not* interested in adopting Adam. Yes, the Saxons do want another child, but we talked about Adam and they know that Adam is happy and secure where he is, and they wouldn't dare interfere with that. So you have nothing to worry about. Adam isn't going anywhere."

Tremendous relief flooded through me. And I also felt stupid that I had allowed myself to dwell so long on the most awful prospect possible. And I felt anger as well at Yvette, who had so casually put us through such trauma.

Worse, this incident exposed to me exactly how vulnerable we were—as foster parents trying to adopt a baby we loved, with the fact of our gay fatherhood giving our vulnerability an extra spin. The scare drove home to Michael and me how vital Adam had become in our lives and how tight we were as family. Vulnerable or not, we knew that if we got through this false alarm, we could endure a five-alarm fire if we had to. Nobody was going to take our son away. Still, the episode was a nasty foretaste of the risks our family would face in the months to come.

Although only seven months old, Adam was bounding around on the furniture like an acrobat, and we were elated. Another fabulous and healthy accomplishment by our infant son, I thought proudly, watching him pull himself to his feet by holding on to the sofa, then take a step before he tumbled.

Wrong. Even though he was trying to walk, Adam wasn't crawling. Michael had been reading news of studies that a baby's crawling abilities related to his or her later skills in math. Kids who crawled longer and earlier did better. But as it turned out, the real issue went deeper than addition and multiplication.

DYFS supplied us with a physical therapist who came to the house,

As time went on, we were able to enjoy those "regular baby" experiences.

a nice woman named Cindy Gannon—middle-aged, stocky, friendly. I showed off Adam's amazing ability as he walked just by holding on to my fingertips.

Cindy shook her head. "That's the first thing you *don't* do."

I looked up at her and let Adam fall into my lap. "Why?" This was the first time we had ever been told we were less than perfect parents.

"Never do that. As a matter of fact, you want to discourage him from walking."

"But why? Isn't it mature of him to be trying to walk already?" Michael asked.

As Cindy Gannon explained, Adam's body might be capable of walking right now, but his brain at seven months was not yet capable of managing the activity. He hadn't developed enough to know how to negotiate a wall, a stair, the edge of the table. His mind couldn't control his body. There's a reason that babies crawl, Cindy reminded us; it keeps them low to the ground and out of harm's way. And let's not forget that he was a preemie as well.

"Look at the muscles in this boy," Cindy said, pulling Adam to her. "He's only seven months old. He shouldn't be hard like this. He should be soft and squishy and rolling around gurgling. But his muscles are hypertonic," Cindy said, sounding knowledgeable and a little amused at the same time at life's ironies. "He's a hypertonic baby."

A hypertonic baby. Because Adam was a drug baby, he had endured various withdrawal seizures in the womb, and he had reacted to the various drugs his mother was taking. Convulsing like that in utero had prematurely toned his muscles. That was heartbreaking to hear. The very thing we had been so proud of in Adam—his Superbaby status— was one more symptom of the trauma he had endured.

Without any hesitation, Cindy Gannon got right down on the living room carpet with Adam and started to teach him to crawl, moving his hands and feet so he would master the motion. It was almost as if she were instructing him in how to swim. We watched what she did, got the hang of it, and practiced it with Adam later on. This along with many other exercises Cindy taught us would be added to Adam's daily routine. For some reason, he got into the habit of crawling not on his hands and knees but on his hands and feet, like a kid trying to be an elephant, which was fine with Cindy.

Whenever Adam would go to the couch to pull himself up, we would go over and pull him down again—which was so sad, since we could tell he was proud of what he could do and puzzled at the new prohibition. After a while he stopped trying, which was also sad; it was as if we'd broken him, tamed him. We also had to get rid of his jumper, which he loved, bouncing in it and laughing hard, because it was building up his leg muscles too much. As it turned out, he wouldn't walk until he was fourteen months old, which isn't that late but isn't early either. For a long time he didn't even attempt to walk again, and I think he had gotten the message earlier that walking was not a good thing to do. His parents, who were teaching him everything else, had been telling him, "No, honey, don't walk, don't walk."

About the time of Kevin and Tim's party in April, Adam's case was transferred out of foster care to the Adoption Resource Center, which meant he had a new social worker and a new set of people involved in his fate—and that we were on what we thought was the fast track to getting Adam adopted, with only the mother's acquiescence in our way. We were wrong. Five weeks went by and we heard nothing. When I called for a progress report, I was told Adam's case was "in transit," which, from what I gathered, meant that neither the foster care division nor ARC had any information on our son. This drove me crazy.

After our scare over the prospect of losing Adam to another family, I would not accept any more stumbling or stupidity from the state. The very next morning I called the Adoption Resource Center and threatened some supervisor that if ARC didn't find the file and assign us a caseworker, I would badger them every day until they did. I even used the gay card: "This case has been 'in transit' for five weeks. Does this have anything to do with our being gay? I can only assume it does." I wanted to make them nervous—that I would call in a horde of civil rights attorneys to beat down their doors until they found his file and assigned him an adoption-placement social worker. If they got their backs up in the process, that was fine with me.

The very next day I received a call from Loretta McCormick, who in a sweet, firm voice introduced herself as Adam's new social worker from the Adoption Resource Center. That she had called and made an appointment on her own made us feel instantly better.

The afternoon Loretta came to check us out, Adam was sleeping, and as Winston and Topaz yapped around us, we went upstairs so she could peek in and see him. "He's beautiful," she said, and Michael and I liked her right away. Fair-skinned, with smart blue eyes, small features, and bobbed light brown hair, it was as if Patty Duke had walked into our house, updated from her television show into the 1990s but perky as ever. She was friendly, caring, professional, and timely in her responses. Immediately we felt secure with her.

After Adam awoke, we all sat down in the living room as he crawled around us on his hands and feet. We told Loretta about Adam's liver, which at this point was a huge concern for us. His enzymes were still high, and we were living with the concern that he might have to undergo a liver transplant. We filled her in on Adam's physical therapy—that our little Bamm-Bamm was so physically developed that he had to go back to learn to crawl. I was determined to impress her with our skills at parenting. I wanted her to walk down our front steps confident that Adam was in the right place and that we would be terrific permanent parents for Adam. I wanted to make her as much an ally as my mother.

We told her that we were adopting Adam together, as a couple, and Loretta, like everyone else we'd dealt with, saw no problem with that. "If that's what you've been told," she said, and shrugged. She went on to tell us more about Diane, Adam's birth mother. "I don't know how much you know about Adam's family. I know that the foster care division doesn't give out much information until the parents are technically preadoptive. But now you're entitled to a little more information."

Loretta took a deep breath. Michael and I listened, tense. "I've built up a relationship with Diane. I was Sean's social worker—you know, the son the Saxons adopted." According to Loretta, Diane was now about twenty-six, a high school dropout, and had already borne five children, the first four of whom she had already surrendered to the state. She was of Irish, Italian, and German descent—which meant that Adam shared an ethnic background with his adoptive fathers; Michael was Italian and I had been told that my anonymous birth mother was Irish. Adam's birth father was unknown—just like mine, I thought. Someone had called the O'Neill Center while Adam was still there, identified himself as the baby's uncle, and inquired about Adam's health status—specifically, if he was HIV-positive. The staff had refused to give that information over the phone, and no one had ever heard from that person again.

Diane pretty much lived on the streets of Paterson, Loretta told us. She was a drug addict, regularly using all the drugs that were in Adam's bloodstream at birth, and she prostituted herself in return for drugs and the money to buy drugs. She wasn't a professional prostitute, exactly—she just did it to keep up her habit, out of necessity, when she needed dope or cash. When Diane was nineteen years old and her sister, Donna, was eighteen, Loretta said, their mother, Agnes, had introduced them to heroin and shot them up for the first time. Her daughters had been into drinking and smoking pot, but it was Mom who'd actually wielded their first needle. When I heard that, I went cold, and I felt a wave of grief and compassion for Diane. She may have been a mess, but she was a victim too.

Diane was introduced to DYFS when her first son was three years old and the police found him wandering the streets of Paterson naked at two in the morning. Apparently Diane was on a drug high and had left her apartment door open and the baby had stepped out for an evening constitutional. After that episode, DYFS handed care of the boy over to a relative of the child's father, and Diane surrendered all parental rights to him. She had another child, who was placed with a foster family. All five of her children had ended up in the state's care.

Because of Adam's medical condition, it was important for us to get health information about Adam's mother—did she have high trigylcerides the way Adam did, for example, and what about her heart, her liver?—and Loretta briefed us about that. She asked us if we were interested in keeping in touch with Adam's siblings, and we said yes, even though we were still residually wary of what the Saxons might want. Loretta promised to write the other parents telling them of Adam's existence and our desire to keep in touch with them. His siblings were spread out across northern New Jersey, from Scotch Plains to Hoboken.

At the time, DYFS's primary mandate was to reunite families, putting siblings in foster homes with other siblings and favoring genetically related guardians for children in the system—including aunts and uncles, grandparents and cousins. But Loretta said in that regard the path seemed clear for us to adopt Adam; no one else in Diane's family, and no other adoptive parents of Adam's siblings, were seeking to adopt our child. The only remaining issue—a significant one—was what Diane would do.

"I think it's highly likely she'll surrender custody," Loretta told us. "She has a history of surrendering her children, and that's in your favor. Most birth mothers either do it for all of them or don't for any of them. Since I have a working relationship with her, I know where to find her. She'll either be at her mother's house or, if she's high, she tends to hang out on the same street corner. And I can find when or where she has to pick up her check." Diane had been in treatment repeatedly—

the state was mandated to try to treat her, and she needed to be registered for treatment to get her relief checks. Typical of many addicts, she had signed up for a treatment program so she could qualify for free methadone while continuing to use heroin, thus getting a double high.

"What's she look like?" I asked.

Loretta told us Diane had dark reddish blond hair, a small frame, and a big warm smile. She was unkempt most of the time and had bad teeth. "She was a pretty woman at one time," Loretta said with a cool wistfulness.

"And what's she like?" Michael wanted to know.

"It depends on whether she's using. And that's easy to tell. If she's on drugs, she's belligerent and arrogant. When I catch her sober, I can see a real mother in there."

Maybe Loretta saw the mixed emotions on our faces. She reached down and touched Adam's blond head. "A real maternal, caring, loving person, who is smart enough to know that the right thing to do is to surrender her children to parents who'll love them."

It would not be a cakewalk, she cautioned us. If she didn't get Diane to surrender her rights, the state would have to go to court to seek termination of her rights. During the upcoming two weeks when Michael and I would go on our first vacation with Adam, Loretta would see what she could do to urge Diane to make a decision.

After hearing from Loretta about Adam's mother, I wanted to believe that Diane was more of a pathetic person than a monstrous one—a woman with a loving soul, even if she was probably messed up beyond repair. I hated her for what she had done to Adam, but I also felt a gut compassion for her. For me, though maybe not for Michael, who she was and what she had done to Adam was a big personal issue. I was realizing I had to draw a line between Diane as an addict and myself as an addict. I felt compassion for her because I had to have compassion for myself as an alcoholic. I knew I could have followed in Diane's path and become a major drug addict and alcoholic who lost everything. I'd been able to turn my life around very early down that road. Still, there but for the grace of God . . .

Even more central for me was that Diane could have been my birth mother, a woman who some thirty-three years before had been unable to care for her child, for whatever reason, and had given him up to parents who could. As Loretta told us more about Diane and about what the next steps were in the adoption, I looked over at Adam playing on his *Sesame Street* activity blanket and felt a curious surge of envy. Even though his birth story was sad and ugly, it was a story; his birth had knowable facts to it, and mine didn't. Diane might not be someone he'd ever know, or even want to know, but he had a connection to his own blood that I had never had.

After I was adopted in 1963, at eleven days old, the identity of my birth mother remained locked in a file cabinet in the offices of Catholic Charities in Kearny, New Jersey. I'd grown up never knowing anything about the woman who had given birth to me, except for a couple raw facts: her last name was Reilly, she had named me Mark Anthony, and I was Irish. Over the years I'd ignored what I didn't know. Or else I'd been so terrified of the idea that I'd not been able to think about finding out if I even could find out about my birth mother. Now, thanks to sobriety and to my foster son, who at this moment was roughhousing with my husband on the carpet beside me, I wanted to know more about where I came from. But what if my mother was as lost a soul as Diane?

Loretta mentioned the corner in Paterson where Diane hung out, and later after Loretta had left, Michael and I talked about the urge we discovered that we shared—to drive by and take a look at this woman for ourselves. It seemed almost a natural thing to do—to get a glimpse of our child's mother, to see the resemblance and maybe from her body language obtain a sense of whether she'd sign over her child. But we were afraid, and we knew better. The smart thing was to make sure that the curtain remained drawn between us—for Adam's sake and for our own. Still, Diane had grown more real for us, someone we could feel both anger and sympathy about. Addicted, desperate, volatile, she still seemed to possess the power to destroy our new family.

———

In late July we went off with Adam to Provincetown, the resort at the end of Cape Cod that is a summer destination for a lot of gay people as well as others who relish being at the remote eastern edge of America. Coincidentally, our trip occurred at the same time as the first annual Gay and Lesbian Family Week, sponsored by the Gay and Lesbian Parent Coalition International, now called the Family Pride Coalition. It would be our first trip with the baby. We packed our cramped little hunter-green Grand Am with just about every baby item we owned, including a playpen and a huge blue stroller with yellow racing stripes and big butch wheels—a Jeep of a stroller—that we'd bought at Toys "R" Us. We'd also bought all new baby clothes for Adam, from floppy hats to sunglasses, so we could show him off in style. To make sure that Adam would not lack for entertainment, we packed our VCR and all our *Sesame Street* tapes as well as his *Barney* videos, so that whether we liked it or not our son could get his fix of the purple dinosaur, as he danced to the sounds and gestures his hero made. Adam would tap his feet and bop his head to the video. Even at ten months old, he had rhythm.

The drive from New Jersey took us eight long hours with Adam mostly sleeping but placidly enjoying the ride in the car. He was a pretty good traveler, and of course we made frequent rest stops so Adam could bound around on the grass or hold himself suspended from a low tree branch like Bamm-Bamm, laughing, as his proud fathers marveled at how tough he was.

We stayed at a two-bedroom condo we'd rented, just off Commercial Street, Provincetown's main drag. Our place was directly adjacent to P-town's premier lesbian hotel, the Mayflower. The Vixen, a women's bar, was just outside our kitchen window. We'd be home by eight-thirty in the evening, keeping Adam to his regular bedtime schedule, and as Michael and I played Scrabble, the crowd outside would be acting up, laughing and teasing each other, aggressively on vacation. We wouldn't go out for a single night on our own until the end of the trip, when our priest friend Punky came up from New Jersey and volunteered to baby-sit so that Michael and I could go sing at our favorite piano bar, take in a drag show at the Crown and Anchor, and get to see the outrageous and lovable entertainer Lea DeLaria back at the Vixen.

In the daytime, when we ventured out onto Commercial Street with Adam in his sports utility vehicle of a stroller, we drew attention from everybody. Sure, there were a lot of parents with children, but not too many with a stroller pushed by two men, and even fewer featuring a baby as gregarious as Adam. As we paraded down the street, Adam would reach out to strangers, laughing and smiling at the lesbians, the straight tourists just off the ferry, and gay party boys staggering home after a long night on the town. "Hi!" he'd chime out to everyone, waving feverishly. "Hi! Hi! Hi!" By the end of the trip everyone would know Adam if not us. "Hi, Adam!" people would cry out as they walked down to Tea Dance at the Boatslip. We weren't individuals with names—we were Adam's Parents, and that was fine with us.

People dressed in their beach-town costume of tank top and shorts would squint at him from behind their sunglasses and either smile and stop or else avert their faces and hurry on. Lesbians adored us. As soon as single women and women couples glimpsed us, their faces would light up and they would squat in front of Adam, play with him, make faces, and nuzzle his cheek. Then they would glance up at Michael and me and see that we were a couple, and their grins would widen. "Where did you get him?" more than one woman would ask, as if it were the most amazing thing in the world for two men to have a baby outside of a Hollywood movie or an ABC sitcom. Two women they could understand, but two men? Was he really ours?

The reaction from gay men was more complicated. Many would glimpse Adam, see us, and burst into a smile, as if they'd just encountered a friend they hadn't known they'd missed. Adam is hard to resist that way, even for those gay men for whom children are as unfamiliar as NASA space capsules. But some other gay men would draw back, glancing at Adam warily, and eyeing the gay couple who were his parents. They would grimace at us and scurry away, as if our little family had somehow violated their vacation sanctum or at least their sense of propriety.

There were too many obstacles for us to go to the beach easily—

we had so much to carry, and Adam would get covered with sand, from his feet to the inside of his diaper to his mouth, which made no one happy. We took Adam to the pool at the Boatslip, one of the main places that people hang out in Provincetown in the daytime, its deck filled with lounge chairs, 90 percent of them occupied by gay men wearing Speedos. It looks like a gay cruise-ship commercial. Adam swam, elated at encountering the water for the first time. The women there would hang out with us and ask us questions about everything from how he slept to what he ate, and some of the men would get their courage up and come over to make Adam's acquaintance, gazing at him fascinated, as if he were an exotic tropical bird.

In spite of Gay and Lesbian Family Week, gay and lesbian Provincetown was not prepared for people with children. One evening as we stopped at a restaurant named Fat Jack's, the gorgon hostess blocked our way. "No room," she told us, staring at our stroller and our sleeping child, her face shutting like a suitcase.

I looked out at the expanse of the room. It was so empty that it looked as if they had posted a sign on the door offering FREE ROACHES. "You've got only four tables full," I remarked.

"All the others are reserved," she informed us.

"Yeah, *right*," I said.

Michael put his hand on my arm. "Jon, honey, let's go."

We ended up at the appropriately named Café Blasé, one of the few restaurants in Provincetown that actually stocked high chairs.

Sometimes the reaction we got was even more cutting. One day as we were crossing Commercial Street, I overheard some overtanned gay male vacationer declare, loud enough to be meant for us to hear, "Oh, isn't that *cute*. They think they're a *family*."

His tone sliced right through me, and I didn't know whether to burst into tears or read him for filth. So much for gay brotherhood, I thought. Later, when Michael and I talked about it, my attitude softened a bit. In a way, I understood the guy's reaction; at a street fair in Nyack, New York, a few years before, surrounded by parents with their screaming kids, I'd muttered the same sort of thing to myself—"Damn breeders . . ." But back then I thought I couldn't have my own children because I was a gay man, and my response was less annoyance than the anger of feeling left out of something basic, energetic, and wonderful.

Men in general, and gay men especially, have been so estranged from children that nobody even has a context for seeing two males in the company of a baby they love. Even the idea of lesbians being parents was new in 1996, and the notion of gay fathers was practically outrageous, even to other gay men. Lying in bed that night, listening to the lesbians carouse outside the Vixen, with Adam asleep in the next room and Michael lightly snoring beside me—my two best men—I found myself with some sympathy for the guy who'd made that bitchy remark. He probably didn't think he could be part of a family.

Michael and I made a concentrated effort to look like a couple during those two weeks in Provincetown. But it wasn't hard. After fourteen years we were the kind of couple who could and usually did finish each other's sentences. And now I was falling in love with my husband all over again. Never had he seemed more masculine and attractive than he did when he cared for Adam. He acted more assured in the world, more bold, as if being responsible for Adam had given him new purpose and greater courage. I loved looking at him, touching him. I think he felt the same way about me. Back when Punky was counseling us on our impending parenthood, she had explicitly told us that we would have to take care to maintain our relationship, no matter how much effort it took. In Provincetown and afterward, it didn't take much effort at all. Adam was bringing us closer together.

Most of the parents here for Gay and Lesbian Family Week were women. We all gathered at a playground on Bradford Street. Many men, and some of the women, had parented their children in previous heterosexual relationships and now had custody or visitation rights. There were about fifty lesbian couples, most of whom had decided to have children with their homosexual partners. Many mothers had given birth to their children, with a male relative of their partner as biological father, or else had undergone in vitro fertilization using sperm from an anonymous donor. Some children had been adopted by single parents, or parents in relationships adopting singly. Two couples from New York State, one gay and one lesbian, were coparenting three kids together.

Another couple, a gay man and a lesbian, had gotten legally married so that they could parent kids as a state-protected family. On that playground were only four or five men with babies, and most of them were older than we were. Other gay male couples had ethnic children, but Adam was white, which made us an oddity. "How did you get him?" people asked us, intrigued. Their hearts would break when we told them Adam's story.

Our vacation culminated at a barbecue on the beach, at Herring Cove, at sunset, for all sixty of the "alternative families" who had come together in Provincetown. The event was a frenzy of people, primarily women, mostly white, with kids of all ages and colors bounding everywhere. So many toddlers! We were all new at this parenting gig, weren't we? Adam crawled among the blankets, happily devouring food offered to him by other families. As I kept an eye on him to make sure his treats were things he could eat, Michael chatted with a lesbian couple who were shop owners in Provincetown and had given us three bags of baby clothes that their son Sam had just outgrown.

I walked a little toward the waves to get a look at the sunset, then looked back at the gathering of families on the sand. It was like a little picnic at Jones Beach or Sandy Hook—the same but different, or different but the same. God, we were a creative bunch, I thought. All these distinctive relationships—all they had in common was that everyone involved loved kids and that all these people would alter the shape of their lives to give their children good homes and lots of love.

Were these children different from the ones Michael and I had grown up with? More colors were represented here than there had been for us in Maywood and Wyckoff. Their parents would raise them to be more tolerant than the norm, and they would have to be resilient when the outside world looked at them with puzzlement or fear. But otherwise it seemed to me that children were children. If these boys and girls were special, it was because their parents had made an extra effort to bring them into the world, to keep them, to rescue them, or just to love them. On that beach, as the sun swept us all with summer light, I knew we were doing something difficult, ordinary, and beautiful.

One afternoon at the beginning of August, while Michael and I were relaxing in Provincetown, Loretta McCormick caught up with Diane as she was waiting in the heat for the welfare office to open. It was apparent that Diane was high. Her hair was snarled, her clothes were unkempt, and she smelled of stale beer. She had a black eye and a missing flip-flop. Loretta knew it was a bad time, but still she had to try to take advantage of the opportunity of actually finding her.

"I don't want to see you!" Diane shouted.

"Come talk to me, Diane," Loretta entreated her. "Why don't you come in the car and I can turn on the air conditioner so you can get out of the heat?" At eight-thirty in the morning it was already ninety-five degrees.

Diane went from shaking and shivering to profusely sweating. She looked at Loretta for a hard moment, then climbed in the front seat. Loretta knew that Diane, her sister, and her mother had been burned out of the apartment that one of them had accidentally set fire to, and Loretta found out from Diane where she and her mother and sister were now staying. As soon as Loretta began gently explaining that Diane needed to consider signing the papers surrendering her parental rights so that her son could have a permanent home, Diane exploded.

"He's my son and nobody's taking him away from me!" She slapped the dashboard with both hands. "I'm his mother!"

"Diane, do you really think—"

"I'm going to get my act together and take him back! He's my son! Who are you to take my son away from me!" She turned to face Loretta, her hair wild, her eyes blazing with anger and addiction. "I'm not signing any papers! You tell them he's mine!"

Before Loretta could say anything else, Diane got out of the car, slammed the door, and stalked unsteadily down the sidewalk.

Two weeks later, on August 14, Loretta went back to search out Diane at the barely furnished apartment her mother, Agnes, shared with Diane's sister, Donna. Both Agnes and Donna told Loretta that Diane wasn't there. Loretta saw a door slightly ajar to a back room. Mother and daughter watched Loretta eye the door, and they looked uneasily at each other.

Loretta raised her voice just a little and told the women that they should give Diane this message: Her son couldn't stay in foster care forever. He required a permanent home where his medical needs would be taken care of. Loretta looked straight at Donna, then at Agnes. "Would you please have Diane call me so we can discuss her plan for Adam?"

The door to the back bedroom opened and Diane emerged. She was crying and her head hung low, but Loretta could tell she was sober. "I'll sign the papers," she said to Loretta.

Later, as Loretta dropped Diane back at the apartment after she'd signed the surrender forms, she said to her, "Please tell his family that I did this because I want the best for him." Her eyes were full of tears.

"How soon can we adopt him?" I asked as soon as Loretta told me the good news. Loretta reminded us that this was not going to happen instantaneously. A judge would have to approve Diane's surrender papers. Loretta would then write up an "adoption plan"—the history of the child, his birth and parentage, and her evaluation of the prospective adoptive parents. The division supervisor of the Adoption Resource Center would have to approve the plan, and then it would be given to us so that our lawyer could file it and ask the court to set an adoption date. DYFS would then submit to the court all its papers and its Consent to Adopt form. It might take time, and if we were to leave the state again for a vacation, we would again have to give Loretta notice so she could obtain appropriate approvals. That we were a male couple who wanted to adopt Adam together did not seem to be an issue.

Loretta was turning out to be a great gift to us—from her persistent work in getting Diane to do the right thing, to her steady guidance as we began navigating the adoption process. Adam loved her too. He had a special smile just for her, as if he knew how important she was to his well-being. It looked as if this adoption would happen with no problem, and what a relief that would be—just to be a private family with no forms to fill out, with only a son to love.

Earlier that summer, at the fiftieth birthday party for Adolph's cousin Bobby, I had sat across from Billy DeMarco, a lawyer who was a good

Little Poppy (Adolph) with his grandson Adam.

friend of Adolph Galluccio's. With his silvery hair, genial manner, and goomba hugs, he could have been Adolph's brother, and like Adolph he knew his way around the state justice system. Michael had known him all his life and remembered him from the church bazaars at Blessed Sacrament in Paterson, a big, bluff guy who would send Michael to fetch DeMarco's beverage of choice.

On the other side of me sat the redoubtable Aunt Angela, Adolph's born-again Christian sister, who had made her disapproval of our parenting Adam evident way back in January when we'd first brought him home. Dorothy had stewed that Aunt Angela would take one look at us and storm out of the catering hall, ruining Cousin Bobby's birthday—that is, if Angela took a long enough break from handing out graphic antiabortion pamphlets in the parking lot to come in and behold us in all our parental glory.

I was in the heart of Galluccio country, which in the past had meant I would feel frozen out, unwanted, not a family member, not even an in-law—more like an outlaw. But this time, because I was proudly showing pictures of their grandson, I was *in,* with Michael seated at my side. I felt a hundred percent comfortable for the first time. In no way was I the "friend" or the "roommate" of the man sitting next to me, to whom I'd committed my life. I was the other father to Michael's child, and no one there could pretend otherwise.

Even Aunt Angela. Dressed in peach satin, and looking as mighty as a duchess, she eyed me, took a decisive breath, and started a pleasant conversation—although she was careful not to acknowledge the existence of our son. She hadn't handed out any pamphlets at this family gathering, and now she was cordial—so we talked like in-laws who meet at weddings and birthday parties. I eyed her suspiciously. Still, what a relief.

As we sat eating birthday cake and watching everybody dance the chicken dance, Billy DeMarco remarked, "Cute kid you got there. Adolph says you need a lawyer to handle the adoption." Before we could wipe the cake frosting off our faces, Billy let us know he had already offered to Adolph to represent us in Adam's adoption at no charge. That was a huge relief to us, because even with the foster-child support the state gave us, having a son was proving a real financial strain. Diapers alone, not to mention cribs, carriers, strollers, clothes, and high chairs, added up enormously. After all, both of us were working, but only one of us was drawing a salary, and the last thing we needed was to pay another x-thousand dollars in legal fees for what promised to be a routine case.

And it did seem as if it would be routine. Audrey Malick, our highest contact at the Adoption Resource Center, had told us way back in April of 1995 that there would be no problem in our adopting Adam jointly; she told us she had called her superiors at the main DYFS office in Trenton, who had no problem with our adoption plan. As soon as Loretta gave us the go-ahead, Billy's secretary Terrie sent all the forms to the clerk at the courthouse. Within a week the clerk called her back to say that everything had been received from ARC—the home study, the adoption plan—except the Consent to Adopt form. Would Terrie get hold of ARC and make sure they sent this last piece of paperwork along?

Terrie called me to tell me, and I called Loretta, who was taking a well-earned vacation. Her superior was busy, and I was bumped up to

Elizabeth McGovern, the office manager, and left a message for her: Would ARC please hurry up and send the Consent to Adopt form to our lawyer so we could get Adam's adoption process into the courts where it belonged?

On a sunny September morning only ten days before Adam's first birthday, the phone rang. Adam was sleeping upstairs and I was cleaning my freshly painted cobalt blue kitchen cabinets. "Mr. Holden? Liz McGovern at ARC. I understand there's a problem."

Wiping my hands on a dish towel, I told her that we had everything we needed from her office but the Consent to Adopt form. "There's been some kind of holdup. If you could just sent it over to our lawyer, William DeMarco, then Michael and I can move ahead on the adoption."

There was a long pause on the phone. "We were hoping that Loretta would be back from vacation to tell you before you found out."

"Tell me what?"

Elizabeth McGovern took a breath so deep I could hear it over the phone. "I know that you and Michael were planning to adopt Adam together, and I know that was our plan too. But we made a mistake."

"What do you mean, a *mistake?* The mother signed off on it, Loretta told us—"

"We at ARC have a policy that prohibits unmarried couples from jointly adopting. That would mean that either you or Mr. Galluccio has to adopt the child as a single parent."

"Wait—" I was feeling terror and fury.

"And since you do not have a salary, that would mean that it would be best if it were Mr. Galluccio who became the adoptive parent."

I fell against the kitchen cabinets. The sun was blaring in through the window over the sink, but I was as cold as I'd ever been. I was stunned. I was stabbed and cut right open. "No," I uttered.

"I'm sorry, Mr. Holden. I know that we had planned it the other way. But we've reviewed our polices and there's nothing we can do."

The standard bureaucratic response. There was nothing she could do, and I was the one who was being told I could not adopt my son, who was sleeping upstairs, whom I had nursed into health and loved more than myself.

I was crying and shaking. I don't know what I said after that to Elizabeth McGovern. I'm sure it wasn't nice. She was sympathetic but cold; clearly she had rehearsed what she was going to say. "Who can I talk to?" I asked numbly.

"There's no one to talk to about it. Do you want me to send the consent form in Michael Galluccio's name, or not?"

"No! In both our names!"

"Mr. Holden, that isn't possible," McGovern said evenly.

"Somebody has to do something! This isn't fair to Adam!"

I may have said good-bye; I know I hung up, then slammed the phone into the wall several times and fell back onto the stairs and started crying hard.

Adam awakened. I could hear him upstairs, crying, his tears matching mine.

At last I caught my breath and called Michael. He was at a meeting nearby. "You have to come home. They won't let both of us adopt Adam." Through my clenched throat I explained to him what had happened.

"I don't believe it." Michael sounded stunned too. "Oh, honey. I'm coming home."

I clicked off the phone and made my way up the stairs, to be with the child who was my son.

FIVE

FATHERS IN CRISIS

Michael Galluccio

Jon was insulted, devastated, and profoundly angry at the state's denial of his fatherhood. Even in how he dealt with Adam I could tell he was making an effort not to show how much pain he was in. I understood it completely. After spending two years preparing to have a child, he receives a baby he falls in love with and spends all of his waking hours caring for, full-time—only to have the state reverse itself and tell him that it will not recognize his efforts as legitimate and worthy of legal recognition. As far as the outer world was concerned, Mr. Jon Holden might as well not have been in Adam's life at all. Their contempt bruised his soul. He felt nullified as a father and as a man.

Yet even as I saw how much agony Jon was in and tried to comfort him, my instinct was to go along with what the state wanted. Wasn't the point just to get Adam into our home, legally? Why did we need to fight this? Wouldn't a fight jeopardize our chances of keeping him at all?

From the start, something in my reflex to accommodate rankled me—not to mention that the state had obviously pulled a fast one on us, doing a kind of bait and switch with our parenting rights, which offended my sense of justice. And Jon was so hurt. Swallowing the reflux of fear in my throat, I was ready to agree to this much: If Jon wanted to pursue a bid to get the state to change its mind, I'd support the decision—as long as we didn't make waves.

As we discussed our dilemma, Jon and I found ourselves increasingly caught between our families' contradictory expectations of us. Jon's mother was telling him that he had to fight this thing—to safeguard Adam and to insure his own rights as a father who had been fundamental in nursing Adam to health. My father and mother were astonished that we were making an issue of it at all. When I first told them about what the state had done, my parents' first question went straight to their deepest fear: "Are you going to lose Adam?" When I explained that the situation seemed to be not whether Adam would be taken from us but that we couldn't adopt him together, my mother didn't understand why Jon and I were so upset. Why did we want to persist in trying to get DYFS to reverse its decision? "Shouldn't you just get Adam adopted legally, any way you can?" she asked. This infuriated Jon, who felt my mother was being insensitive to his own fatherhood. Adolph felt the same way Dorothy did—and so did our lawyer. Why fight city hall—in this case, Trenton, the Adoption Resource Center, a state bureaucracy, and for that matter an American culture that didn't exactly embrace gay men or lesbians as parents—when we could just go along and get along?

When Jon said he wanted to fight this, Billy DeMarco gave a defeated shrug. "Okay," he said, "see what you can do." Jon called Audrey Malick, at the Adoption Resource Center, because she had obtained clearance from Trenton for us to adopt Adam jointly in the first place. Jon wanted to know whom she had talked to so that we could ask them why they had said yes then and were saying no now. He also called Lynn Amsterdam at the Division of Youth and Family Services in Hackensack, because she too had approved us as joint foster parents for Adam, way back the previous November.

Jon didn't get a call back from Audrey Malick or Lynn Amsterdam early on; it seemed as if they were avoiding us in the wake of Elizabeth McGovern's call telling us Jon was out of the picture as Adam's legal dad, because they didn't know what to say. This made Jon crazy, and he made it clear that he was not going to give in to this quietly. "You know they're hoping we'll go away," he told me. "I don't care if I have to sit on the phone all day, every day—I'm getting an answer."

I understood this, but the more I told the other people in my life what Jon was doing, the less support I received for our actions so far. And it wasn't only my parents. Donna, the administrative assistant for our group at Nokia and one of my best friends at work, had followed the entire saga of our deciding to have a baby and then bringing Adam home. She had a daughter a year older than Adam, and we often compared child-rearing experiences. Donna just wrinkled her brow when I told her how we were trying to get DYFS to allow a joint adoption. Like everyone else, she was worried that we'd lose the baby. When I told her that Diane had surrendered her rights and the issue was joint adoption, not keeping Adam, she said, "Yeah, but you never know."

I had to admit that she was right. You never do know—the state had just shown us that. One of Diane's relatives could descend on us and seek to take Adam away, or DYFS could pluck him out of our house and place him with a family where one parent wasn't badgering them every day. I began to nurse a fear that we could lose Adam after all.

In the midst of this family trauma we had to prepare for Adam's first birthday. We could pursue an appeal of DYFS's capricious reversal of their early approval of us, but this birthday was an important milestone, one that we had never even been sure we would reach. Nothing would stand in the way of that.

Except my job, of course, and the travel it required. On the actual day of Adam's birthday I was scheduled for a mandatory meeting in Dallas; we were introducing a new state-of-the-art cellular phone, and fourth-quarter budgets were being set. While snow didn't fall this time around, a freeze sure occurred in our household when I told Jon that I had to be out of town on September 18. Jon vehemently didn't want me to go, and I countered by saying that I had no choice if I was going to bring home the income that made our lives possible. I justified it because we would be having a party on the weekend that I wouldn't have to miss. It killed me not to be there for Adam's actual birthday, but I was trying to do the balancing act that working parents have attempted for generations. We tried to have fun with it. Two weeks earlier, we sent out invitations—diapers onto which we had glitter-glued "Adam's First Birthday." When you opened the diaper up, you found the date, time, and place for the party, together with a Tootsie Roll.

The night of Adam's birthday, in Dallas, I excused myself from the festivities and went back to my room at the Westin hotel to call home. Jon had made Adam pasta and sauce, which he loved—low fat, of course—and Jon had set up the high chair at the end of the table and put Bette Midler's *Gypsy* in the CD player. While Adam ate, Jon lip-synched the whole thing to him while Adam laughed and gurgled along, delighted. Our son was such a huge success story. Miraculously, the hole in his heart had healed on its own. He still had his HIV antibodies, but otherwise he was healthy, robust, happy, his liver stabilized. For months we hadn't known if he would survive. Now he was a happy, triumphant year-old baby. And I wasn't there to share in the celebration and thanksgiving.

Later that night, my entire family and Jon's joined the two of them at the house for cake. Jon called me in my room when everyone was ready to sing "Happy Birthday" to Adam. I was a mess, trying to sing and sound cheerful as I sat there crying. I felt like a failure—how could I possibly be away from my son on his birthday? I hung up the phone and sat on the edge of the bed, my head in my hands, thinking. I didn't want to be the kind of father who misses his son's birthday, his first step, his first day of kindergarten. My family was being abused externally by DYFS and I felt I was abusing them from the inside, because I just wasn't there enough.

I wasn't putting Jon and Adam second; I just wasn't putting them first. I had a work I loved and I made a good salary, but if this was what I had to sacrifice, then it was time for me to get a new job.

———

Adam's birthday party that weekend was hard for all of us. I felt emotionally wrung out, flying in from the Dallas event and then dealing
with all the continuing fallout from DYFS's denial of Jon's parentage.
At Adam's actual party that weekend I told everyone we didn't want
to talk about the uproar over the joint adoption. We brought in an
entertainer who dressed as Barney, which turned out to terrify Adam—
a hulking, honking purple dinosaur looming in his backyard. Jon had
baked a low-fat sheet cake, covered in blueberries, which everyone
agreed tasted great. Even as we ate cake, we were busy avoiding the
subject on everybody's mind: Whose son was Adam, anyway?

No one mentioned it, but I could see concern on the faces of our
families and guests. I could see it in my mother when she looked at
Adam. Having grown up hearing her imagine the most awful outcome
possible in any situation, I could tell that as far as she was concerned,
the state had already ripped Adam screaming and flailing out of our
arms and delivered him back to the slums of Paterson. And when I
walked up to chat with small groups of people, they would quickly stop
talking, put on forced smiles, and make polite conversation. "Great rock
garden!" somebody exclaimed. "You move all those rocks yourself?"

Only my grandmother Grace had enough courage to disregard our
request for silence. Short, only four feet ten inches, and a classic round
Italian grandma, she scooped Adam out of the grass and said, "Little
Adam, don't you worry—you're our baby and no one will ever take you
away! They'd have to get past me first!"

Our honored guests at the party were Joan and Paul Saxon, who
arrived with Adam's two-year-old brother, Sean. They were a gentle,
tweedy couple, and their son looked exactly like Adam, except for his
red hair. The two boys shared the same huge, dark, delighted eyes. "I
can't believe I'm finally meeting you," I said to Mrs. Saxon. "I was
scared of you for so long."

"Why?" Joan asked.

"We thought you wanted Adam," Jon said.

"Oh, you heard that from our social worker?" She patted my arm.
"No, we never had any intention of doing that. Look at him—he's so
happy."

The yard was packed with children—Adam's cousins from both

sides, my sister's kids and Jon's cousins' kids, neighborhood children, children of friends—but as soon as Adam saw his brother, he froze. On some primal level he was recognizing the bond between them. He crawled and tumbled as fast as he could to his brother's side. With lumps in our throats, Jon and I stood alongside the Saxons and watched as the two boys, so clearly brothers, romped through the yellow and red Fisher-Price tunnel we'd given Adam to crawl through. Adam would follow Sean everywhere that afternoon, from pulling the presents off the table to climbing down the slide behind his older brother. How far these two boys had come, I thought as I watched them. And how much they each deserved to have the parents who loved them.

Later in the party, after Adam had smeared cake all over Kevin, Tim, Punky, and two sets of grandparents, I was standing by the ice cream station talking to one of our guests, Vicky, an old friend of mine from the days when Jon and I had lived north of where we were now, in Rockland County, New York. She is a tall, blond woman with a smoky voice and a killer figure. On a dare, she had once actually picked me up, thrown me over her shoulder, and carried me down the street. Naturally, I respected her. Vicky was telling me that she had just accepted a new job at Sprint PCS. They were starting up their New York operations.

"Oh *really?*" I said, suddenly enormously interested.

"Why?" she asked, slowly looking at me with bewilderment. "You'd consider leaving Nokia? I thought you loved that job."

"I do. But I hate the travel. I need to be able to have dinner with my family."

"You know," she said thoughtfully, "there's a position open that you'd be perfect for." She promised on the spot to set up an interview for me.

I got the job. After six years with Nokia, which has been in the wireless communications business from the start, I was the most senior salesperson in the company. I would leave a position I adored to join Sprint PCS, with the oddly melodic title of director of indirect sales. I would assemble and command a sales team selling Sprint PCS phones and accessories through retail chains. I was giving up not only a lot of seniority and a first-class expense account but the flexibility and freedom that came with being based at home. At Sprint PCS I would make a good salary—although we remained a one-income/stay-at-home-parent family, which meant we'd still have to exclude everything extravagant from our lives—and I wouldn't have the grueling travel schedule I'd endured at Nokia. Even though I'd have to get up before dawn to catch the bus to New York City, I would make it home in time to spend the evening with my husband and son. It was a giant adjustment, and sometimes I feel some sense of loss around it. But once again, being father to Adam had led me in a brave new direction.

The week after Adam's party, Jon finally cornered Lynn Amsterdam on the phone and got a straight answer from her. We were told that in spite of all the positive talk at DYFS and ARC, only my name had appeared on all the official documents sent to Trenton from their offices. I had signed all the documents. Jon and I had always assumed, rather naively, that because mine was the first signature on the original paperwork, only I had to sign the forms that covered us both. However, we quickly realized that every document that DYFS sent us had *both* our names on it as approved foster fathers and preadoptive parents. So we had had no early warning that the bureaucracy was about to screw us, *and* we had written proof that both parents were recognized by the state as Adam's caregivers. Everything had gone along beautifully, with the social workers and administrators treating us like real people and a qualified two-adult family, until some homophobic rules had kicked in. Now people were no longer listening to their hearts—or heeding their common sense, or recognizing the best interests of the one-year-old Adam. They were just belatedly, foolishly, painfully following procedure.

At the start of our bid to be foster parents, we had no illusions about what we had to prove as gay men. We had to be extra perfect—as a gay couple we felt we had a lot to prove to the state and had to cross every *t* and dot every *i* in our lives to make sure that state would find us acceptable foster parents. "Remember, all through this process they are going to see you as two gay men," our friend Kevin had warned us even before Adam arrived. He and his partner, Tim, had gone through the system to adopt their boys. "You can't give the state an excuse to turn you down. Don't let them hang anything on you." Following Kevin's advice and our own instincts, Jon and I had changed our lives completely, studied hard and been tops in our parenting class, quit smoking, childproofed our house even before we had to, renovated it, and designed a nursery. We'd done everything we could to prove to the state that we were ideal parents, both before and after Adam arrived. We'd nurtured our child, monitored him, stayed home on Saturday nights to watch him breathe. Now, in the eyes of the state, our only failing was Jon's and my greatest success—the relationship we'd built up over fourteen years, which in our view was integral to the love we could provide a child.

Loretta returned from vacation and was stunned to hear our news. She was speechless. She had to tread carefully, since we were challenging her bosses, but on her visits to check up on Adam she would make sure we knew exactly whom we needed to write to and how, in general, the system worked. She went over the chain of command with us and pointed out the officials she thought would be the most knowledgeable, reasonable, and sympathetic. She was terrific to us, hopeful but cautious, and rightfully loyal to her employer, yet facilitating our case in every way she could, from telling us who was who at DYFS to making sure that we received Adam's clothing allowance and WIC support checks. She helped us get copies of letters on state letterhead that approved both of us as a foster family, so that we would have written proof of our status.

But any of us could only do so much as we plodded through the state bureaucracy. It was an accomplishment even to get a phone call returned. Even setting aside all moral or ethical issues about what was the right thing to do for us and for Adam, we thought we had them nailed legally. Yet as we struggled with these issues as privately as we could—in calls and letters to New Jersey state bureaucrats, in discussions with ourselves and with our families—I felt increasingly alone. Jon did too. Billy DeMarco could not be helpful until we had actual adoption papers to file. We were two parents caught in a battle we hadn't wanted to fight, and we were being buffeted on all sides, and no rule book was out there for what felt like the right thing to do.

"You've done so well with Adam that we have another child for you," Jean, the DYFS placement counselor, said on the phone to Jon one day in late October. "His name is Andrew, and he needs a family badly."

I was in Boston, finishing up work for Nokia, so I didn't see Jon's mouth drop open in astonishment when Jean proposed we take in a second baby. Jon called me immediately to tell me that we'd been offered another child. The irony was not lost on either of us that the very state agency that wanted to deny us joint custody of our son would recommend another child to our care. DYFS was ratifying our healing of Adam by offering us another grievously ill, abandoned child who needed care and love.

"Wait," I said. "They won't let us adopt Adam and they want to give us another baby?"

"You sound surprised," Jon said dryly. "You've seen how DYFS works."

Andrew, like Adam, had been born with heroin in his system and was HIV-positive. "He's a crack baby, he's HIV-positive, he was born very premature, they had him on a ventilator until two weeks ago, and he's been alone in the hospital for two and a half months," Jon said, keeping his voice as steady as he could. "His mother gave birth to him and then checked out of the hospital and left him there. Nobody has come to visit him. No warm comfy Joanne at the O'Neill Center."

I gazed out at the red and yellow leaves of the trees on Copley Square. "God, honey, I don't know. Adam still needs so much care, and we're not exactly on great terms with DYFS and ARC right now—"

"Which is why this might be our last chance to have another child," Jon finished. "They think he'll become open for adoption."

He was right. Jon and I had talked about adopting more than one child; I knew Jon was eager to do it soon, but we'd never made a decision to go ahead, and I had assumed we'd wait until Adam was totally stabilized. But if we antagonized the state any further in our quest to adopt Adam, they might push us to the bottom of all their lists and we'd lose our chance to have another child. "Do you *really* believe you could handle this? Two little kids, and one of them so sick? We've been really fortunate with Adam," I said.

"Remember, God doesn't give us more than we handle."

"Okay, now let's think about this. This is very sudden. Let's hang up and *really* think about it. I'll call you back in a little while."

Jon agreed, and I called the office and spoke with Donna to tell her the news. "Oh-my-God," she said, as taken aback as I was. "So what are you going to do?"

"I don't know. It's really important to Jon. He's always wanted more than one child, and he doesn't like to wait."

Would Jon have been so eager to take on a new and very needy baby if the state hadn't nullified his parenthood of Adam? I wasn't sure. And could he really handle caring for another desperately sick infant? He was the stay-at-home parent doing the primary caregiving, and even if I'd be around more, thanks to my new job, the diaper-changing and phenobarbital-giving and baby-soothing would mostly fall to him. I sat on my too hard hotel bed and thought about all this. And I thought about baby Andrew, sick and alone and alive enough to be scared, a baby it seemed that nobody loved.

I called Jon back. "Are you sure that you can do this?"

"*Yes.* I can."

I took a deep breath. "Okay. I'm scared. But this baby needs a home. Why don't you call them and say yes." I had no idea if I was doing the right thing, but I could hear Jon's voice quicken in excitement as he started telling me his plans for getting Andrew into the upstairs bedroom, pronto.

Two days later, Jon and I drove back into Paterson—not to the O'Neill Center this time but to St. Joseph's Medical Center, the hospital where both Adam and I were born, and where Andrew had lived his whole life so far. After we had waited in the lobby for the social worker, who was late, we went up to the nursery and waited some more, until the head nurse finally noticed us and instructed us to put on gowns, to protect these immunosuppressed babies from germs on our clothes. She led us past the glass windows where all the healthy newborns were on display to a small room off to the side that housed the HIV-positive babies. The room was gray and smelled of antiseptic and nothing human; the only sound was the humming of machines that cleaned the air and the steady beep-beep-beep of heart monitors.

Three babies lay in little clear cribs, tilted up. They were wrapped in white blankets so that only their heads showed. They looked like irregular items at a white sale. One was a little African-American girl, peaceful, sleepy. Another was adorable; he looked just the way Adam had at the O'Neill Center, only healthier. The third was Andrew.

Andrew was wrinkled, his skin a reddish brown-gray. Nearly all of him was covered by a pebbly white rash. His skull was shaped like a book, flat and long on the sides, his face narrow with a misshapen mouth. His nose was nothing but two nostrils, flat against his face. His eyes bugged out like a cartoon character's. Parts of his head were shaved bald. The rest of his skull had thick black hair, pretty long for a baby.

This had to be the saddest, ugliest infant I had ever seen. Jon and I watched him a long time as he slept and as the gray room hummed. We looked at each other in shock we could not admit. Okay, he's a preemie, I said to myself; that must explain the shape of his head, and the tubes he'd had in his nostrils since birth must have pushed his nose in. They would have had to shave his head to do tests on him.

"No eat yet," said an older, friendly woman nurse in broken English. "You want to feed?"

I carefully lifted him out of the crib and felt him stiffen, as if he wasn't sure about having human contact. There was nothing to him—he couldn't have weighed more than seven pounds. He was far littler than Adam had been when we had met him, and yet he was almost the same age. He looked at me and began uttering thick grunting sounds I'd never heard a baby make before. His eyes were wide and unfocused. As I brought him close to my face, he nestled against me, suddenly comfortable, as I started to feed him. Otherwise, he didn't react much to me, except for his look of alarm when I lifted him away from my body to hand him to Jon. Jon's face was grim. This child had *visibly* been done wrong by the drugs in his system—far worse, it seemed, than Adam had been—and he was unhappy and hurting. He would need a lot from us—from a high-fat formula to loads of close attention. God, who wasn't supposed to give us more than we could handle, was giving us a *lot* to handle.

"Poor boy, no one ever comes to see him," the nice nurse said sympathetically.

"They don't come too often, huh?" I asked.

"No, no one ever comes to see this boy. Only us." She pointed to the other nurse.

After several hours of feeding, holding, and talking to Andrew, we put him back in his washtub of a plastic crib, kissed his scaly face, and walked in silence out of the hospital and toward our car. "Are you thinking what I'm thinking?" I finally asked.

"He's *so* ugly." I could hear tears in Jon's voice.

"He really is." I tossed Jon the car keys. "He really needs us."

We got in the car. "Are you sure you can do this?" I asked.

"I'm sure." Jon's voice was clipped and resolute, and that left me worried.

We brought Andrew home the next day, October 22, and installed him in his own room, our former guest room, in Adam's old crib. Adam was sleeping in the bed we'd bought him for his birthday. Just as they had nearly ten months before when Adam arrived, all of our friends and parents trouped in to see the new baby. But as they reached into his crib to hold him, I could detect a kind of trepidation on their faces I'd not seen before. It wasn't just that Andrew was so malformed looking, although that didn't help. It was how little he reacted the way we all thought a baby should: he didn't seem to respond much to care, comfort, or cooing words.

And he cried. From the first moment he came home, Andrew cried nearly all the time. He began crying the moment he woke up. He cried until he was fed, and then after he was fed, he cried some more. He wailed except when he slept. Even though he was no longer addicted to drugs, some pain in him was so profound and basic that he had no choice except to wail it out.

We held Andrew. We sang to him. We cooed, we walked him from room to room. We played music. He just cried. Nothing helped. We could not console him. It was hard even to get close to him, to play with him, because his shrieking was so loud. When he wasn't crying, he would grunt like a pig, the way he had that first day. Dorothy or Ann Mary or Grandma Grace would hold him, then hand him off to one of us when his face became a weeping fist. It was hard, to be a mother holding a baby you cannot comfort. He was making us all feel helpless.

We were in baby boot camp. At 4 A.M. when I woke for work, the house would be blessedly silent, and I would creep out, relieved to be able to go to work. Two hours later, Andrew would awake crying. His wails would wake Adam, who would climb out of bed and demand attention. Jon would attend to the now very mobile toddler while holding a screaming infant in his arms. By eight Jon would call me at the office, holding back tears, as Andrew screamed in the background so loud we could barely get words out to each other. I would come home in the evening to find Jon pale, Andrew crying, Adam pulling at my leg, and Winston the Pomeranian yapping and nipping dangerously at Adam's fingers. Jon would hand the boys off to me and go off to a twelve-step meeting. I would get to hear Andrew cry all evening as I tried to play with my newly confused and anxious older son.

Because he was no longer king of the hill, Adam was understandably jealous of Andrew. With his infant schedule of feedings and diapers and his immense hunger for simple human comforting, Andrew was demanding attention that Adam needed, and all of us knew it—including Adam. We caught on quickly. "Hey, Adam," Jon would sing out. "We're helping Andrew now. You want to help out helping Andrew?" Adam would hold Andrew's bottle as he sucked on it, studying this little baby gravely, as if recognizing a version of himself. Adam had been a very different baby, and actually a lot more had been wrong with him inside than there was with Andrew. But whenever we had given Adam some kind of treatment, such as phenobarbital, or drawn blood from him, he just bore it silently and seriously, like a wounded soldier biting on a leather strap. Poor Andrew just screamed.

Once we tried to go out for a family dinner at the local shopping center, propelling our big double stroller down the mall's main thoroughfare toward Ruby Tuesday's, with Adam in the front and Andrew bringing up the rear, sleeping. Passersby would glimpse Adam and exclaim, "Oh, what a beautiful, beautiful baby! Let me see your other one!" And they'd pull the cover back to see Andrew's squashed eggplant of a self. It was grimly amusing to see their shocked faces. They couldn't even lie. See what crack does? I wanted to say.

That night Andrew woke up during dinner. He screamed so loudly that I had to take him out of the restaurant and roll him around in his stroller as he cried, while Adam and Jon finished dinner inside. People would look at me as if I must have dusted my son in itching powder to make him scream like that. I got so many looks of disapproval that night, as if I obviously did *not* know how to be a parent or comfort my child. Then Jon spelled me with Andrew while I swallowed my cold dinner, with Adam squirming, perplexed and rambunctious, at my side. This kind of evening sure did a lot to advance our family togetherness. "It will get better," I said loudly to Jon, trying to console him as he drove home that night, the car full of squalls.

"It will get better," Dr. Fenkhart told us, "but not for a long time. He's a crack baby." He shrugged. "Crack babies cry."

Some things in this broken world cannot be amended, and we learned one of them is a crack baby's awful lament. I hate crack. I despise what it does.

I called my mother to say I understood why an unstable mother would throw her baby in a Dumpster.

"Michael, honey, I know what you're feeling—firsthand." She went on to tell me something I had never really realized. She had had to contend with infants and toddlers at the same time: my sister Karen and my brother Mark were born only thirteen months apart, at the time I was six and my sister Terri was four. "I wanted to throw you all in the Passaic River more than once. Michael, you wouldn't be normal if you didn't feel that way sometimes."

My mother's sympathy made me feel closer to her; she was treating me like a fellow parent who needed some good advice. But I was feeling less connected with Jon, who increasingly resented my low tolerance for Andrew's crying. It drove me crazy. Jon could shut down, white-knuckle it, when he had to. For him our frustrations with Andrew were part of a larger difficult picture, namely how the state continued to give us the runaround about our status as joint legal fathers. He found some solace in the hands-on practice of parenting, which even at its worst distracted him from the stonewalling he was getting from the state.

And even more was on his mind than Andrew and our battle with the New Jersey social services gulag. During one of Loretta's visits shortly after Andrew's arrival, as we tried to fill her in on the latest effort with our appeal to her employers at DYFS, Andrew lay in Adam's old baby basket on the other side of the living room, crying so loud we could barely talk. Loretta had brought us Adam's lifebook, a kind of scrapbook that ARC puts together for each preadoptive child. Even though we didn't know if we would be able to adopt jointly, the process was continuing at this level, and we now had the right to have more details of Adam's parentage and family medical history—and so would Adam.

With its colorful paper and carefully worded descriptions, the life-book was sweet and comparatively gentle in how it presented Diane, her family, and why she had had to give up a baby she loved and couldn't care for. The book also contained medical information about all of Adam's known relatives, which would be helpful later on if Adam had any further family-related health concerns. Also included was a photo of Diane—reddish hair, pretty, worn. She was sitting against the hood of a car wearing a T-shirt. Her body language said, "Okay, take the picture already!"

Jon looked up from the book and I saw he was crying.

"What's up, honey?" I asked, looking at him, then glancing at Loretta.

"Adam has this and I don't."

Ever since I'd met him back in college, a shining, sarcastic little guy—we'd spent all our free time together having fun and trading stories in the frat house about who we were—I'd known that Jon had been dogged by the fact that he didn't know anything about his birth parents. It was as if he had been plucked out of space as an infant and plopped down like an alien with a loving adoptive mother and father. On the other hand, as a son of a sprawling Italian family, with grandparents and great-grandparents in my life, I had so many family roots that they sometimes threatened to strangle me or trip me up. And now here was baby Adam, an adopted child just as his father Jon had been, but with one notable difference. Not only would Adam know at least part of his medical history, he would know—for better and for worse—where he came from.

Jon didn't have that, and I could tell how much it was hurting him early that fall. Even as Andrew cried and the state stalled us, Jon's quest to answer questions about his parentage would change our lives profoundly.

In his dogged quest to adopt Adam, Jon kept trying to reach Michelle K. Guhl, who was head of the Adoption Resource Center, but he was repeatedly diverted to a secretary at ARC, who listened with real compassion in her voice and promised to talk to someone named Charles Venti, who was Guhl's assistant and responsible for coordinating policy at ARC. Right before Thanksgiving he and Jon finally spoke on the phone. Venti had a lawyer on the line with him, and they heard Jon out and sounded sympathetic as he explained how the documents we'd received made it look as if we were approved. Our friends Kevin and Tim had previously been allowed by ARC to adopt their second son together, so there was precedent for our bid. And of course, Jon said, it was quite obviously in the best interests of Adam Galluccio to have two loving, legal fathers. "Mr. Venti, I have not yet heard anyone give one good reason why it's not in Adam's best interests to have two parents. If your department can give me *one good reason* why this is not in Adam's best interests, then I'll back off. All we are challenging you to do is to live up to your own mandate—the kids' best interests." Venti agreed that an exception to the rules was more than reasonable and left Jon with the impression that this was doable.

For three days we were hopeful, and the weather inside our little house cleared considerably, even as Andrew yelled out his pain and Adam became more and more active. Then Venti called back to say there would be no exception for us.

Jon lost it on the phone; he got pleadingly angry, amazed, and appalled that the state would thwart us. He composed himself and said, "Look, we just need to get this done. Do we have to get a lawyer?"

Venti seemed prepared for the threat. "You should be very careful about saying or doing that. There's a lot of opinionated people who might rise up and find you and cause you a lot of trouble."

This pierced Jon where he lived. "Don't even *try* to push that homophobia button on me!" Jon shot back. "Charles, don't think for a *second* that you're talking to some faggot who's so ashamed of who he is that he's going to run away and hide! I'm not ashamed of who I am, and I'm not ashamed of my family! Both of us adopting Adam is in Adam's best interests—that's just common sense. So if you think you'll stop us by talking about crosses getting burned on our front lawn, it *just won't work.*"

Venti was silent. "Well, I guess there's nothing more I can do for you. I'm sorry."

Jon took a deep breath, banged his fist on the kitchen cabinets, and called me to vent. We talked for a little while until he calmed down. "Go over their heads," I told him. "No sense holding back. Go to the top. Who's the head of DYFS?" So Jon called Patricia Balasco-Barr, the director of the entire Department of Youth and Family Services, and the boss to Malick, McGovern, Amsterdam, Venti, and Guhl, the people who had turned us down so far. But he couldn't get through to her either. Several times a day the phone would ring at my office near Rockefeller Center, and Yvonne, my assistant, would pick up and hear the furious disappointment in Jon's voice. "Hi, honey," she'd say, and put him right through. Jon always had the same news: he couldn't get to Patricia Balasco-Barr. Jon would get bounced back to Charles Venti, who didn't exactly want to hear from him. "It just *amazes* me that a system that wants to protect children *won't even take our phone calls* and we're foster parents!" Jon yelled into the phone—with me, not *at* me.

Patricia Balasco-Barr seemed as remote as the Wizard of Oz, and, we worried, she was probably about as effective to our cause. Totally disillusioned with the system, eventually we decided to circumvent her too. Although I was getting more and more nervous about challenging the higher-ups, I agreed that we should write directly to her boss, William Waldman, the state commissioner of human services, who reported directly to Christine Todd Whitman, the governor, explaining our situation in what we both agreed was a businesslike, commonsense way. For days and then weeks we heard nothing from Waldman's office.

Needless to say, it was not a happy Thanksgiving, even as we counted our considerable blessings—especially Adam's blossoming health. Invited to my parents' house in Wyckoff, we decided not to mar the occasion by discussing where we stood with the state—as Andrew screamed, Adam threw food and laughed, and we declined to eat the turkey. Being vegetarians was one more thing that separated us from our parents, and as we ate the side dishes and fed sweet potatoes, corn, and tomatoes to Adam, my mom looked put off and puzzled. Who were these people sitting at her table, and why were they risking such wrath from an unkind world?

"I have some sad news for you two," Loretta said to us during a visit the first week in December.

I tensed, and I could see Jon's eyes narrow. What now?

"Diane died last week." Loretta's eyes were cool but sad. "They found her, frozen, dead, in her boyfriend's apartment. She overdosed." She did not need to tell us it was heroin.

Our son's mother. I took Jon's hand, and he squeezed it hard. An odd kind of grief flooded through me. Jon felt something of the same thing. Diane wouldn't cause us trouble now—we'd always had nightmares that somehow she would come charging back for her son and make our lives a living hell. But any hope that she could become a positive part of our son's life was gone now too.

Donna, Diane's sister, would overdose and die a month later.

What would we tell our son about his mother's fate? We knew we would have to explain it to him someday. That will be the hardest conversation I will ever have. She suffered from the sickness of alcohol and drugs, a sickness that she couldn't bring under control, we'll tell him. She may have been too broken to do what she needed to do, and she didn't have people in her life to help her to grow stronger and rescue herself. But she loved you, Adam, and so she made you free. You can love her for that. And even as you love her, you don't have to *be* her. Her fate is not yours.

A week before Christmas, Andrew's caseworker, Jim, stopped by for his monthly visit. We sat in the living room, as usual, and went over the standard questions: health, development, milestones. During this normal conversation, Jim threw in, "By the way, I received a call from Andrew's grandmother this week."

Andrew was quiet in Jim's arms, content with a bottle in his mouth. "Andrew's grandmother? I didn't know he had a grandmother!" Jon finally pushed out.

Jim shrugged, as if this were routine news. "Well, he does, Jon, and she wants to have custody of him."

Andrew's grandmother had already taken in her four other grandsons when her daughter got in trouble with drugs and the law. While not a done deal, it was likely, Jim said, that she would be granted care of a child we weren't sure she had ever seen.

Over the past two months we had nursed Andrew into something resembling normal human babyhood; his weight was close to normal and he had become chubby and pink, with hair that grew in over a regulation-baby-shaped skull. His face had become actually cute—long eyelashes framing strong black eyes. His temperament was mellowing, and the crying, thank God, was much less frequent. Now he was going to be taken away from us. "Why her?" was Jon's first reaction, and mine too, along with "How dare she!"

Jim explained that the hospital in Paterson had screwed up—Mrs. Alvarez had gone to the hospital to see her grandchild, had discovered that he was not there, and reported him kidnapped, claiming that Andrew had never been supposed to leave. Naturally we were mad and disturbed by what was happening, first at the grandmother, and then at DYFS, which had led us to believe that Andrew would be ours. With their resistance to our joint adoption of Adam and now with their hurtful mismanagement of Andrew's case, our good experience with foster parenting was rapidly turning sour. We'd put out a lot of effort to bond with our difficult baby.

Jim didn't defend DYFS. "You should know," he said simply, "that Andrew's grandmother is a tough and caring woman. She's working full-time while raising four boys well, alternating the childcare with her husband. She doesn't have to do this, you know." The policy of DYFS was to try to keep siblings together, which we could understand, even though that prospect had spooked us so much six months before, back at Kevin and Tim's party, regarding Adam and his brother. "Mrs. Alvarez deserves our respect," Jim told us firmly. "And it's probably hard for you to hear this, but she deserves Andrew."

Neither of us was ready to hear that right away. Jon was angry and ready to fight, but we were already tangled in our battle to adopt Adam, and we probably couldn't win anyway. Moreover, as foster parents we'd been trained for this possibility—that a child could be taken away from us without notice and without our having a say in the matter. And I had to admit Mrs. Alvarez had to be a pretty caring woman in her way, if she was willing to keep working in her sixties so she could take on raising four—now five—boys. It seemed we had no choice except to defer to the rights of Andrew's closest caring relative. Jim would start establishing officially that it was in Andrew's best interests to be returned to his grandmother; in the meantime, we would take care of him and do our best to wipe away his tears. Getting him healthy so he could return to his birth family may have been the role in Andrew's life that we had been meant to have.

Whose son was Adam? Jon and I had gone to the top and had no special reason to hope. Should we just give in, let me adopt Adam as a single parent, and try to have a nice Christmas?

During the countdown to the holiday, I could see Jon's pain and frustration growing. He was the one being turned down every day, told that in the eyes of society his fatherhood didn't count. But even though I was deeply pained by what I saw Jon going through—and even as Jon vented his anger and his grief on me, in our late-night conversations and terse phone calls during the workday—I was not committed to fighting this at all costs. How could I get this issue resolved, I asked myself, and still keep everybody happy?

I'm from a big, genial family, and I had been bred to compromise. When we had first told my mother and father about what the state had done to us, my mom said, "Oh, I was so afraid this would happen. Why do you boys need to draw more attention to yourselves? *You* know you're both his fathers. Well, I guess the point is just to get Adam adopted, isn't it? You don't want to do anything to risk losing the baby, do you?"

My dad echoed that view. As a criminal defense attorney, he's seen the worst of what the world has to offer, and by temperament and profession he was inclined to settle for what he could get. Jon could maybe do a second-parent adoption of Adam later on, to cement his legal relationship with his son—assuming, of course, that he would qualify; we'd already seen the problems Tim's partner, Kevin, had encountered. But why draw attention to ourselves and maybe incite the state into taking Adam away from us after all? What if the news got out that we were two gay men trying to adopt a little boy? Maybe Aunt Angela would start handing out anti-gay-adoption pamphlets at the local Shop Rite supermarket, or her son Bob Enyart might decide to broadcast one of his hyperconservative, antigay radio talk shows from our front lawn—and then where would we be?

Jon's mom kept telling us just the opposite. By nature she was confrontational and bluntly honest about everything, and she had instilled a lot of that attitude in Jon. "What if Michael adopts him and Michael dies?" she challenged us, making a point that already haunted both Jon and me. "What right would Jon have to his son then?" What if Jon and I broke up as a couple—would Jon even have the right to see his son? We had read about several nightmare cases where lesbian or gay couples had split and the nonlegal parents found that they had no right even to see children they had helped to raise. Such scary scenarios did not happen to straight people, since even nonbiological parents would enjoy a presumed legal right to custody, visitation, and the accompanying responsibilities. But gay people had no such rights recognized. Jon's mother was right to be worried and defiant.

I was trapped between my husband and my family. I'm my father's boy, my mother's son. But I was bonded to a man who liked to fight.

We talked late one night, sitting side by side on the living room couch, after Jon had been stymied all day with phone calls to the state politely trying to get through to the elusive Patricia Balasco-Barr. "Do you understand how much this hurts me?" he asked. "*Your* name is the one on all the forms. *You* can legally be Adam's father, but I can't, and *I'm* the one who's with him all day, the one he calls for in the middle of the night when he's got an earache or he needs his diaper changed. How would you feel if the world erased *you?*"

"Jon, we've still got a shot at straightening this out, and if we don't, then as soon as Adam's adopted we can—"

Jon's eyes were afire. "Are you ashamed? You may be gay and okay that everybody knows it, but when it comes to defending our rights, defending our *son* and his right to have a secure family with *two* legal fathers, you can't just give in!"

"That's not fair. I'm not giving in. I want what you want—"

"Do you want Adam to grow up ashamed? But if we don't fight this all the way, look what we're telling him! We're telling him to lie about who his fathers are. Do you want that?"

I was silent.

"You can't let fear rule your life."

Jon was right. It hurt to say it because I just wanted the whole issue to go away, so I could concentrate on being a new father, on enjoying my son, teaching him his ABCs, his numbers, singing along with Barney. Slowly, over those hard autumn months, Jon had helped me to realize how much of my life was based on my fear of what I thought might happen. Now I was having to make some hard decisions: Who did I want to be as a father? I didn't want to teach my son to roll over. I'd been taught to do that, and it had held me back, left me feeling fearful and illegitimate when I had to interact with the outside world.

It did all come down to doing what was right for Adam. Legally and ethically, we had to make sure that we weren't going to lie to our son, to submit to the state's fake version of our family truth. Not only would acquiescing to the state do him a legal injustice, it would be a fundamental warping of the openness and no-lies attitude we wanted to instill in him.

And we would never let ourselves lose Adam. If we had to, we could run; we could go to England with Adam, the way we'd considered doing that spring when it had first seemed possible that Adam would not be our son.

"No," I said. "I want Adam to be proud of us."

"Well, Michael," Jon said, "we've come this far. Honey, we have to be ready to do what it takes."

Adam's adoption thwarted; Andrew crying constantly, yet on his way to leaving us; Diane dead; conflict and stress between Jon and me and with our families: It was a dark Christmas at our house. Compounding our pain was the loss that fall of my gruff and wonderful former boss Mike Losee, who died in an airplane crash. We were physically, emotionally, and mentally exhausted. I was still getting used to my new job and my new routine, which had me rising at four in the morning so I could take the bus to work and arrive at six to do paperwork, so I could feel justified leaving at five to come home to Jon and my children. I was helping to start a brand-new wireless business, hiring a staff, and setting up Sprint's relations to the stores that sold the company's digital service. Jon was being ground down by the uncertainty of our situation with DYFS and the stonewalling we kept facing.

This was one holiday where we would go through the motions of being a father and a daddy—not to mention being a couple—sleepwalking through the holiday, from open house to Santa's visit. Not until two days before Christmas did we finally get our act together. Just as with Adam's birthday, we were not going to let the actions of others ruin this Christmas. It was Andrew's first, and Adam's first at home. We decorated the house and shopped in a rush, spending more money than we had planned. We sang Christmas carols, hoping that our melodies could drown out Andrew's cries. We made each child his own Christmas stocking—red velvet, to which we hot-glued jewels and a pile of plastic candies. We bought Andrew gifts and clothes in a bigger size to extend our presence in his life beyond the time he would leave us, which puzzled some of our relatives, who wondered why we were spending so much effort on a child we knew we would lose.

It was a year since we had met our pale, geriatric-looking baby, swinging in his swing in that roomful of abandoned HIV-positive children at the O'Neill Center. This Christmas would be Adam's first in our household. He had bloomed so much in a year. Not only had he thrived, he had *excelled* at thriving. He was a goodwill ambassador for babyhood. Jolly as Santa, delighted at life, he was calling on us to recognize the gifts he had brought us.

One morning that Christmas season at a hospital just ten miles east of where we lived, a fourteen-year-old girl named Rosa would look through the reinforced glass of the nursery window to see her mother, wearing a surgical mask, holding up a newborn infant, tiny, bald, shriveled, and wailing.

This was Rosa's new sister, arrived just in time for Christmas. Rosa had stood at the nursery glass before, and she knew what to expect. Her life had been hard. She'd grown up fast—abandoned, abused, sexually assaulted by a grandfather, all before age eleven. The state had plucked her away from her mother. Now she was living in a group home, with other girls whose lives had been as brutal as hers. Visiting her mother was a special occasion, one full of both hope and disappointment even when there wasn't a newborn sibling to meet.

Rosa looked through the glass with a combination of excitement and sorrow. The new baby was quivery, premature, sick, full of drugs and who knew what else. She would need a lot of care, which her volatile, druggy mother couldn't give. Rosa understood what would happen to this baby. She would be detoxed in the hospital and then disappear from Rosa's life into a foster home, just as two younger siblings already had. They would not be a family. Rosa didn't even really know the woman waving at her, who came and went in her life at will.

Rosa knew the baby would disappear, a Christmas gift that had been misaddressed to her and then returned. She raised her disposable camera and snapped a picture, to say good-bye.

SIX

BIRTH FAMILY

Jon Galluccio

Adam was lucky in one way I was not. As he grew up, he would have access to at least half of his genetic medical history—the identity of his birth father was never known—so he'd know a lot more about what illnesses and medical conditions, from cancer to heart and liver disease, he might be prone to. Although his mother's life history would cause him pain, he would have some sense of where he began in the world. Unlike Adam, I never knew the identity of my birth mother. While we were trying to persuade the state to allow our joint adoption of Adam, I had a lot of moments like the one when I first looked at Adam's lifebook and saw his problematic past laid out—and found myself jealous of my baby son.

For years I had been barely curious about the identity of my birth mother—maybe because I'd always known I'd been adopted. From childhood, my mother, Ann Mary, had supplied a happy version of my nativity story: my three-year-old brother, Stephen, wanted a brother, and so they went to Catholic Charities, the adoption agency from which Stephen himself had been adopted, and he picked out the cutest baby brother available, who was me. Until I was ready to enter my teenage years, I didn't even think about having birth parents. I had enough other things to deal with. My father, Donato (Danny) Dell'Olio, had a fatal heart attack when I was ten years old. My grandmother died the next year. My mother's second husband, Joe Holden, died, also of a heart attack, when I was twelve. All three of them had died in our house. Even more than I knew, I grew up haunted by the prospect of quick death close to home, and I expected to be abandoned by people I loved.

Also around age ten or twelve, I began to be bothered by the medical forms I had to fill out in school, asking me for my family medical history, when I signed up to play a sport. All I wanted to do was to run track, in school, and here I found it frustrating and even hurtful to put down the answer "not applicable" or "no information available" and then explain why to a doctor, nurse, or coach. At the same time, I decided I had something wrong with my heart—no wonder, with two fathers dying of heart attacks in bedrooms across the hall from mine: my bedroom was next, I thought. I grew convinced I would die of a heart attack too, and I demanded to be taken for an echocardiogram. It turned out I was right, sort of: I had a mitral valve prolapse—wherein a flap in the heart ventricle falls forward and can accumulate bacteria, getting infected even after minor procedures, like getting a tooth filled. I would always take preventive antibiotics before going to the dentist. The condition was minor, it was treatable—and it was genetic. For the first time, I saw how an anonymous birth parent had affected my fate.

I first seriously considered seeking out my mother when I entered high school, because at age thirteen I was still so short, not even five feet tall. I had left grammar school as the shortest kid in my class and entered high school as the second-shortest among five hundred students. Would I ever grow tall, or even normal-sized, or was this it for me? Everyone else in my family, including my brother, Stephen, was regulation height. If I knew who my birth mother was, I told myself, then maybe I'd be able to forecast how tall I might grow, and I wouldn't feel so alone.

And I did feel alone. I wasn't just realizing that I was adopted and a leaf on some unknown family tree. I wasn't just suddenly fatherless.

Baby Jon.

I was gay too. Even though I seemed to be the perfect little kid, I decided that something had to be wrong with me, if all these people were forsaking me, and if I had these secret feelings for other males. By age thirteen I felt isolated, miserable, and sad. I started drinking. Wandering the Bergen Mall unbeknownst to my mother, I started having sex with grown men, all of them married to women. Sex made me feel like a real person.

And I underwent a bout of serious depression. That same sadness would come back in college after I met Michael, when I'd become so paralyzed with alienation that I couldn't function, for reasons I couldn't begin to locate. Even as I became more comfortable as a gay man, I wondered if I was gay because of some twist of my anonymous genes. More important to my immediate well-being, was I prone to depression because my elusive birth mother was too? How healthy was my heart, genetically? From mind to body, what unknown legacies did I carry?

Preoccupied with my career and with building a bond with Michael, I didn't think about my birth family too much in our early years together. Sometimes, when Michael's mother would trumpet the genealogical discoveries she had made about the Galluccios and show us the latest additions to the family tree she kept, I would feel hurt—not only because as Michael's partner I was left out, but because I could never explore such a tree myself. By 1994, at the time I got sober, a year and a half before Adam arrived, the ghost of my anonymous birth mother would begin to haunt me in earnest.

Our friend Kevin, a therapist, and his lover, Tim, had done a lot of work with Michael and me as we prepared to become foster parents. During a fall 1994 retreat at their shore house on New Jersey's Long Beach Island with some other friends and strangers, we participated in an exercise where all of us role-played significant people in our lives, the last one being a surprise guest. When Kevin told me that my guest was my birth mother, and a woman in the group began to speak to me as her—apologizing for leaving me behind, saying she just had to do it—the experience was so intense that I felt as if my brain had opened up and the sun was pouring in. Then clouds came, and darkness, and I became angry. My birth mother had given me up, and I was mad! How could she have done this to me? How could she have abandoned me! The rage I felt during that encounter awed Michael and scared me.

I'd never known that my feelings ran so deep. Up until now, the woman who had given birth to me had always been a fictional character in my life, an excuse for not feeling complete, a reason to consider myself a victim of fate. Now in her absence she was beginning to be real. But if she was real, who was she? Where was she? Could I run into her on a street corner, in a car wash? What if she was a drunk? If I discovered her and she was poor and needed my help, would I aid her? What if encountering me upset her and she abandoned me all over again—could I handle that trauma? What if she was dead?

One day in the winter of 1996, as I lay on the floor with Adam on my chest smiling and cooing as I talked to him, I was overcome with a real, crisp visual memory of myself as a young boy, lying on my father's chest, eye to eye with him, in the hearty grasp of a man who breathed beneath me with assurance and love. The vision shocked me: for many years I had had no true memory of my first adoptive father. Danny was just a series of stories and a few color-saturated photographs my mother would show me. Because he had died on me, he'd been too painful for me to remember, and I'd blocked him out.

Again and again when I held Adam, I felt that startling connection to Danny, the father who had held me as an infant, fed me, cuddled me, cooed with me, just as I was doing with Adam. The more I cared for Adam, the more memories would come flooding back to me of my own childhood—of riding my bike to meet my dad at the bus stop, or cuddling with him to watch TV. On some level, adopting Adam was making my own adoption right. Once I'd been the adoptee; now I could be the adopter.

But accompanying these fresh memories was a new, recurring, somewhat irrational but very real fear: that my son might lose his father at a young age, the way I had. What if I had some silent, treatable genetic defect that would rise up in me at age forty and kill me? Even though I wasn't biologically related to Danny Dell'Olio and Joe Holden, they had died without warning, and their fates tainted my own. Would I somehow bequeath fatherlessness to Adam? Was there some way I could ensure that he wouldn't go through what I had?

When Adam's case was transferred to the Adoption Resource Center and Loretta McCormick started telling us about Adam's birth mother, her sister, and their mother, my urge to reconnect with my own birth mother escalated. Yet the more I started to get a picture of Adam's birth mother, the more I realized that I didn't have any clue to what my own mother's picture might be. By that August, after Diane had signed off on the adoption for Adam and we got all of her medical history, that was it for me. Here was my son with all this medical information, all these pictures—and I had nothing. I didn't even have the sort of problematic mother Adam would have. As personal and scary as it was, I had to deal with my own origins if I wanted to be a good father. Because now I had a larger responsibility—not just to my own well-being but to establish as many connections as I could with my son.

At the very time these feelings were growing stronger, Elizabeth

McGovern and all the bureaucrats at DYFS were trying to block me from adopting my son. As my legitimacy as a father was being challenged by the state, I was spurred even more to find out and establish my own place in the world. Thanks to confronting the state week after week, I'd grown more fearless. And if I was fierce enough to stand up to a whole state bureaucracy, then I was bold enough to explore my own parentage, no matter where my searching led. Besides, Michael would be there to support me through it all.

My first tentative phone call was to an adoption-support group, to a woman named Jane Nast, whose voice exuded nearly angelic care and love, which, given the state I was in, was exactly what I needed. She seemed to know that I was calling from a spot of pain, and she was soothing, giving me answers before I could even ask the questions. "What information have you been living with so far?" she asked gently. I told her about Catholic Charities, and that my mother, Ann Mary, had a piece of paper, a court document, that had made me legally theirs. The document listed my birth date, the hospital where I was born, the law firm that had handled my adoption by the Dell'Olios, and my birth name, which was Mark Anthony Reilly.

"Oh, Jon, you are so fortunate!" Jane exclaimed. "You have so much more information than so many people! And to have an adoptive mother who is willing to help you out in your quest—that's rare. You know—I'm not sure you're ready to hear this, but . . ."

"But what?" I coaxed her.

"You'll be able to find your mother if you want to."

Jane knew immediately that the law firm that had handled my adoption was now defunct, and she told me that Catholic Charities had become helpful at reuniting children with their birth parents. She suggested the name of a private investigator, Joe Collins, whom she thought would expedite my search—that is, if I really wanted to continue with it. "Jon, it can take a lot of time and it can cost a lot of money, and there's a lot of bureaucracy to contend with. And you never know what truth you are going to find. Are you ready for the truth you think you want?"

I thanked her profusely and got off the phone and started thinking hard. Did I want to go through with this?

Without telling Michael, I called the detective, Joe Collins, a really nice guy, who agreed with Jane Nast that I had a lot of information— and a lot more would easily be available. "With Catholic Charities you're going to hit pay dirt," he told me. I could hire him, he said, but I could also go through Catholic Charities, where he had a contract; they would almost certainly hire him to take the case and give him a lot more information. Since I had a birth name, he was pretty sure he could get a first name of the birth mother and be able to locate her, or at least find out what had happened to her.

I waited a couple days until I could take a deep breath without trembling, and then I called Catholic Charities. Lisa Roser of the organization, based in Kearny, New Jersey, just outside Newark, explained to me that the group had what she called a "donation scale" that for different costs would provide me with different levels of information, depending on what I wanted to know and what information could be found out. For $75 I would receive nonidentifying details about my birth parentage—my mother's first name, her approximate age when she gave birth to me, where she was from, the names of her siblings, and any medical history they had in their files. For $425, Catholic Charities would also conduct a search for the identity and whereabouts of my birth mother, based on their records, and contact her, telling her that her son wanted to be reunited with her. That search could take up to twelve months. For $625, they would do an expedited search and hire an outside investigator, whom I knew to be Joe Collins; within six months, if possible, they would find her.

I sent the check for $75. Three afternoons later, after gnawing through all of this in my mind, I sat down at the dining room table and called Lisa Roser back to go over the schedule of fees. Michael was working back in his office. "Oh, by the way, Mr. Holden," she said, "we already have the information you've asked for. I was just about to put it in the mail to you. But I can give it to you over the phone if you want."

I went cold and hot and dizzy. "Why don't you just give me the information right now?" I heard myself say.

My birth mother was named Nancy. She had moved here from Ireland when she was twenty. She got pregnant a few months after she arrived. She had one sister, Regina, and two brothers, Frank and Conor, over in Ireland. She was five feet tall. She had dark hair and blue eyes and weighed one hundred pounds in 1963. One brother had a history of asthma.

She had lost her father when she was young.

"And your birth father's name was Richard," Lisa said. "He was born in Germany, and he was twenty-four when you were born."

When I heard that, I felt a new chill. In my years of drama over the identity of my mother, I had never imagined myself having a father. Somehow, having a birth father shocked me even more than the details of the identity of my mother. Ann Mary had been told by Catholic Charities that I was 100 percent Irish, and here was a little bit of an ethnic surprise.

I thanked Lisa Roser, lied to her and told her I was fine, hung up, and sat at the table until I stopped crying. After I'd collected myself, I went to the back of the house where Michael was working. He listened seriously as I told him what I had found out—that I'd not gotten all the medical history I'd wanted, but I knew the first name of my birth mother. She was out there, and somewhere out there was a father as well. It was as if they were beacons of light in the distance that I had to follow. I told Michael about the fees for the yearlong search and the expedited search.

Michael had supported my search all along. He had seen how I'd reacted at Kevin's retreat on Long Beach Island where I had encountered the apparition of my birth mother in the voice of another woman. He knew well what Adam had stirred in me—from the intense memories I'd reclaimed of my father Danny to my own fears that, like Danny, I would fail Adam by dying. So Michael's response didn't surprise me: "I know you. You're not going to stop now with this. You'll have to follow through to the truth."

"I don't think I can do anything else."

"Honey, you may not like what you find out. We've talked about the sweet girl who couldn't keep a baby. That may be true, based on what they said. But your mother could be someone like Diane."

"I know. I think I can handle it though. Still, it's a lot of money."

"Well, your birthday is next week. The money for the search could be your birthday present."

"You mean the money for the quick search, right?" I asked, all cute and coy.

Michael smiled. "Yeah, for the quick search. Happy birthday."

I called Catholic Charities and told them to hire the private investigator and seek out this woman Nancy.

What was I getting into?

I also had an issue even closer to home to deal with: my mother, Ann Mary. Understandably, she had been thrown off-balance and hurt when I began to tell her that, first of all, I felt angry that I had been abandoned by my birth mother. Ann Mary bristled. How could I have such ugly feelings for a woman who had suffered by giving me up at birth? Ann Mary had invested a great deal in creating a compassionate picture of the woman who had given birth to me. And how could I feel abandoned when I had been brought up with such love from Ann Mary herself? These were difficult questions to answer. But Ann Mary is a sensitive and thoughtful woman whose mind and opinions evolve. The more I talked about trying to seek out the anonymous Reilly woman who had given birth to me, the more Ann Mary came to understand that I loved her and that for my own sake and for Adam's, I needed to know the truth.

Whatever the truth was.

Both Ann Mary and Michael were right to be concerned that I would find not the mother of my dreams but somebody who would give me nightmares. "If she is a Diane, you can't go on a mission to save her," Michael told me. He was concerned I would be scorned, rejected because I was gay, or hurt or used. I knew he was right. What would happen if I expended all this time and energy to search out my birth mother, only to discover she was some aging alcoholic sitting on a barstool somewhere?

But if someone like Diane was my mother, I told myself I could deal with that. If I had to, I could keep her at the proper distance from our lives, and I could refrain from tumbling into the trap of being a child caring for a needy mother. Even though I was still furious about what the real Diane had done to Adam in the womb, I knew I had compassion for her—for what she'd gone through, the pain she'd endured. I respected that she'd been able to give up her son to people who loved him, the way Ann Mary had loved me. If I had charity for Adam's mother, I could have charity for my own.

My mother as Diane was the second-worst scenario. The worst was that I would search her out only to find she was dead.

On November 9, Lisa Roser called me to tell me that they had found Nancy. They were about to send her a registered letter saying she had a son who wanted to contact her. They needed to have a letter from me, as a follow-up for her to read, if she decided she wanted to. That night, after I had put Andrew in his crib and sung Adam to sleep in his bed, and with Michael reading over my shoulder and stroking my hand when it shook, I spent hours poring over what I had waited thirty-three years to say.

On November 13, at noontime, Nancy Henson heard the front doorbell ring at her large colonial home in Chappaqua, New York. It was the postman with a registered letter from Catholic Charities. Nancy had an unnerving idea of the letter's contents. She signed for it and, while the postman stood there, opened it and read it.

"A relative of yours," it read, "born October 26, 1963, is trying to contact you. Please reach our office immediately to advise us on whether you wish to be contacted."

Nancy was so shocked she staggered backward onto the steps in the foyer and slumped into them. The postman looked at her, concerned. "Are you okay, Mrs. Henson?"

Mrs. Henson didn't know yet if she was okay. Neither her husband of twenty-eight years nor her son knew that she had given birth to a baby thirty-three years before. She had set the trauma of her first pregnancy aside, but only with great difficulty. Now, one way or another, she had to face it again.

When she was twenty, far from her family in Ireland and working as a social secretary for a wealthy woman in Rumson, New Jersey, Nancy Reilly had begun dating a young chemist born in Germany. After two months of dating, they slept together, once. Nancy felt so guilty about having sex without being married that she would no longer return his calls. Then she found out she was pregnant. A good Catholic girl, embarrassed and humiliated, Nancy had nobody to turn to. Nancy couldn't burden her mother with what had happened to her. Better to go it alone.

When Nancy contacted the baby's father a month and a half later to tell him what had happened, he didn't want anything to do with her. Sally, another Irish girl who was a friend of Nancy's, confronted him, insisting that he pay for room and board at a home for unwed mothers run by Catholic Charities, in Newark, New Jersey. It was there, in October, that Nancy had a baby boy. She named him Mark Anthony. Eleven days later, she was told he had been adopted.

After the birth, Nancy sank into sadness that she countered for a while by swallowing Valium. Then she met a young Scandinavian immigrant named Roger Henson, who was starting his own car importing business and who rescued her from her stagnant place in life. They married in 1968. It took them two years before Nancy conceived a son, Donald, born in 1970. Nancy had thought she would never get pregnant again, that she was being punished by God for having a child out of wedlock.

She led a comfortable life, working as an office manager in a Westchester County law firm, playing bridge, gardening, raising her son. Yet every fall she would grow depressed, starting in late October and lasting through Christmas and the New Year. Her family and her friends noticed how shut down she could seem, especially at that time of year, but they didn't know what caused it, and Nancy hadn't acknowledged its source to herself. Her grief was more an absence than a presence.

She had no idea what this man, her son, would want from her. She didn't know how she wanted to respond. Her husband didn't know she had given birth to a son and allowed him to be adopted. How would he react if her past became her present?

In the twenty-four hours after she got the letter, she couldn't sleep, and when she was alone, folding laundry, raking leaves in her garden, she found herself crying. She called Catholic Charities. A woman named Lisa Roser told her that she had a letter waiting for her from her son. It was unsealed, and a copy of it would be kept on file by the adoption agency, but could they send it to her?

"No!" Nancy said. "I'll come for it." Because she didn't want her husband to know her son wanted to meet her, she would have to travel to Catholic Charities to pick up the letter. So Nancy, whose life seldom required her to get on a highway, drove from Chappaqua down through Manhattan, across the Hudson River and onto the New Jersey Turnpike, over to the industrial town of Kearny, near Newark. Looking over the carefully printed letter in a bare office, she was shocked first of all to find out that her son's name was Jon Holden. For the last thirty-three years she'd thought of him as Mark Anthony, a name Catholic Charities had told her he would keep even after his adoption.

"Dear Nancy," the letter began. "For as long as I can remember there has been a place in my heart reserved for the young Irish girl who gave me life. They tell me it is you. You see, you have always been a part of my life—a wonderful life—but there have been mysteries that only you can solve." Jon Holden wrote that he had been pondering a lot of questions major and minor, from the truth of his medical history to whether he had siblings, to how he came to be named Mark Anthony.

My guess is that I was named after Richard Burton's role in *Cleopatra,* which premiered in October of 1963. Many times I thought to search for these answers, to search for you, but I always put it off. Until now. Something has changed in me, and now I have found the courage and determination to follow this through. One thing that has changed is that I am in the process of finalizing my son Adam's adoption. Somehow I feel that I owe it to him to find you, as he will never have the opportunity—his birth mother is very ill and will not live until he's three, let alone thirty-three. Another change, possibly more important, is that I no longer need any of these answers or these mysteries solved. There were many times throughout my life when I thought having these answers would somehow help define me. Well, I'm a man now, and happily I know who I am. Finally, I believe there is a higher power that is the driving force behind my search for you— something I just can't explain, something from within. Well, it's getting late, so I will close now. I'm here when you're ready, Nancy.

Lovingly, Jon Holden, your Mark Anthony

It was strange to hold the letter in her hands, but it felt like reality too. And it intrigued her that this son had adopted a baby boy.

What would Nancy say to me? Would she even respond? Waiting for a response to my letter, I lived with unnerving uncertainty.

I talked to Adam about how I felt. At fourteen months old, he was not about to hold a conversation with me about the perils of reuniting with your long-lost mother, but I would sit holding him on my knees, facing me, and tell him how scared I was. "Am I doing the right thing?" I asked Adam. "What's she like?" I knew Adam himself would be asking these questions in a decade or two about the mother he could never find. After I'd written my first letter to Nancy, we would find out Diane had died. I didn't want Adam to be mad that I hadn't done what he could never do.

Adam would cock his head at the sound of my voice and look as if he understood. The more I talked to him, the more I was convinced I was truly searching for my mother not just for myself but for my son. He'd already been a catalyst for my quest, and maybe, thanks to my search for my own family, he would end up with a more complete sense of himself as well.

Two days later, Lisa Roser called to tell me that Nancy had come to Catholic Charities to pick up my letter. "What was she like?" I asked Lisa.

"She's like all of them," Lisa said. "Frightened, shaken up."

"Is it a good sign that she came in person for the letter?"

"I suppose. You never know." Lisa Roser was professionally reticent; she wasn't going to build up my hope, only to have to manage the fallout if things went wrong.

"What does she look like?"

"Pretty. Black hair, very fair skin. Nicely dressed. Healthy looking."

"You think she'll write me back?"

"Jon, she said she'd write you back."

Now I was more nervous than ever, waiting for her response. It came via Federal Express (Michael had supplied his company's account number, which we would reimburse). After signing for the letter I hurried to the dining room table and tore it open. Okay, this is real now, and I'm ready for this, I thought. Then I thought to myself, Maybe not. So I picked up the phone and called Michael in the city. "No, I didn't read it yet, but it's here," I blurted out as soon as he answered the call.

"Do you want me to come home now so I'm there when you do?" he asked gently.

"No, I just wanted you to know that it's here and I'm going to read it now."

"Do you want me to hold on while you read it?"

"No, honey. I have to do this by myself. But I'll call you right back. Please don't go anywhere. I might need you."

Michael agreed and I hung up and began to read.

"I have been on an emotional roller coaster since receiving your letter," she began. She introduced herself to me, describing her brothers and sister, and told me that she had not informed her husband that the son she'd had adopted had contacted her. He had heart problems due to a congenital defect—which freaked me out as the son of two fathers who had died of heart ailments—and she implied that this news would kill him. She gardened, she said. She liked to play tennis and gin rummy. Naturally, she was curious about the reaction of my adoptive mother to my search, and she seemed to want to be reassured that she would not upset the family balance if she met me. And she wanted to know more about Adam. That I was adopting my own child fascinated her.

She was testing me out, taking steps to show she was interested in connecting but was still tentative, and I understood that. Immediately I hopped in the car with Adam and Andrew and drove to Ann Mary's house, calling Michael along the way. "She's curious! She wants to meet!" I cried, promising to tell him more later.

From the start, Ann Mary's reaction to my quest had been complex, a combination of encouragement and anxiety. Probably few things are more threatening to an adoptive mother than her child's pursuit of his biological roots. Together we examined Nancy's letter like a Talmudic text, reading every line for clues to who this woman Nancy Henson really was.

"She gardens, she plays gin with her friends," Ann Mary pointed out. "That means she's got some money. A good life, probably." Ann Mary was right; Nancy's life had a Martha Stewart aura to it, which suited me just fine. One of my main nightmares had been negated, because it was clear my birth mother wasn't exactly living on the streets of New York City in a cardboard box, with a bottle of Thunderbird in one hand and a hypodermic needle in the other.

I searched Ann Mary's face for signs of what she was feeling. "You've got to have some feelings of jealousy," I said. "This has to be threatening to you."

"Oh, no, no, no. Don't be silly. You know I'm fine with it," Ann Mary said, too fast to be believed.

"You're sure?"

"Jon, this is what you need to do. I'm behind you, the whole way. Really."

"Okay," I said dubiously.

Ann Mary had to have trouble with what was happening, I told myself. Should I really push the subject with her, get her to react? "Let it go," Michael said. "She's feeling what she's feeling. Don't force her." As usual, he was giving me good advice. I took Ann Mary's words at face value. If she said she was fine with it, then she was fine with it.

One risky issue I hadn't yet brought up with Nancy was that I was gay. "Don't come out to her right away," Lisa Roser had advised me. "Birth mothers are very vulnerable during this stage in the reunification process, and you don't want to scare her off." I'd followed her counsel, and in my first letter to Nancy I hadn't even mentioned Michael's existence even as I told her about Adam. It hurt a lot to do this, because I'd spent so much of my adult life getting the world—and my own heart—to acknowledge the legitimacy of my relationship. In the past month I had been doing the same thing with DYFS nearly every day, calling foster-child officials in an attempt to get them to realize that they should recognize the bond between Michael and me for the sake of what were obviously Adam's best interests. After all that, what if Nancy abandoned me once again, this time because I was gay?

I called Lisa Roser and told her that in my next letter to Nancy I was going to come out. "Better to freak her out now rather than hit her with it later," I said. And better—less painful—to have her deny me now rather than once I'd met her and the truth came out, I thought to myself. In my family and Michael's, I'd seen mothers react different ways to their son's homosexuality, from denial and fury to grudging, growing acceptance, and I had no idea where in that continuum Nancy would fall.

Not that Nancy wasn't prepared for my coming out, as I would find out from Lisa Roser. "Jon, fact is, she's already asked me," Lisa said a little reluctantly. "I didn't answer her, of course, but the fact that you didn't mention you were married but did say you have a son—well, that may have tipped her off a bit."

I went ahead and wrote my letter, telling Nancy the core truth about myself: that I was gay and always had been, that I was lucky in having a marriage of nearly fifteen years to a wonderful man, and that we wanted to adopt our son, Adam, together and were seeking to win that right from the state I lived in. You're only as sick as your secrets, the twelve-step programs tell you, and because I didn't have any more secrets from a birth mother I had never met, at least I felt healthy. The rest was in Nancy's hands.

She wanted to meet me. Lisa Roser forwarded to me Nancy's next letter suggesting we meet face-to-face, on December 16, at Catholic Charities. As I searched the friendly but cautious phrases of her letters for their true meanings, I still wondered if I was going to meet a woman who would give me a cheery, political-wife smile, shake my hand, and say, "Nice to meet you—now go have a nice life." Yet would I want more from her than that? The more I pored over these questions, the less I could answer them. I wouldn't know what I wanted from Nancy until my eyes met hers.

The night of December 15 I couldn't sleep. I was going over in my head all the possible scenarios for my meeting with Nancy Henson. Still, I got out of bed full of energy and dumb hope.

"I'm so jealous I can't be there with you today," Michael said as he ran for the bus to Manhattan that morning. "Call me first thing when you get back, okay?"

"Yeah, if I don't drive the car over a cliff afterward."

Michael laughed. "You do that and I'll kill you."

Ann Mary came by to look after Adam, who had pulled me out of bed at seven this morning to be fed, and Andrew, who noted the momentous occasion by falling asleep after breakfast without crying. I could tell Ann Mary was as nervous as I was. Over the last couple weeks as I'd corresponded with Nancy, Ann Mary had become more short-tempered and abrupt, and her protestations that she was fine with my search for my birth mother had grown a little thin. Now as I left the house, my stomach too knotted to eat breakfast, she handed me an envelope. "Read this and then give it to Nancy. It's a letter welcoming her into your life." She kissed me and smiled. "Good luck. We love you." I was more grateful than I could say.

Dressed in khakis and a blue, button-down shirt, I got into my kid-battered hunter-green Grand Am and drove down the New Jersey Turnpike to Route 287 as if on autopilot and made my way through the region's warehouses and rusty factories. Beside me was a photo album that Ann Mary had assembled for me years before when Michael and I moved to California after college. Determined not to let me forget who I was or what family I had come from, she had put together photos of me from age eleven days to age eighteen—my first day of kindergarten, crew-cut and scared; my first Communion, looking more impish than pious; various birthday cakes and candles; my father and stepfather; and a picture of me from junior year in high school sporting a huge blond Afro of a perm, which I wasn't so sure I wanted to inflict on Nancy Henson. And in my wallet were photos of Adam,

Andrew, my parents, and Michael, which I hoped I would want to show.

Catholic Charities was located in a defunct Catholic high school, at the top of a hill, surrounded by winter-bare trees. I drove into the parking lot and pulled in next to a hunter-green Volvo sedan. It had to be hers, I decided; I could feel it.

I was buzzed in and walked down the main hall, getting directions from the receptionist to Lisa Roser's office. I was just seconds away from meeting my birth mother, and I had never been so nervous in my entire life. Carrying the photo album in a canvas tote bag, and wearing the brown overcoat I'd worn the day I'd met Adam at the O'Neill Center nearly a year before, I made myself knock on Lisa Roser's door. Just on the other side of it . . .

Lisa Roser, small, perky, opened her office door. "Jon?"

"Uh, yes."

"Come on in."

I stepped inside. The office was empty. No Nancy. Then whose hunter-green Volvo was that in the parking lot?

"You okay? You sleep okay?"

"No." Where was Nancy? Oh, of course: Lisa Roser was going to prep me first.

"Okay. Well, she's here. She's in the next room."

I could have wet myself. This was really happening. "Now I know you're both nervous about this, so just take it easy, relax, see what happens, okay?" Lisa patted my arm. "You feel you're ready?"

"Ready as I'll ever be." I popped a breath mint into my mouth.

"Then let's go."

Lisa led me to the next door on the hallway and opened it.

Nancy was sitting and rose to her feet. She looked at me and cried out.

She took two steps, I took steps, and before we said a word we were hugging. She was sobbing, and I guess I was sobbing too, but I couldn't hear myself over what sounded to me like wailing—a combination of grieving and celebration. She was shaking, trembling in my arms. I trembled in hers.

We held each other for whole minutes, hours it seemed. The entire time as I stood there crying, feeling Nancy's keening, I saw in my mind's eye the brief glimpse I'd had of her face, the instant before we hugged. Framed in silky black hair, her face was full of pain, her mouth open in the beginning of her cry—and in the middle of her face were my eyes.

Had I seen right? Had I really seen my own eyes? I wanted to step back and gaze at her, but I couldn't let go of her. I've always been told I couldn't hug people, that I had to let go of them before they let go of me so I wouldn't feel abandoned. This was the first time I wanted to hold someone and not let go. And she was squeezing me as if she'd never let go of me ever again.

We broke apart enough to step back, holding each other's hands. I slowly lifted my head and so did she. I looked into her eyes. She was crying. In that small portion of her face, I could have been looking into a mirror. Her eyes were mine.

For the first time I understood what biology meant, how our common blood calls us back to each other. It wasn't just my medical history that I was after—I'd always known in my heart that my worries over my heart's health were a pretext, a metaphor for what I really sought. What I was hoping for was this very thing, this dramatic, electric connection. As we looked at each other, another vision flew into my head: to my shock, I saw myself actually being born—emerging from the birth canal into the world. This was something that quite simply I had never thought about.

Her breath was sweet, minty. She'd done what I'd done—I had to chuckle. We sat ourselves down in a couple of drab institutional-green leather chairs and started to talk, still holding hands. Lisa Roser receded. Now, after the initial rush of contact, Nancy was coming into focus for me as a real person. She was wearing a charcoal gray suit and a blue silk blouse—very Ann Taylor—that brought out her eyes, complete with a black patent leather purse and shoes. They were perfect, unsmudged, which made them appear strange to me, coming from a house of infants and toddlers where everything has fingerprints on it. Delicate but athletic, she was naturally pale, very Black Irish, and paler than usual of course today, except for her reddened eyes, which were still a brilliant blue. It would be several meetings before I could handle the truth of her eyes.

To this day I'm not sure exactly what we said to each other—our words were halting, tear-choked exclamations, punctuated with laughs and sighs of shock and relief. I do remember saying what I felt—"I can't stop looking at your eyes."

"Why?" she asked, but I think she knew what I was going to say, because she was looking at me the same way. "Is there something wrong?"

"You have the same eyes as me. No," I corrected myself, "I have the same eyes as you."

She just kept gazing at me. After a while we took deep breaths and began to make words and sentences, like normal people, trying to manage the charge between us and our huge disbelief that this conversation was even happening at all. She told me that her husband knew about me now and knew she was there. "I just had to tell him I was coming here. He's not happy about it—this whole thing has made him very nervous. But nothing would stop me from being here today." She looked at me and smiled. I could hear only the faintest Irish lilt in her voice. "I think my husband is going to understand."

I told her about Michael, opened my photo album, and flipped through it as Nancy blinked at the pictures, trying to absorb some thirty-three years in almost that few seconds. I told her about Ann Mary, what a wonderful mother I had, how I'd grown up knowing I was loved. Nancy listened carefully, pondering all this, still crying. I handed her the letter from Ann Mary, expressing her support for my search, which Nancy examined thoughtfully and then put in her purse to read later.

I told her about Adam and Andrew and showed her pictures of them. "It sounds like you have a handful at home," she told me. "I remember what it's like having a small child in the house." She looked stricken when I told her we were losing Andrew, that within a few weeks we would return him to the care of his grandmother. I realized that it made sense that it would bother her so immediately—after all, she could recall something of the pain that comes when parents have to give up their children. Then she asked more about Adam, listening carefully to every detail of how he had come to us, and how his birth mother had died two weeks before. That pained Nancy. When I told her I was having trouble adopting Adam, she didn't comprehend at first why Michael didn't adopt him alone and let me join in later. I let that concern pass for now, because I had so many other questions. "Why was I named Mark Anthony?" I asked.

Nancy smiled, almost girlishly. "Oh, it was my favorite name. No other reason. Why did you choose the name Adam?"

"I named him after my parents and Michael's parents. Adolph, Dorothy, Donato, Ann Mary."

My parents: a myriad of expressions crossed her face when I told her that. I almost wished I hadn't.

"You know," she said, "I admire what you are doing with Adam. And Andrew. It's a very hard thing, very brave."

There were volumes in her words. "Thank you," I said.

I had to go; she had to go. We said good-bye to Lisa Roser, who looked relieved to see us arm in arm, and walked into the parking lot together. "There are Christmas presents for you in the trunk," she said, pointing toward that hunter-green Volvo sedan parked right next to my hunter-green Grand Am.

"Well, this is already a typical mother-son relationship, because I don't have anything for you," I said, chuckling through my embarrassment.

She smiled, opened the trunk, wearing her dainty leather gloves, and handed me a number of wrapped boxes. "These are for your children, and these"—she gave me two book-shaped presents—"are for you. Now, don't you open them until you get home!"

"I won't, I promise." I stashed the gifts in the backseat of the Grand Am and straightened up to meet those amazingly familiar blue eyes. "Well, I better go." I didn't want to leave.

"I better go too." I could tell she didn't want to leave.

"Well, then, I guess you have to go," I said, gulping down tears.

"And I guess you have to as well."

We waited a second. Nobody moved. "Well, then, go!" she said, laughing.

"Okay, I'll go!" I laughed too.

We parted, hugging, hugging some more, and promising to get together and talk soon. I think we both realized that we would each need time to absorb the implications of our reunion and figure out how we could relate to each other from here. I drove out of the Catholic Charities parking lot, waving good-bye the whole way, made a right-hand turn, drove five blocks, pulled over, reached into the backseat, and ripped open my gifts. So much for waiting until I got home.

She had given me a copy of *The Christmas Box,* a tale of holiday reconciliation between parent and child, and a book of short stories by Irish writers—Nancy was reminding me where I came from.

I called Michael from my mobile phone. "Well, I did it. I have a birth mother."

"Oh, honey, terrific. Details! Give me details!"

"It just kind of happened." I could hear the dumb awe in my voice. "Mostly we just looked at each other." I couldn't explain it to him yet.

"And how do you feel?" Michael's voice was tentative, concerned.

"Wonderful. Exhausted. Thank you, honey."

I drove home on autopilot again. The world I was returning to had its wearying difficulties—the struggle with the state to get their consent for our joint adoption of a child who had just lost his birth mother, the impending sorrow of having to surrender our difficult, lovable Andrew—but now it all felt different somehow, clarified and renewed. Ann Mary heard my car and met me at the door; she had just put Adam and Andrew down for a nap. Her face was full of tenderness and also worry—for me, for herself. I hugged her hard before I said a word.

"Well, is she rich?" Ann Mary joked with a nervous laugh.

"No, but we did get Christmas presents."

As I told her about my reunion with Nancy, I opened the kids' presents. Nancy had given Adam a Fisher-Price basketball set and Andrew a *Sesame Street* activity blanket. As I finished my story, Ann Mary looked thoughtfully down at the gifts. "The kids can call her Nana," she said. "I think that's what the Irish call their grandmothers."

I looked up at her and smiled, then hugged her. Our family had just grown.

———

I called Nancy to wish her a Merry Christmas, then met her briefly just before the New Year, when she and Roger Henson were about to go away for a winter vacation in the Caribbean. We met at the Westchester Mall for a casual, conversational lunch and an exchange of gifts. I gave her a gold bangle bracelet Nancy swore she would never take off. As I had suspected, we both needed some space to put our experiences into perspective. We knew we had plenty of time, and that was a huge relief. We would meet again after her return from Jamaica. Then the slow and tender business of introducing each other to our families and our lives would begin.

In the weeks after my first meeting with Nancy I had grown increasingly hung up on the identity and whereabouts of my father. Nancy couldn't be much help beyond providing his name, which I already knew, nor did Catholic Charities have any further information about him. But assuming the man still lived in New Jersey and still worked as a chemist, I was able to narrow down the list of possible candidates to one. What was harder was coming up with the guts to make a cold call to the man I was sure had fathered me.

On the afternoon of January 3, I found myself sitting on my bed, dialing Richard Hartman's telephone number at work. The receptionist put me through.

"Hartman!" a voice barked into the phone.

I went cold and almost hung up the phone. "Is this Richard Hartman?"

"Yes, it is," said the voice—tough, no-nonsense. "Who is this?"

"Hi, this is Jon Holden." I rushed the words out. "I'm afraid this is a difficult conversation to start—but did you know a Nancy Reilly?"

"No, I don't think I do."

"Well, it's not someone you know now. It's someone you would have known thirty-three years ago."

"That was a long time ago." Richard Hartman's voice was wary now. "I'm not sure."

"I'll refresh your memory. And I'm sorry to be calling you at the office, but I didn't know how else to reach you. You see, I was adopted, and I decided last fall to search for my birth mother because I really wanted my medical history. I was successful, because I found my birth mother, Nancy Reilly. She's been very good in supplying me the medical information I wanted. But now I have only half of the history, because I need information from my birth father too. And that would be why I'm calling you."

There was a pause on the line. "What do you mean?"

"Well, you're my birth father."

"How do you know that?"

"From talking to Nancy and from talking to Catholic Charities."

"That was thirty-three years ago. I don't know who you could be talking about. And how do we know that it would be me?"

The man was grasping, I could tell. "For one thing, Nancy claims that she slept with only one person, a man named Richard Hartman who worked at your firm and who lived in Edison, New Jersey. And there's only one man with this name that has lived and worked in the same place then and now."

"My memory's not very good for events back then," Richard Hartman said evenly.

I could feel him receding from me. I knew what he was thinking—this voice on the phone was an unwelcome blast from the past, one that could cause him all kinds of uproar. "Listen, I just want you to know I'm not some sort of crackpot. I just want my medical history. I know this is a shock, sir. It was a shock for me too. So can I give you a little time to think about it? How about I call you next week?"

"You can call in a week, but I can't guarantee I'll remember anything."

"Okay, well, I'll call. Thank you very much."

I hung up the phone, felt my heart spinning in my chest, stewed for three days, and called him again. "Hi, this is Jon Holden again. We talked just a few days ago? I said I'd call back in a week, but I couldn't wait."

"Like I told you—"

"It seems odd that you wouldn't remember, since you had to pay Catholic Charities for Nancy's room and board."

"Yes," he said simply. "I remember."

"I'm not looking to cause you any trouble," I rushed to say. "I just really would like my medical history." I wanted more than that, I knew, but that was all I could tell him.

Richard Hartman rattled off some rough information. His parents had divorced and remarried and gone to separate European countries. He hadn't talked to his father in over thirty years—another lost father, I thought—but he had heard that the man was still alive. He hadn't seen his mother in a decade, but she was healthy too. No cancer, no heart disease, no mental problems. The internationally dysfunctional family he described was alive and well.

All this was hard to hear. The door that I had managed to pry open with my questions about my genetic background was about to close—I could hear it creaking. "I know I said what I just wanted from you was my medical history," I said, my throat tight. "But that's not the whole truth. I would very much like to meet you."

There was a pause on the line. "I don't see why we would need to meet," my father said.

"What do you look like?" I was getting desperate, trying not to cry or yell on the phone. "Could I see a picture?"

"No, I don't think so."

"Would you think about this? You're my birth father. It would be nice of you to do." I had another thought. "By the way, you haven't told me—do you have any children? That kind of medical-history stuff is especially important if one of them needs a kidney or bone marrow. I could match." I was straining, I knew it.

"I don't want to get my children involved in this."

"Could you at least promise me that you'll think about it? If only for a kidney?"

"Okay."

"Well. Okay then." I couldn't think of anything else to ask for. I gave him my name and phone number. We said good-bye.

I hung up the phone and flopped back on the bed. Adam and Andrew were napping, Michael was away at work—I would call him in a minute, and he would comfort me as he knew so well how to do. Richard Hartman had admitted he was my father. I had wrested a barely useful medical history from him. But the longer I thought about this, staring at the silent phone, the more my anger swelled. I felt angry as well for Nancy, who had been more or less abandoned by this man the way I had been moments before. I had lost my adoptive father and my stepfather by the time I was twelve; now I'd lost another, sort of, whom I never knew I had.

When I told Nancy about my conversations with Richard Hartman, she was hurt that he had hurt me. So were the other loved ones in my life. "Focus on the parent who wants you," Bill W., my twelve-step sponsor, encouraged me. And whenever I think of my birth father, I recall the precious advice Michael gave me that night, after I had put Andrew and Adam to bed for the night and was trying to sing Andrew from tears into sleep: "You can be the father he wasn't. You can be the fathers you've lost."

On January 14, 1997, I looked out the window and saw a hunter-green Volvo sedan pull into our driveway. Just back from Jamaica, Nancy Henson was here to meet Michael, Andrew, and Adam.

Michael peeked through the curtain of the front window, anxious and excited. "Oh, she's tan," he said. "And she's got more gifts!" He turned to me grinning. Michael had told me I had become a different man over the last few weeks. It was as if a light had gone on in me, he said, and I had won a new kind of serenity. Now he was about to meet the woman who had helped me complete my life—who for him was "one more mother-in-law," as Michael had slyly put it.

Nancy entered our house a little tentatively, as if she wasn't sure she yet belonged here. In her arms were Caribbean souvenirs—T-shirts for the kids, coffee for Michael and me—that I took from her so that I could hug her. I could feel her tremble just a little; her nerves matched my own. I introduced her to Michael, and I could tell by the spontaneous smile on his face that he felt an immediate connection with this woman as he took her hand. And I saw him see my eyes in hers.

In her face I could see the beginnings of a bond with him too; she already knew enough from me to be grateful for all he had done for me, working so hard to build our relationship over the last fifteen years, standing by me when I went into recovery, and coparenting the two babies who were now clamoring for attention.

Andrew sat in his swing, making something like laughing sounds. Adam, now sixteen months old, eyed this new woman in his life as he stood and gave her a widening smile.

"Adam, this is your Nana," I said.

"Hello, Adam," said my birth mother, kneeling down and opening her arms. Adam burst into motion, running and tumbling across the room, his face alight. Maybe he too recognized his father in her eyes.

Adam fell into her embrace and she hugged him. She looked up at Michael, then at me, and I watched her face grow from grandmotherly delight to maternal command. "You have to adopt this child—both of you," she said as her grandson nestled against her.

SEVEN

EXTENDED FAMILY

Michael Galluccio

"DYFS policy limits the consent to adopt to one person when two single or unmarried people are seeking to adopt," wrote Division of Youth and Family Services director Patricia Balasco-Barr to Jon and me on February 20. There was no way—no way—that she or her boss, Department of Human Services Commissioner William Waldman, would make an exception that would let us adopt Adam the way a married heterosexual couple could.

Even amid the joy of Jon's reunion with his birth mother, everything was so heavy for us that New Year. Our son's birth mother, Diane, had died, which was very sad; we were preparing to return Andrew to his grandmother and grandfather; and now we had to figure out how we would handle this final no from the state.

Don't fight this, Billy DeMarco was advising us. He could do little anyway. Dorothy and Adolph agreed with him, smothering us with their fear masked in sympathy. In the kindest tones they would tell me, Don't risk any more; just get your son into that house legally.

Should we just give in? If we challenged the state further, would

Adam be taken away from us? The state's pronouncement was a contradiction of all we had worked to accomplish, both in bringing Adam into our home and in developing our lives as a proud and assured partnership. The more we discussed it—with Adam bouncing in his chair held by a spring in the archway between our living room and dining room—the more we felt we just couldn't accept this decision without fighting it to the bitter end. To give in, to have me adopt Adam singly, with Jon to join in a so-called second-parent adoption at some vague later date—it wasn't fair to Jon, who was now spending all of his time teaching our son to feed himself and talk. But even more than that, it wasn't fair to Adam. An orphan who was a ward of the state, Adam deserved two parents who were legally recognized as his guardians. If I, his legally "single" parent, were to die suddenly, Adam would be orphaned once again. In the eyes of the law—as personified by the judge who had given Tim and Kevin such a hard time in adopting Corey—Jon, the man who raised Adam, would have no right to his son.

Nor did we want to bring up Adam in secrecy and shame. From the beginning, we resolved we would always be open and honest with our children. When they were of an age when they could understand it, we would tell them about where they came from, who their birth parents were, and what they themselves had struggled with as infants. We would also tell them the truth about their adoptive parents. Now DYFS was asking us to agree to a lie. As we played in our family room with Adam and saw how within just a few years he would begin to ask us some hard questions, we realized we had no choice but to fight to reverse the state's decree.

But how? We didn't know where to turn. As a resource we went to Lambda Families of New Jersey, a group of lesbian and gay parents who got together to provide each other with social and moral support, as well as a chance for their kids to play with children from like-minded families. Tim Fisher, chairman of the executive committee, advised Jon to call a professor at American University, Nancy Polikoff, the leading expert on adoption case law for lesbian and gay couples. Professor Polikoff referred us to Matt Coles, the executive director of the American Civil Liberties Union's Lesbian and Gay Rights Project. Jon left a pleading message with Coles.

Matt Coles called Jon back that day. After Jon told him the entire misadventure of Adam's adoption status, Coles said, "Well, if everything you say is true and you have the documentation you say you have that lists you both as preadoptive foster and adoptive parents, then we'd be more than interested in helping you out and taking the case." When Jon called to tell me, he was practically dancing.

Michael Adams, a lawyer with the Lesbian and Gay Rights Project of the ACLU, called Jon the next day, saying he would be our lawyer on the case if the ACLU took it on, in concert with Lenora Lapidus, of the New Jersey state division of the ACLU.

I was not at all thrilled that the ACLU wanted to come to our rescue. I'd been taught at my lawyer father's knee that ACLU attorneys were out to make waves and news, their clients be damned. Still, I realized I didn't have too much of a choice. Billy DeMarco wasn't charging us anything; if we wanted to pursue this with a private attorney, we would have to pay for it, and we were under severe financial constraints despite my new job, with a house to pay for and a lot of bills. Moreover, at least an advocate attorney would believe in our case.

Even though I was uncomfortable with getting the ACLU involved, I was getting more comfortable with letting Jon take the initiative. Jon was receiving a lot of help from Bill W., his twelve-step sponsor, as he had all fall. "God didn't bring you this far just to let you down," Bill W. told him. But I was also able to give Jon greater support than I had, because I felt more resolved than I had before the holidays that we were doing the right thing.

Jon had really impressed me over the previous months with how well he had been able to *manage* our parenting challenges. As a father, he had taught Adam to walk and to eat with a spoon. He could hold a wailing Andrew to his chest and smile at the same time. As hard as it was, he'd agreed to surrender Andrew and had not fallen apart. He'd taken a huge risk in seeking out his birth mother and reconnecting with her. And he had been persistent in the grunt work of challenging a sluggish and callous state bureaucracy. In our nearly fifteen years together I'd seen Jon go through a lot of trials and grow as a result, but in the last twelve months I'd witnessed his nurturance, his smarts, and his grit and determination more than I ever had before.

He had done a tremendous job taking care of his family, without losing any of the sensitivity I'd always valued in him. He didn't need to be taken care of more than your average human being did, and he was able to minister to others. Together with the unconditional love I gave him as my husband, I felt a new kind of bond—the love earned from hard work and crises faced. I trusted him to lead the way.

On February 27, a clear, cold, windy day, I stayed home from work to meet with the ACLU people and to return Andrew to his grandparents.

It hurt just looking at Andrew that morning, dressing him and packing his baby toys and clothes. Jon had just bought him a lot of clothes to grow into in his new life, and we'd provided him with new bottles as well as rattles, teething rings, and a teddy bear. His Christmas stocking, a red velvet affair with a huge letter A written across it in glitter glue that matched Adam's, was the hardest thing to pack. In his future Christmases, Andrew might not remember us, but he would know we had given him something. I wrapped it carefully in tissue, put it in a department-store shirt box, and taped it shut.

Jon was in bad shape that morning, maybe because he'd already met Andrew's grandmother in preparatory visits at DYFS headquarters and the impending transaction was more real to him than it was to me. "We knew this could happen. This is part of foster care," I said, trying to comfort him. "He'll be with his birth family, and they love him."

"Those people are too old—in their sixties, with four boys to take care of already. How can they give Andrew the attention he needs?"

I couldn't answer that. Maybe our role was to make Andrew healthy, in a home without a lot of children where he could get a great deal of special care, and then return him to his blood family.

Andrew was so darn cute—finally. He was much chubbier, up to twenty-two pounds by now. At last he looked like a real baby, smiling and laughing, and he was Adam's best pal. He was still testing HIV-positive and was on Bactrim to prevent pneumonia, but like Adam his overall health suggested he was on the way to losing his HIV antibodies. As I put him down for his morning nap, I realized how central children

were to my life's purpose—which made me feel even more determined
to do whatever was required to protect Adam.

The doorbell rang precisely at 11 A.M. I dashed downstairs to greet
the ACLU lawyers. Michael Adams was a severely handsome man, his
speech rapid, cool, yet urgent. He wore a lawyerly tie knotted at a
collar that rather endearingly looked to be one size too small. Lenora
Lapidus, from the New Jersey ACLU office, was sleek and compact,
sporting a black pantsuit and blessed with a pair of sensationally pronounced, manicured black eyebrows. In contrast to Michael, she
seemed gentler and less urgent, but I knew immediately she was not
someone to mess with. "Can we meet Adam?" Lenora asked immediately, which made me feel good.

We led them upstairs so that they could admire the napping child
whose rights they'd be defending. And we explained about Andrew as
well—that this was his last morning in our house, and that we were
sad. Michael and Lenora listened sympathetically.

Gay protocol would have us serve a fabulous tea to our guests, but
Michael and Lenora had to settle for coffee and an Entenmann's
cheese roll, the kind of thing a harried parent picks up at the 7-Eleven.
As Jon finished packing Andrew's clothes, and we signed papers officially designating them our lawyers, I got down to business right away.
As uncomfortable as it made me feel, I had to be honest with these
civil rights activists and tell them how I felt about their organization.
"I'm glad you want to represent us," I began, "but you need to know
up front that I don't trust the ACLU—nothing personal, but my per-
ception is that the ACLU takes a case and then throws your name
around the media and exploits you for their own causes. My father's a
lawyer, and that's what I grew up believing. But Jon thinks this is a
good idea, and because I love and trust Jon, and because I don't know
how else we can do what we need to do, I'm going to go along with
this."

Michael and Lenora were listening.

"And I'm telling you right now," I went on, "you are not going to
put me or my family in the media circus. This is about my child and
his best interests, and this is going to be a private, family matter." I
knew I didn't sound like my usual conciliatory self, but this was vital.

Michael Adams looked me in the eye and nodded. "I understand your reservations. This is your family, and you have a right to remain private—that's part of what the ACLU fights for. And we agree with you totally. Lenora and I have discussed this, and we believe we can make our point with the state and get them to change their policy without making your name public in any way."

Those forthright words relieved me. With Jon interrupting to comment and elaborate, I smoothed my feathers and went on to explain the history of our foster parenting and adoption appeal. We showed Michael and Lenora the letters from the state that showed Jon and I were an approved foster family and later an approved adoptive family. We showed them Adam's foster-parent identification letter, which listed both of us as Adam's foster parents, and Adam's plan from Loretta McCormick, which declared we were both going to be adopting Adam. And beyond our legal foundation we felt we had a compelling moral argument: we had taken an unwanted, deathly sick little baby, nursed him to health, and provided him with a stable home that gave him nurture and love. Wasn't it in Adam's best interests for the state to give him two parents to provide him love and security?

Michael and Lenora were clearly impressed. "You have a strong case," Michael told us. "With what you're telling us, we can make an incredibly persuasive argument to the Division of Youth and Family Services that their policy makes no sense, that they *know* their policy makes no sense, and that they have to change it. And besides, in New Jersey we have a legal precedent." Lenora went on to remind us of a case we already knew: two years before, a lesbian named Joan Garry had appealed to the New Jersey State Supreme Court and won the right to adopt her partner's biological child as a "second parent adoption." Her case was one reason we'd felt comfortable moving to New Jersey.

"Now you've got to get them to change the policy on joint adoption, both for Adam's best interests, and because you might want another child, and for other parents like yourself—and their children," Michael said. "We have the compelling evidence to make them do that." They wouldn't need to start by filing a lawsuit. We would have to remove Billy DeMarco from the case, which we already knew, and bring in someone else in concert with the ACLU strategy. Michael suggested a lawyer from the Joan Garry case, who could serve as our private attorney in concert with the ACLU.

Taking what we had been saying to DYFS and putting it into legalese, Michael and Lenora would jointly ratchet up the pressure on the state and, if necessary, lobby Peter Verniero, the state attorney general, to get the joint-parent prohibition rescinded. That would be a victory for lesbian and gay rights. However, just as Joan Garry had won her victory as the anonymous plaintiff "J. M. G." (later, as executive director of the Gay and Lesbian Alliance Against Defamation, she would make known her role in the case), we too could remain private in our success. We knew our case would set an important precedent. That suited us just fine: The ACLU would get the policy changed for unmarried parental couples in New Jersey, and we would get to adopt Adam together without having our names or faces, or Adam's, out in the world.

By now Andrew was out of his crib, sitting on the floor, as Jon dressed him in a green jumper and dress shirt, with little blue shoes, so that he would look sharp when he joined his brothers. Jon was trying not to cry, but his hands shook. The phone began ringing. Nancy called to give moral support for our return of Andrew to his family and to tell us she was there if we needed her. My mother phoned, wringing her emotional handkerchief on our behalf, and then my sisters called, Terri and Karen, one right after the other—everyone trying to ease us through the shock of returning Andrew, even as we had lawyers in the living room preparing to fight for Adam. When the phone rang a fifth time, I told Jon to let the machine pick up. But he sighed and heaved to his feet and apologized to Michael and Lenora, who watched in awe as he handed off Andrew and his bottle to me as efficiently as a football.

"Hi, Jean," Jon said, loud enough so I could hear. I knew that this had to be the placement specialist from DYFS who had called to offer us both Adam and Andrew. I thought she must be calling to see how we were doing with returning Andrew. But by the bewildered look on Jon's face, I knew something was up.

"I have some babies you might be interested in," Jean was telling Jon. Before Jon could interrupt her, she added, "Four infant boys. Each one has special circumstances."

Andrew, transformed from such a horribly ill infant to a regular baby boy. This photo was taken during our last hours with him.

"Jean—"

"The first one, six months old, born with drugs in his system, HIV-positive, three months premature, much more premature than Adam. He has four siblings, all positive. I'm afraid the last two developed full-blown AIDS."

"Jean, we're just getting ready to surrender one child. Right now I couldn't possibly consider taking a baby that could die." Jon was seeing Abdulla, the baby he and I had encountered, his eyes huge, in the rocker at the O'Neill Center the day we'd picked up Adam—the child we had left behind. But Jon and I had agreed that before we considered taking in another foster child we would both need time to work through the pain we felt around losing Andrew.

"Well, there's another baby boy, two months old, HIV-indeterminate—antibody only, no evidence of the virus—low birth weight. His records look good. However, there's definitely some neu-rological problem. It might be Down's syndrome—it's too early to tell."

Jon leaned his head tiredly against the kitchen cabinets. "Jean, we can't. Adam is so active right now, and he needs so much attention from us, that I don't see how we could give both him and another *really* medically fragile baby the care they need. I'm sorry—"

"Okay. Well"—Jon heard papers rustling—"then this next one's out."

"Thank you," Jon said.

"Thank me for what?"

"For sparing me the details so I don't have to say no again. I hate this."

"I only have one more," Jean said hopefully, forever the saleslady of abandoned children. "This one's a child who's easier to manage because he's older, eight months. He's testing well. But his problems are going to be in the future."

"Why?"

"His left leg is significantly shorter than his right, but with some physical therapy he could begin to move around. He's got HIV but the signs are good he'll test negative."

Jon pictured a child on crutches, with Adam bounding around him. "Jean, I'm tempted. But I don't think we could manage a child like that and deal with Adam at the same time. Adam's needs have to be primary—especially after all we've gone through with Andrew. You're making me feel awful. Don't you have any girls at that place?" Jon asked jokingly. "Is it a gay thing that you don't offer the gay couple any girls?" He knew the answer to that question—there just weren't that many girls in foster care.

There was a pause on the line. "Isn't that funny." Jon could hear some more papers shuffling. "They just put a file on my desk, and it's for a baby girl."

"Oh *really*."

"She's in pretty good health." Jean began reciting from the file. "Two and a half months old. Latino, born premature, very low birth weight but thriving, tested positive for heroin at birth but had no physical withdrawal symptoms. She's HIV-antibody-positive, but they just did a PCR test for the actual virus and the results haven't come in yet. The mother has had five children in the system. One of them, a teenage girl, is in the foster care system and another is an adult on her own.

The last two have been through DYFS and have been adopted. This new one—she's a beautiful, stunning little girl."

"Michael!" Jon cried to me.

I excused myself from our very patient legal counsels, grabbed Andrew off the carpet, and came in to see what Jon was yelling about. He quickly explained what Jean had told him: There was a baby girl for us. I couldn't believe it.

Jon filled me in on the baby's vitals while Jean waited for our answer. "What do you think?" he asked. He tried to keep the question neutral, but on his face was the most imploring look I had ever seen, a look that said, *Please, can we?* I had heard that tone of voice when he'd called me in my Boston hotel room that October to tell me about Andrew.

"Do we have to do this today?" I asked. I was holding the child we had to give away, and now here was another one who could come into our home—and then leave it.

"Michael, it's a girl. She's healthy, she's probably going to be available for adoption, and you know how rare a girl is in the system. We need to make a decision now."

A little girl. After we sicced the ACLU on DYFS, we might never have a chance to receive another foster child. Loretta McCormick had assured us that she would not allow DYFS to threaten Adam's foster placement in our home. "If they wanted to take Adam away, I would be the first one to know," she told us. "And I just would not let that happen. Even if it cost me my job." But DYFS could certainly withhold another child from us. Maybe this baby would be only a foster child; it seemed that day as if children went in and out of our house at will and left us wounded, but we would have to handle that. And yes, we were about to lose Andrew, and even in considering another child we couldn't help but react to the hurt we felt. But maybe this was God's way of healing us. Here was a child who needed parents and a home, and we were parents who had a home to offer. It felt right.

"Okay." I nodded. "Let's do it."

Jon beamed. He hunched over the phone to make the arrangements with Jean for us to pick up the little girl after the weekend—at the

O'Neill Center, where we had first met Adam. That seemed like a good omen. Still, I couldn't believe what we had just done. By now I knew that everywhere I went with Jon, I would be jumping off a cliff. I felt that the first day I saw him, or the day we decided it was time to tell my family about us, or when we decided at age twenty to go to California, or the afternoon we first saw this Maywood house and bought it on the spot. Or how we felt the morning we'd first seen Adam, knowing instantly he was our son.

We got off the phone and floated back into the living room. "Guess what? We've got a daughter," Jon announced with ironic excitement. Lenora Lapidus looked at him as if he were suddenly speaking Phoenician. We explained our decision to her and Michael Adams even as we were explaining it to ourselves—that a baby girl in the system needed us, and we were going to take her in.

"In all the hassle about adopting Adam jointly, they're going to let you take in another baby?" Lenora asked.

"Yup, seems that way," Jon said. At DYFS, the right hand didn't know who the left hand was slapping. "We meet the baby on Monday. She's at the same place where we got Adam—this home for HIV-positive infants in Paterson."

Our new lawyers were dumbfounded. The two of them left, promising us an action plan on how they would challenge the state. I felt much better about them. Their professional attitude—not to mention their patience with our phone calls—encouraged me to believe that they would keep their commitments to us. For the first time in weeks I felt hopeful that Jon and I would get to adopt Adam together. How could we fail when our joint adoption was so obviously so good for our son?

Ann Mary arrived to baby-sit Adam, who had just woken up from his nap. She would give him his sippy cup of juice and his snack and soothe him as he realized that he wasn't hearing Andrew's cries—or laughs—from the next room. "Adam, it's time to say good-bye to Andrew," Jon told him. We had spent some time preparing Adam for this day. "We're going to take him to his family," Jon said carefully, "to a place where he'll be very, very happy." Adam looked at us puzzled. What were we doing with his good buddy Andrew, who'd made him laugh so much? He thought Andrew was his brother.

We packed the Grand Am—which at this point in its strained life was cramped with kid debris and sticky with two children's fingerprints—loaded Andrew into his car seat, and drove numbly onto Route 80, then made our way through the poverty-stricken streets of Paterson, to the DYFS facility, housed in an abandoned factory built during Paterson's days as "Silk City," now converted to a train museum with a floor reserved for state social services. Here Mrs. Alvarez would take custody of her grandson.

Jon had been here before to meet Andrew's grandparents and mother during earlier, get-to-know-you visitations. Andrew's mother, Anna, was a young woman with dark hair, respectable looking but with youthfully haggard features, wearing a pink parka and checked, pleated pants, surrounded by four little boys that her mother managed and had legal custody to. We'd been told that Anna was a heroin user, but she had seemed pretty clean to Jon. Meeting the son she had delivered and left behind in the hospital, she seemed remote, treating him more as an infant brother than as a child she had given birth to. She spent more time yelling at the older kids than visiting with Andrew; Mrs. Alvarez had kept bringing Anna's focus back to her littlest baby. Anna hadn't shown up for any of the other visits Jon had made.

My mother had accompanied Jon on this first trip, to manage Adam—and to manage Jon, who was still angry at having to return Andrew. Even as she was maternal and caring toward Jon during these difficult meetings, Dorothy was quite unnerved by this foray into the world of foster parenting. "I don't know how you guys can do this to yourselves. I could never do it." Her son and his family were leading her to places that as a suburban wife and mother were totally unfamiliar to her.

We extricated Andrew from his car seat but left his stuff there and met Jim, Andrew's social worker, in the lobby. Together we made our way up to a conference room on the top floor. As we opened the door, an older woman looked up at Andrew cradled in Jon's arms, then softly met my gaze. She was stout with muscle and looked determined, vigorous, and weary, with a worn face and a bouncy ponytail. She was the rock in a sea of scampering preschool boys, all four of them with hair combed and slicked down as if for Sunday school. This was Mrs. Alvarez and her family. Her husband and her daughter were nowhere to be seen.

The boys looked at us full of wary suspense, then jumped up and ran to us to see the new, younger brother entering their lives. Jim made introductions, and then Mrs. Alvarez firmly took Andrew from Jon's arms and looked him over, as if examining his vital signs. We sat with them at a conference table. "He looks very good. You've both taken good care of him," she said to us in broken English. "But you shouldn't have had to." She fixed a harsh look on Jim the social worker and I could tell that in her eyes he represented everything that had gone wrong with the social service agency that had misplaced her grandson. Mrs. Alvarez went on to tell me that when Andrew was a newborn, she and her husband had visited him every day. Somehow DYFS had made a massive glitch and handed him over to foster parents. To her, DYFS might as well have kidnapped him. "We've always wanted Andrew," she said to us, defensive and gentle at the same time. She was steamed enough to sue the state, but mostly she was glad to have her grandchild back.

It hurt to see Andrew in Mrs. Alvarez's arms, no matter how much she deserved him. Jon had told me that she and her husband worked opposite shifts—Mrs. Alvarez cleaned offices—so that they could afford to bring up these boys and have someone at home to care for the children. It had to be an incredible challenge for her and her husband. I looked at the other boys, bounding around the room. The youngest one, just learning to walk, seemed frail and jaundiced. Adorable as they all were, they were a handful for any caregiver, no matter how vital and committed.

"Where's Anna?" Jon asked gently. "And Mr. Alvarez?"

Mrs. Alvarez's face tightened. Then she looked from Jon to me and decided to speak. "She's at the hospital, in the ICU. My husband is there with her. We may lose her today."

I glanced at Jon and felt fear and sympathy wash over me. I didn't know if it was a drug overdose or HIV that had landed Andrew's mother in the hospital—all I knew was that their daughter's predicament had to be added grief for Mrs. Alvarez and her husband. I thought about Diane, how drug addiction had kidnapped both these young mothers and left devastation behind. I looked at Mrs. Alvarez, who had put her cheek next to Andrew's, then raised her face to monitor two of her grandsons as they went wild the way little kids do, bouncing off each other and laughing and yelling. Whatever had gone wrong with her daughter she was trying to repair. At age sixty, she was working hard to make a life for five grandsons. She could have taken the easy way out, but she hadn't. We were doing the right thing, I decided, returning this child to a woman whose love was worn but true.

As we filled out all the transition papers, writing down information about Andrew's eating habits, his last medical checkup, his vaccination records, and drug regimen, I saw tears begin to course down Jon's face. "I'm sorry," he said, wiping at his eyes. "This is just very hard."

Mrs. Alvarez put her hand on Jon's forearm. "I know. Thank you," she said in her tripping accent. "I'm sorry this had to happen to all of us. You are good men. I'm sure there's another baby out there for you." I thought of the little girl waiting for us just a few blocks away at the O'Neill Center. Holding Andrew, Mrs. Alvarez looked as if she were going to cry for us—even as we both felt as if we were going to cry for her.

Outside in the parking lot, we transferred the four bags of clothes and baby supplies from the trunk of our Grand Am into Mrs. Alvarez's cluttered car. Then I strapped Andrew into her well-worn infant seat, kissed him, and shut the door. I stood looking at him through the window for a second and wished him well. I told him I loved him. The rest of the children crowded into Mrs. Alvarez's car as we quickly got into ours.

Jon and I pulled out of the parking lot first. Through the rearview mirror I saw our empty infant seat behind us in the backseat, as I watched Mrs. Alvarez and the child who'd been our foster son drive off into their own lives and fates. It was right, it was right, it was right, I told myself. Just as we were fighting for the right of Adam to be ours, so Mrs. Alvarez had fought the state to claim the child that was rightfully hers.

———

My mother called that night to sympathize with us about the wrenching return of Andrew. "A few other things were happening as well today," I said. "First, Jon and I met with the ACLU. They want to take Adam's case. That means we have to unretain Billy. And Daddy won't be happy with that."

"The ACLU! Why?"

"We decided that if we're going to get this joint adoption through, then whoever is handling it has to believe in it."

"What are you going to tell Billy?"

"We'll tell him the truth. It's the right thing for our family."

"What are you going to say your father?"

"What I just told you. But that's not all our news. It looks like you and Dad are going to have a granddaughter."

"A granddaughter!"

I explained to her that there was a little girl waiting for us at the O'Neill Center. "Oh, Mike," she sighed. "Are you sure you're doing the right thing?"

"No. I *believe* I'm doing the right thing, but I'm never sure of anything anymore."

"Adolph!" I heard her shout to my father. "Come talk to your son! Mike and Jon are getting another baby!"

"What? But they just had to return a baby today," I heard my father say. When he got on the phone, I filled him in his impending new granddaughter. "Why another baby?" he asked. "You know what can happen."

"It seems like the right thing to do. And I have to trust my heart."

"All right." I could practically hear him shrug. Then I told him about the ACLU and he got very quiet. I knew he was worried about his relationship with his friend Billy. And of course to him the ACLU were radical kooks. "They're not going to spread you around in all the newspapers, are they?"

That, I knew, was his big issue. God forbid I should in any way sully the family name. "I made them vow not to. No media. This stays private. It's a family matter."

"Okay. But you call Billy and tell him." Fifteen years ago, on a topic this touchy—say, being gay, moving to California, wearing a lime-green jacket—he would have screamed and yelled and demanded I do exactly what he thought I should do. Now, his attitude seemed to be, My son's gonna do what my son's gonna do. Along with resignation I was sensing a new respect from him—respect for what we were trying to do as parents and how we were fighting for Adam. He might still be grumpy, but it was progress.

That evening, as Jon and I talked over our roller coaster of a day, I realized all over again what a balancing act I was performing. Jon has always been a confronter. I'm a conciliator. For my first thirty-some years, I'd made a vocation of keeping everyone in my life happy. Now it was harder than ever: I had to keep Jon happy, please my parents, preserve Adam's family, and all the while protect us from the cruelty of the outside world, from hardened state bureaucrats to nasty press people to Aunt Angela and Bob Enyart, always there looming in the background. If the state said no to our joint adoption, how long would the balance last?

Late on the afternoon of March 3 we made a return visit to the O'Neill Center, Adam squirming in Jon's arms, to meet our new daughter. I had taken off work to meet our baby and to bring her home.

It was such a different visit from our first one. Even the weather seemed to be on our side, spring suggesting itself in the air. Joanne Harraka, the head nurse who had introduced us to Adam fifteen months before, met us at the front door with her familiar big smile. "Welcome home," she said, "And hello, Adam, you big healthy boy!" She led us up the stairs we had once climbed to Adam's nursery—this time helping our toddler son navigate the steps.

Upstairs we were stopped in every doorway by nurses and staff people who wanted to behold their O'Neill Center success story. Adam was returning in triumph like a one-man World Series winner. Having encountered so many new people in his life already, Adam was open to the hugs and exclamations of strangers. He took it as his due. With every fresh person who picked him up, Adam would smile, reaching for her hair, pulling at her glasses in total delight. He has always especially loved women, of all shapes, colors, and ages. "You men are doing a great job," Joanne told us as Adam bounced on her lap in her third-floor attic office. "Every one of my babies should thrive like this." Joanne was right, and I was proud. Dressed in a flannel shirt, jeans, and new little work boots, our affectionate, vital, ruddy, strong little boy was far removed from the wan, drugged, blue-veined baby who had spent his first weeks in the nursery downstairs.

As we waited for the arrival of Gary, the baby's social worker, Joanne asked us about the story about our tussle with the state to gain a joint adoption of Adam. "They still haven't let you adopt him?" Joanne asked as I grabbed a stapler from Adam—the kind of parental action that was second nature by now. "Amazing. What are they waiting for? Adam's high school graduation?" She looked at Adam face-to-face. "Every baby I know should grow up to be just like you. Including this new baby. Would you like to meet her?"

"Right this instant," Jon said.

Joanne made a call, and within moments a nurse bought up a little blanketed pink bundle and handed it to me. Wrapped in the blanket lay a baby—olive pink, fat-cheeked, bald as could be. My first thought was, God, she's fat! She didn't look sick or puffy, though, just well-fed. She had chins, she had cheeks, she had tiny, pudgy fists. She was quite a contrast to Adam and Andrew, who at the same age looked too sinewy and taut for their own good. For a premature drug baby, she was as close as you get to looking like a normal infant. A serious look dwelt in her dark brown eyes.

"She looks like Otis from the *Andy Griffith Show*," I said.

Jon laughed. She mewled against my cheek. "I don't have a cold this time," Jon said to me. "Let me hold her. Go chase your son." Adam had discovered the play space beside Joanne's office and was furiously excavating a huge trash bag of donated used toys—plunging in among them to pull out a teddy bear, a Nerf football, and a truck, examining them and then throwing them aside to see what other treasures he could find. He acted as if it were Christmas all over again.

"Her PCR just came back this morning," Joanne said after I had retrieved Adam and sat him squirming on my lap. "No evidence of the virus. She'll still be on Bactrim prophylaxis for a while. And no evidence of drug withdrawal. Her mother must not have been using anything for the last months of the pregnancy."

"Can we give her a name?" I asked.

"Well," Joanne said, "based on her history and the fact her other siblings were adopted, I think you can name her, just the way you did with Adam."

Jon and I exchanged a glance. The baby's mother might allow an adoption, but would the state? Any day now DYFS and the state attorney general would be hearing from the ACLU, and they would not be happy with us.

Jon peered into the baby's face. "Hello, Madison," he said into her serious, round eyes. Madison stared up at him thoughtfully, as if pondering her new name.

We had decided to name her Madison because we had once met someone named Madison Adams and thought Madison was a beautiful name for a girl.

"Look, Adam, your new sister!" I said. We wanted to make sure that Adam was part of this meeting from the start, since he was most surely reacting to the disappearance of Andrew. Adam reached to grab her as if she were a toy he'd found among the charitable donations in the trash bag. Jon reared back a little, worried that Adam might scratch her. But, no, he touched her face gently, gave her another investigatory look, and then bounded off my lap to play with a purple Nerf football.

Madison regarded him dubiously, then looked back at Jon and me. She seemed to be scrutinizing us, as if to say, So who are you? Can I trust you? It appeared she was looking not at us but *into* us, her eyes calm yet intense, innocent but deep. So you're my family? her gaze was asking. How are we going to work this?

Gary, the social worker, still hadn't shown up, so we couldn't sign the baby out. Frustrated, Jon commandeered the phone and called Jean, who apologized for whatever schedule confusion had occurred and promised to dash over to the O'Neill Center. Meanwhile, Joanne gave us basic training in girl-baby care. As Joanne watched Jon change

Adam meets his little sister.

the diaper, she relayed feminine-hygiene training that could be summed up in one phrase: front to back. "That's the secret no man knows," Jon declared. He knew about this already, which impressed Joanne.

He gave Madison to me and I fed her. As I held her, I knew she was my girl. She was my daughter, absolutely, already. I had felt that same certainty the day I'd met Jon more than fifteen years before, at a fraternity rush party one spring evening at college. A cocky, skinny freshman, all blond hair, had swaggered up to me. "So why should I join your fraternity?" he demanded. "You shouldn't," I shot back. But even though I didn't know him, I somehow knew I would see him again. It took us another two months to get together, but from that first encounter I felt there was something about him. I'd had that same absolute knowledge in this very building when I'd first beheld Adam. Now I knew without a doubt that I was the father for this baby girl, who had decided to trust me enough to fall asleep on my chest.

Thumping up the old wooden stairs, Jean appeared, out of breath,

Meeting Madison: Daddy gets a lesson in "girl stuff."

her coat flapping, a tall, efficient woman with short red hair. "I'm so glad to see you guys," she panted. "It looks like we found you your baby girl." She apologized for the inconvenience and completed the paperwork so we could take Madison home.

We gathered up what few clothes the baby had, then wrapped up Madison in a white snowsuit we had brought for her. It had a big snowflake on the front and fur around the face, and she looked like a little pasha princess, regally regarding the world from her infant seat, with Adam wrestling with Big Bird in the car seat beside her, as we drove home to Maywood with our baby, to begin again.

"She's a beautiful little girl. I hope you get to keep her," my father said sympathetically. Both Jon's and my family were very loving with Madison, but a little bit more guarded in connecting with a new baby than they had been with Adam. As much as we loved her from the start, we felt the same way. We'd put Madison in the guest room at first, and we didn't decorate it the way we had Adam's room. Somehow, it still seemed as if this baby could be taken away from us at any minute. We didn't prepare for permanency. The problems with the state and jointly adopting Adam, together with the uproar over Andrew's arrival and abrupt departure, had short-circuited a lot of the joy you're supposed to feel when you bring home a new baby. Our families felt the same way, pleased but wary.

Except for Nancy. Jon's mother and Madison were the new females in our lives that spring, and she embraced Madison with great enthusiasm. She'd had two sons—Donald Henson and now Jon—and to have a little girl in her life was an extra reward for her reconnection with her son. For his part, Jon now had the birth mother he had always dreamed of having. On the day he and Nancy had met for the first time, I'd returned home to find my husband already a different man. It was as if a cloud had lifted from him, a cloud we had never known was there, or as if a film had finally been wiped away between him and reality. He could breathe better.

I was so relieved for him. Like Jon, I'd worried that his birth mother would be dead or would deny him somehow—as his birth father had— or else be so damaged by her life and her choices that we could never grow close to her. I have to admit that when I first heard that Jon wanted to meet his birth mother, my joking thought was "Yikes! Another mother-in-law!" Early in my relationship with Jon, Ann Mary had challenged me to prove that I was worthy of her beloved son. I'd risen to the challenge, and now the two of us got along well. Nancy and I had hit it off right away. The first moment I saw her that January day, I thought, "Wow, he's right—here are Jon's eyes on another human being." She was sweet from the start and gave me a huge hug. Just as I had felt Jon's sense of completeness the day he'd met her, I could sense her own relief and joy now that her past and her present had so richly converged.

That spring Nancy came to visit us more and more. She was still tentative with Jon—both mother and son were still feeling out the dimensions of their new bond—but she went ahead and introduced the two of us to her husband, who shook our hands heartily, picked up the dinner tab, and made easy, open conversation. From the look in his eye I could tell he was ready to fall in love with his new grandchildren. Adam and Madison have always been our ambassadors of love.

From Nancy to the other grandparents, everyone warmed to Madison from the start—except Adam. He would try to push Madison out of her swing or scratch at her and try to hit her, and we had to watch the two of them all the time or else keep them separated. It was scary, as if he felt on some primal level that this new creature was a threat to his hard-won security. It took us a couple of days to realize that this might not just be a toddler's jealous reaction to a new sibling. He was also grieving the loss of Andrew, his best friend. And here was this new blob of a baby who needed a lot of care and who wasn't as much familiar fun as Andrew had been at his best. But just as we had done when Andrew had arrived in the house, we tried to get Adam to participate in the new baby's feeding, care, and play. We were a team, the three of us, and within a week or so Adam began to get over his grief and anger and embrace his new sister. Soon he would even be gentle with her, treating her the way his fathers did. It would be the beginning of a beautiful sibling relationship.

The children were the only ones not worrying about what the state would say in response to the ACLU's appeal of the DYFS fiat that we could not adopt Adam jointly. It was on everyone else's mind. Jon had made the call "unretaining" Billy DeMarco, who had been extremely gracious and understanding of our situation. My father was still grumbling that the ACLU was going to lump us in with the communists, Nazis, and pornographers they represented and leave us abandoned and exposed. Ann Mary sat back and relaxed, satisfied with the direction we were taking. Nancy worried about us a lot, that we would be hurt or have to make a public event out of our claim to joint parentage of Adam.

Michael Adams would call us every Monday and Lenora every Friday to give us progress reports about their efforts. They notified DYFS and Commissioner Waldman that we had retained them as our legal representatives, and they brought in a lawyer named Barbara Fox, who specialized in adoption cases and had worked with Joan Garry and her partner, Eileen Opatut, in their successful appeal for second-parent adoption. Michael and Lenora would later show us drafts of letters they would send to DYFS and to the state attorney general. Michael Adams was especially deft at filling us in on the procedural stuff. Lenora was good at keeping us calm. "You just focus on Adam and Madison and be the best parents you can be," she told us, "and we'll deal with whatever we have to, when the time comes." I found myself trusting their judgment. Still, I worried.

Looking at my daughter serenely smiling at me, watching Adam at play, I felt we had more reason to fight than ever—for not one but two children we adored. It gnawed at me even more that if the State of New Jersey had its way, conceivably Aunt Angela could have more legal right over my children's fate than Jon would. If I ended up dead or in ICU, she and her born-again sons could sweep in and make a legitimate claim for custody of Adam, rescuing the poor child from that awful homosexual, Jon, who had helped to bring him up and make him healthy. It wasn't that any such scenario was likely, of course—at worst my parents would have first dibs, and they were sensible—but the fact remained that Adam would have a perfectly fit surviving parent in Jon Holden. How could I look at Jon or watch those kids and give in to allowing the state to tell me what was right for my family?

My fear dueled with my protectiveness. Jon was becoming more sensitive to the issue because he knew how afraid I was. One evening after we had sung Madison and Adam to sleep, we sat quietly in the living room. "What if we have to sue?" Jon asked without warning.

"I don't want to. I really don't want to. I'm so scared."

Jon seemed struck that I would even admit my fear; I wouldn't usually do that. "We might have to," he said carefully, "if the attorney general says no."

I was quiet. "Would that mean going public, telling everybody about us?"

"It could. If the ACLU felt it was the most effective way to get the policy reversed."

"I don't want that. Two gay men raising a boy? There are too many crazies out there. What if one of those crazies comes and grabs one of them?" I thought of what our friends Kevin and Tim had gone through in our own town when they had made public their battle to get their

HIV-positive son, Lee, enrolled in school. Grown men would yell at their kids on the street and say cruel things about their gay fathers. And the words that Charles Venti of DYFS had said to Jon—about how we shouldn't risk having a cross burned on our lawn—still echoed in my head.

I didn't worry only about the cross-burners. I had worries closer to home, thanks to that lifelong balancing act of mine, which could get even harder than it already was. I was growing more and more concerned about the reactions of my family. Even though they had come to accept my couplehood with Jon, anytime in the past that the fact of our gayness had become public news, everyone in the family had gone ballistic, as if in telling the world I was gay I had violated the family code of honor. I was certain they would become thermonuclear if they found themselves the publicly revealed parents of not just a gay son but a gay son with a son.

In June 1995, just after Jon and I had bought our house in Maywood in preparation for adopting a kid, I was interviewed by a reporter for the New Jersey daily newspaper *The Record,* in a story Tim and Kevin had arranged. Kevin, in psychotherapist mode, had thought that coming out in print would help me resolve my problems with my parents. He wasn't exactly correct about that. Complete with photograph, my coming-out tale explored my tough relationship with my parents—who at one point when I told them about Jon had all but disowned me—and how, after a lot of hard work motivated by love, we had reconciled to the point where Jon and I had come home to Maywood and to Bergen County.

My parents' initial reaction to the story negated the truths I had tried to tell. It was one thing to be out as a gay man in the family and another thing to announce it to everybody in northern New Jersey, not to mention my father's law colleagues and their horde of close friends. "You've taken so many steps back," my mother told me flatly. I had sullied the family name by linking it with *that* in the newspaper.

What made it worse was that the story had appeared just a day before my sister Karen's wedding, which meant that the entire clan could move directly from exclaiming over Karen's gorgeous gown to groaning at how her brother had shamed the family. Or so my mother thought. "None of my friends knew about Jon and you," she whispered tragically. "Now they all know."

When my mother mentioned this, Jon and I were at Karen's wedding brunch, with all of my parents' pinochle-playing pals, nice respectable suburban couples every one. The men were all down in the lower yard playing boccie when my mother started complaining about how embarrassed she was by that article. "Excuse me." I raised my voice. "Could everyone listen up for a minute?" A dozen middle-aged women turned my way. "Anyone here who knew about Jon and me *before* the newspaper article came out, please raise your hand."

Every single woman raised her hand. "Mom didn't think you knew until now," I said. Every single woman laughed. "Mom, I haven't had a girlfriend in thirteen years."

My mother was abashed but not convinced. It was the night before, at Karen's wedding reception, that Jon had told Aunt Angela he was going to stay at home to raise a child full-time, and Aunt Angela had stalked off. After that she cut her father, my grandfather, out of my life. Granddaddy just stopped speaking to me. Now, nearly two years later, whenever Jon and I greeted him at my parents' house, I would kiss him hello as I always had, and his face would shut like a garage door. He wouldn't even touch Adam. For Aunt Angela, saving Michael Galluccio became her life's new mission. She told my mother that she, Angela, was the only one in the world who truly loves me, "because I'm trying to save him from the life he's chosen."

For a family that had always kept every joy, tragedy, and secret within the tight confines of the clan, going public about my adoption battle would cause an incredible uproar—no matter how much they loved me and loved Adam. I didn't want to have to choose between the family of my parents and the family I was making with Jon and my children. But more and more, if it came down to it, I knew how I would choose.

One warm spring evening Jon met me at the door and yelled out as he did every night, "Hey, Adam! Father's home!" Adam gave me a big smile as he trundled precariously across the living room, tripping over the cuffs of his Ralph Lauren overalls and plopping down on the carpet. A look of consternation crossed his face, to be replaced by resolve as he got himself up and made his way toward my open arms. "Come on, you can do it!" I said, squatting before him, and Adam laughed as I gathered him into my lap and kissed him and said, "Hiya, Son."

Son. What a small, huge word that is for me. For a long time after Adam came into our house, it was a weird word for me to say aloud. For a gay man to call a child "son" might seem at first like an outrageous thing to do—illegitimate somehow, as if the child squealing in my arms was not mine somehow but a rental, on loan from central casting. The very strangeness of the word was one reason I used it so often. It still seemed strange to say it when I came in the door. Then I would pick Adam up and he was mine.

"Hiya, Son." I'd heard those words all through my childhood—from my own father, as he'd swing open the front door and bellow, "Daddy's home!" Karen, Mark, Terri, and I would abandon our kid games in a mad dash to meet him at the door, mauling him like puppies. I would always make it there before the others, and my father would pick me up and hold me tight, my face jammed against his awful, late-1960s necktie. Then he'd lift me up all the way and I'd be looking into his direct, fatherly gaze. I felt such a sense of completeness in those moments. He was strong, he was my protector, he was a good guy. I aimed to be all these things for Adam. "Hiya, Son."

Jon kissed me hello. "Adam had some good news today. The latest test results came back today. Liver's good, heart's good, triglycerides are lower, and . . ."

"And?" I was pretty sure I knew what he was leaving out.

"He's officially HIV-negative. You know what that means after eighteen months of negative tests, right?"

"He's no longer medically fragile. And he's out of the woods on HIV."

"You got it."

It wasn't a surprise, but I was still surprised to hear it. After our hard start at the O'Neill Center, after all those scares over his liver and the hole in his heart, after a radical change in his diet (and ours), after seventeen ear infections in eighteen months that ultimately required second-level antibiotics, our son was safe now. Whatever challenges he would face in the future, right now he was just a delighted and delightful boy, his mind spurred by *The Cat in the Hat Comes Back* and the Berenstain Bears and every kind of pop-up book imaginable, a boy who was terrific at making animal sounds—mooing, oinking—and happily driving us wild as he romped through his newfound toddlerhood. What a relief.

I kissed him again. "Congratulations, Son."

On May 1, Michael Adams sat in his lower-Manhattan office furnished with exotic Turkish carpets and Mexican wall hangings, sorting through his mail. A letter had arrived from the office of Peter Verniero, the New Jersey attorney general. Opening it, Michael carefully studied its contents, ran his fingers through his red hair, and then called Lenora Lapidus at the New Jersey ACLU. When Lenora answered, all he said was, "Either Michael and Jon accept a onetime exception for Adam, or we have a lawsuit on our hands."

"What's wrong?" I said as soon as I came in the house on the evening of the first day of May, back from another wild day directing indirect sales at Sprint PCS, and saw Jon's face.

"Nothing, I'm fine," Jon said in a tone that made clear that nothing was fine.

Even Adam seemed to know what was going on, scurrying to me with more neediness than usual, and Madison had a severe expression on her round face as Jon put dinner on the table. By the way he held Adam tight, I guessed that something had happened with the ACLU's appeal and that Jon was stiffening his spine so as to tell me.

"Michael and Lenora got a letter from the attorney general's office," he said after a battle-weary breath. "They won't contest the joint adoption of Adam but they won't approve it either. That would be up to the judge. And they won't change the policy. There's nothing else the ACLU can do, short of a lawsuit, if we still want to jointly adopt."

I felt cold, exposed, as if a gust of public wind had coursed through the dining room. Jon and I had created a private comfort zone for our family where we were just ourselves, two men with two children, and no one else could interfere. But if we did something that made the world recognize us on sight, that zone of safety could disappear. And then what would happen?

Still, even with all our trepidation, the decision was inevitable. We'd lived with this so long, and our cause was so vital and so right. "Well, then we have to sue," I said. "Let's talk to Michael and Lenora and see where we go from here. We'll do what we have to do."

Jon just looked at me as he put Adam and Madison in their high chairs. "I am so in love with you right now," he said.

The following evening, Michael Adams and Lenora Lapidus returned to our house. Madison had just learned to crawl, and she and Adam rolled around the living room carpet as Michael gravely told us that he and the ACLU were stalled with the state. "The time for private negotiation is over," he told us. "You have two choices. The first is to accept this onetime exception and seek to adopt Adam together, without the official consent of the state. You might win at that; you might not. It could depend on the opinion of the judge, especially without a recommendation from DYFS. Along with Barbara Fox, we would handle that adoption bid for you, as we agreed from the beginning."

Then Michael glanced at Lenora and set his level gaze on the two of us. "The second choice is to file a lawsuit that would reverse the policy that prohibits unmarried couples from adopting. That would clear the way for you and for lots of other parents."

Jon looked down at our daughter as Adam curled up alongside her, patting her belly as if he could burp her, the way he'd seen his daddy do.

"If we go to court for Adam jointly without having DYFS stand in the way, would we be able to do the same thing later for Madison?" I asked.

Michael looked at Lenora, then at us. "There's no guarantee of that."

"So we'd have to go through this whole thing again in six months," I said. "And a lot of other couples are going to have to go through it all the time."

"That's right. And hard as it is, if you choose to be the public face for this lawsuit, that will make a huge difference in garnering public support for your case."

"Yeah, I know we maybe should do that," I said. "I know it can make a difference. Maybe some more of these babies would be adopted if the state made it easier."

Jon and I looked at each other. It was an awesome moment. I could see his mind move from his "I told you so, I knew we'd have to sue" stance to "I know how hard this is—how can I support you in this?"

"Then I think we should go ahead with the lawsuit," I said. Jon nodded. "And I'm ready to make my own case to the media in person, if you think it's important. Jon will too, I think." Jon nodded again.

We told Michael Adams to draw up the papers to petition the court to adopt without consent. From this point on we referred to our plan as our hostile takeover bid for our son. Michael told us that for the class action lawsuit we had to garner the support of other gay parents—the wronged class—which meant recruiting support from other fathers and mothers who were, or could be, discriminated against by the state. Jon agreed to set this up.

After Michael and Lenora left, I called my mother to tell her what we had decided to do.

"Oh my God," was her reaction. "Do you realize what this will do to your father? Your grandfather? And wait until Aunt Angela—"

"I have to do this for my family," I interrupted. "It bothers me I have to do this. But I do have to. Let me talk to Dad."

My father just listened. I heard him let out a breath. "I guess you have to do what you have to do," he said.

Over the next weeks Jon worked hard to recruit other lesbian and gay parents to the cause, so that the national and state ACLU could put forward a strong contingent of couples to challenge the state policy, claiming that being forced to do single-parent adoptions was not in the best interests of their children. We couldn't ask Kevin and Tim because their case would be one that the lawsuit would refer to, since DYFS had violated their own policy and more or less accidentally given them a onetime exception, back before our bid to adopt Adam had begun. Jon contacted people he knew from Lambda Families of New Jersey, the group of lesbian and gay parents whose board he had joined recently.

All the gay male couples immediately bowed out from participating in the lawsuit. A man who was part of one couple had adopted a baby girl from abroad and was adopting another; he and his husband were afraid that officials in her country would find out their sexual orientation and deny the adoption. Another father of a five-year-old girl worked in a social services capacity for the state and decided it would be a conflict of interest to sue his employer. Some other gay fathers weren't out at work as gay men or as fathers.

Every single one was afraid of being seared by the public spotlight. Some worried about the ancient libel hurled against gay men—that society would tag them as pederasts, predatory homosexuals abusing the toddlers they had adopted. I understood that, and it strengthened my resolve that Jon and I would put a face to the issue, even if it meant taking on some risk.

We made an appeal to the board of Lambda Families that the organization as a whole come on as plaintiffs in the case. The board talked with Michael and Lenora and then met in the Morristown living room of one lesbian couple, without Jon or me present, so that they could talk freely and take a vote. Except for one person who declared that Lambda Families was "a play group, not a legal group," all the board members voted to join the suit. Michael Adams needed someone from Lambda to give a face to this issue. Vicky Riggs and Daphne McClellan, two mothers representing two more families, would become spokespeople for Lambda Families and speak at an ACLU press conference in Newark announcing the suit, along with Jon and me.

Even though we would be putting our names and faces out there, we could still protect Adam from any media glare—in fact we were required not to use his name or likeness, since as his foster parents we had to protect his confidentiality, as well as Madison's. With

Michael Adams's agreement, in all court papers we referred to Adam as "Mark"—a bow, of course, to the name that Jon had been given by Nancy right after he was born, before Ann Mary and Danny Dell'Olio adopted him. Nancy, who had been upset that her son had been given a new name after his adoption, was touched by our homage.

That this case involved a child put it into an entirely different and uncertain realm. Many brave parents had gone ahead of us, including lesbian mothers defending their rights to custody and visitation of the children they had had with their husbands. Sometimes winning, sometimes losing, always suffering, they had all blazed the way for parents like Jon and me. In going public, in connecting the words *gay* and *father, homosexual* and *child,* we knew we were venturing into volatile, scary territory. We had no idea whether the media would care about our case or whether there would be vehement or even violent opposition to it. Strangers might attack us in word or deed; Aunt Angela might picket our house; Cousin Bob could broadcast his cable show from our front yard. Yet people needed to know that we weren't two anonymous, random faggots. We were a pair of gay men dedicated to a son we loved and wanted to protect.

"We'll do what we have to do," I told Michael Adams. And I believed it completely. And then to Jon I said, "We need to install an alarm system in this house—and we need to do it today."

EIGHT

GO, DADDY!

Jon Galluccio

"Oh, Lord, we ask Your blessings this day for all parents and their children everywhere, especially those facing trial, poverty, abuse, and injustice," prayed the Reverend Canon Elizabeth Kaeton at the regular Oasis communion service for lesbian and gay people at Christ Church, Ridgewood, the Tuesday night she announced in church that Michael and I were going public with our lawsuit that Thursday.

I felt a chill shoot down my spine. Adam wriggled in my lap, and Madison dozed calmly in the infant seat beside me. "And especially keep in Your loving care Jon Holden and Michael Galluccio, and their son Adam, as they seek justice and security for their son," Mother Elizabeth intoned.

"O Lord, hear our prayer," the congregation murmured back.

"Open the hearts of the people in places of authority, that they may see that family comes in all forms and that love for Your children exists among all Your people," Mother Elizabeth continued.

"O Lord, hear our prayer," the congregation repeated. Adam gave a yelp of approval. I whispered along with them. At Communion, I sipped the sacred wine for the first time in my sobriety; it seemed important to have that extra spiritual sustenance. Mother Kaeton laid her hand on Adam's and Madison's heads, then hugged me and whispered a prayer in my ear, asking God to support Michael and me in our time of trial.

The morning before our ACLU press conference, the Slomin's security-alarm people arrived with a truckload full of dials, drills, and motion sensors to put an alarm system on our house, pulling aside the furniture and taking down the pictures to drill holes in the walls.

At the same time, three towns over in River Edge, my mother, Ann Mary, was sitting in a doctor's office undergoing a routine mammogram, a procedure she approached so casually that she told her husband, Herb, just to wait in the car for her; she wouldn't be long. After all, Ann Mary was a survivor, solid and strong, and nothing ever dared go medically wrong with her. She took care of everyone else; she never needed to be taken care of herself. That was the plan, anyway.

But as she stood in a cold examining room while a young and quite beautiful radiology technician took more and more film, and as the clocked seemed to tick slower and more loudly, she began to suspect that something was wrong. Before she was to speak with the doctor, she went and retrieved Herb from the car.

Sitting in the doctor's office, holding her husband's hand, Ann Mary was told that she had three large malignancies on her left breast and two questionable spots on her right. She had had lumps on her breast before, but they had always turned out to be benign. She had to come back for a final determination the next Monday, but based on what the doctor told her, she realized that she did have cancer and would require a mastectomy for one breast and at least a lumpectomy on the other, and soon.

Right after the alarm people had cut a hole in the plaster next to the back door and sprayed plaster dust all over the kitchen, the doorbell rang. I was on the phone with Loretta McCormick, giving her a heads-up on the ACLU press conference. I recognized what a difficult position Loretta was in, with clients she liked suing her employer, and I didn't need her to tell me I was doing the right thing. I just needed to hear her cool and caring voice. "No one is going to remove Adam from your home," Loretta reiterated. She grounded me.

At the door was the Reverend Kevin Coffey, one of the priests at the Episcopal Church of the Atonement in Fairlawn, which Michael and I had started attending a couple months before. Wearing his collar and his black shirt, Father Kevin was breathing hard and dripping sweat, his thick salt-and-pepper hair nearly drenched. Behind him on the front walk was his bicycle. He'd ridden over from his house on what was turning out to be the hottest day of the year so far. I hung up with Loretta, promising to report back on how things went, and let him in.

"Sorry to look this way," he said over the buzz of the drills from the alarm people. "But Cathy has the car, and I have good news I just had to come in person to tell you," Father Kevin panted. "I've just spoken with Bishop Spong, and he wants me to tell you that you have the complete support of the Diocese of Newark. The bishop and all his clergy will stand behind you one hundred percent—to make statements, appear in court, talk to media people. Whatever you need us to do, we're there."

I felt incredibly warmed by what Father Kevin was telling me. My last reservations about becoming an Episcopalian seemed to dissolve all at once. Our bishop, John Shelby Spong, had been a leader in bringing gay and lesbian people into the Christian flock, and he was one of the reasons Michael and I, raised Catholic, had been comfortable darkening the door of a church again. Along with the possibility of parenthood, belonging to a church had been one of the things we'd thought we'd have to give up when we acknowledged our gayness. But the Episcopal Church—as shown every Sunday by the good people at the Church of the Atonement—had given us a place to be spiritual again, a place to belong.

Damp as Kevin was, I hugged him. Before he left, I got him—and the security workers—tall glasses of Adam and Madison's apple juice.

———————

Michael walked in that night from work, saw the security alarm pad on the kitchen wall giving him the evil eye, and blanched, as Madison squealed a greeting and Adam clambered across the carpet to hug his legs and beg to be picked up. When I saw the expression on his face, I said, "It's a good thing. This way, if they want to burn a cross in our living room, we'll know." Michael just grimaced and went to play with Adam and Madison, to rebalance himself.

That evening, having worked myself into a nervous frenzy about the press conference, I was cleaning up after the security people as Madison kept herself busy on her activity blanket. Adam was reacting to all of our clamor, more rambunctious than I'd ever seen him before. The phone rang. It was my mother.

After asking about our press conference preparations and sympathizing with the mess the alarm people had caused, she got to her news. "I went to the doctor today," Ann Mary said casually. "I wasn't going to bother you just before your press conference, but Herb made me promise to tell you."

"Tell me what?" I plucked Adam off the dining room table.

"They found something in my left breast."

"What do you mean? A little lump?"

"There are three large areas of malignancy on the left breast. And two little ones on the right are suspect."

"What are you talking about? Is it cancer?" I grabbed Adam around his waist and removed him from the dining room curtains.

"Yes."

"What—what happens now?"

"I find out more on Monday. Probably they'll tell me I'll lose the left breast, maybe the right one. I'm not dying," she added, half in explanation, half in command. "It's a routine surgery these days, it really is. You and Michael need to stay focused on your press conference. Herb's going to take good care of me. And we're going to get through this. Okay?"

I told Michael as soon as I hung up the phone, then grabbed Adam off the top of the couch. Michael seemed as stunned as I was.

Granny (Ann Mary) with Madison at a Little League game.

"I just realized something—I mean, *really* realized it," I said to Michael as I lay on the bed after having finally gotten the children to sleep. Michael was pacing the bedroom. "We're going to speak at a press conference tomorrow morning."

We had no idea what we were getting into. Would this be a small incident without much fallout, or would the media swarm all over us? A story was coming out in *The Record* that we had set up with the same reporter, Ruth Padawer, who had written the story about Michael and his family; she had been following the saga of our attempt to adopt Adam. Denny Lee, the publicist at the ACLU, had told us that whenever he publicized an ACLU press conference announcing a lawsuit, the case usually attracted just local newspaper reporters. Because our petition involved a child, there might be a few more, but there was no telling.

Using our names in public was one thing—but we would be connected to our lawsuit by our faces as well, which meant everyone in north Jersey would know that we were two gay men with a little boy at home. We were even listed in the phone book! Over the last few months I'd been feeling more trepidation than usual, partly because Nancy was so worried. For a change I was the one who was reluctant to step forward, not Michael.

"Do we have to be there?" I asked.

"We told them we would," Michael said.

"Maybe they could just use our names, just have Michael Adams and Lenora and the Lambda Families people make the statements." My stomach felt hollow.

"We should call them and ask." Michael looked hard at me.

"Yes," I said, considering the option. "Yes."

We phoned Lenora at home. She couldn't have been more steadying and serene in the face of our last-minute jitters. "We want you there, and it would be good for the case, but it's totally up to you to come or not," she said immediately. "We can do it either way. Just call me back and let me know."

Now we had an out. Damn. Michael paced; I got up and paced too.

It came down to this, we decided: What would be the best thing for Adam? There would be more of an impact if the public could see not just a couple of lawyers but the gay-father plaintiffs for whom this wasn't just law but life. This was our son—could we really just turn it over to lawyers and reporters and just sit still?

"I'm too scared to do it and too scared *not* to do it," I said.

"And not just for Adam but for Madison," Michael added. "We have to think big. Also it's for Vicky and Jill's kids, Daphne's kids, for Stan and Hal's kids, all the other kids. Awesome."

We called Lenora back and said we'd be there, then went to bed. I lay awake staring at the ceiling. So did Michael. "My mother has cancer," I finally said. That news was just sinking in. "What are we going to do?"

Michael pulled me closer, held me. We didn't get much sleep that night.

The next morning, Nancy came to baby-sit Adam and Madison, arriving just while we were reading *The Record*'s nicely positive story chronicling Adam's life with us and our attempt to adopt him together. When my mother saw the photo of the two of us, and the back of Adam's head, her face grew knotted with worry. When we explained the alarm system to her, she grew even more grim.

Dressed in our usual chinos and polo shirts, the right clothes for this hot weather, we drove down to the ACLU offices in Newark via Route 21—in our brand-new, sensible replacement for the Grand Am, a bright white Chevy Venture minivan, which made me feel like a soccer mom. When Michael flicked on the radio, the news announcer led off with "Two gay men are filing suit to adopt a baby boy, because the state won't let them do it together. Today in Newark . . ." We looked at each other, surprised.

We arrived an hour early, and the drab conference room at the well-worn ACLU headquarters was already crammed with people—reporters with notebooks, reporters with microphones, photographers with a forest of tripods, cameramen with massive video cameras propped on their shoulders. A lot of the TV reporters looked familiar from local newscasts, but shorter and shinier than on the screen. Phones were ringing nonstop. We hugged Vicky Riggs, the earnest lesbian mother who worked at Lucent Technologies and would speak on behalf of Lambda Families. When Michael and Lenora greeted us, looking professional and severe in their lawyers-meet-the-press suits, I realized Michael and I were dressed all wrong. In our short-sleeve shirts and khakis, we looked like golfers. But maybe that wasn't so bad—maybe we also looked like Dads.

Terrified Dads. The sheer number of the press people and their equipment had both surprised us and scared the hell out of us.

As the press people eyed us neutrally, Michael and I wedged our way through the crowd to take our places at a table in the front of the jammed room. The cameras clicked on and we were blinded for a moment by the glare. Michael Adams and Lenora delivered their statements announcing that we would defy DYFS and seek joint custody of Adam without the consent of the state, and that along with Lambda Families we would be party to a class action suit that would seek to overturn the policy prohibiting unmarried couples from adopting together. Vicky spoke next, firm and forthright, on behalf of the other lesbian and gay parents in our predicament. Then, steeling ourselves and squinting in the hard television lights, we began to speak, in a short statement we'd worked on the night before, in the midst of our anxiety.

Our voices determined but quivering in fear, we addressed the crowd in alternating paragraphs, first Michael, then me, in a way that represented how we were truly cofathers to the son we demanded to adopt together.

"Michael and Lenora spoke to you about a lawsuit," Michael began. "They talked to you about statutes and constitutions . . . about plaintiffs and defendants. So now it's our turn to speak. But I don't want you to see a plaintiff or a party. I want you to see a father. Well, actually, two fathers," he said as the cameras clicked away. "Two parents who are frightened and fighting for what is best for their child. That's what parents do.

"My name is Michael. For as long as I can remember, I've wanted to be a father. Everyone I've known has said it was what I was meant to be eventually, and what a pity that I never would."

"I am Jon. And I too have always wanted to be a father, and, yes, people who knew me thought it was a shame that I never would be, either." I kept my voice strong and even. "However, we believe that God had other plans. That it was intended that we be parents all along.

"And so it was about three years ago that we found out that we could be parents. We could have a family," I said. The reporters were scratching down notes, the cameras were whirring. It was unreal.

"To hear it was not enough. We needed to be sure that it was not only good for us, but that it would be good for our child as well." This was an important point—no one listening to us should believe we just up and decided one day to become fathers.

"Off we went. We began researching options; reading books and studies; talking to family, friends, psychologists, clergy, and other gay and lesbian parents and their children. The point is, we knew this was a big decision and a huge responsibility. Although in our hearts we knew this was right, our minds needed reassurance."

Michael picked it up from there, telling the assembled reporters how we had bought a house in the suburbs, packed up the pets, and moved in, then were approved in December 1995 by the state as an adoptive family. "We were welcomed," he said. Holding back tears, he told them about the day we first met our son—two days before Christmas.

Michael looked down at the table. Shielded from the press in his cupped hands was a framed photo of Adam at six months old, wearing blue overalls and a bib that said I LOVE DADDY, and he gazed at it for support and focus. "For nearly two years we have been living as a family. A child born medically fragile is now a thriving toddler with two parents, grandparents, great-grandparents, aunts, uncles, cousins, friends, a house, and dogs," Michael declared. "Everyone we know recognizes us as a family . . . as his family. However, New Jersey state policy will not."

We made our case as succinctly and as sharply as we could, that the state policy denied Adam the chance to have two parents.

"Let us end by saying that we have faith in our justice system—that the best interests of our child will prevail," I stated. If the state and the press would retain anything from that day, we wanted it to be that phrase: Best Interests of the Child.

"We have faith in our attorneys that they will represent our children and serve their best interests," I continued.

"And we have faith in you, the media, that you will serve the best interests of our children," Michael added firmly, "that you will allow our lives to go on without disruption and report only the truth." For us, this was as much a challenge as a hope.

"We have faith in all people, that their hearts will be open to support all the children of New Jersey, regardless of what their family looks like," I told them. "We have faith in our families, friends, priests, and neighbors, those who have supported us all along, that they will continue to be there for our family and others." Thank you, all six grandparents, Mike and Maria next door, Bishop Spong. And thank all of you standing in the back of the room, sending me divine vibes: Father Kevin, Mother Elizabeth, and Mother Linda Strohmier, whom we knew from the Church of the Atonement.

"We have faith in ourselves. We would not be here if we weren't sure we were serving our children's best interests."

And I concluded: "Above all, we have faith in God, that His will is being carried out today—and that all of His children will be cared for."

We finished, took a breath—and a torrent of questions descended on us. Actually, just one question, in a dozen variations: "Where's your son? Why isn't he here?" We told them why, and the reporters seemed to understand this, even seemed impressed by how we were shielding our son and protecting his confidentiality. We answered the questions in as measured a way as possible—about Adam's HIV status, why exactly we wanted a joint adoption from the state, about our foster daughter, what "Mark" called the two of us, and who was pictured in that framed photo in Michael's hands. The more we talked, the more respectful and understanding they seemed. We might not have been able to persuade the state bureaucrats that our case was right—obvious, even—but it seemed that the television and newspaper reporters who quizzed us that day were impressed with what we were fighting for.

Still, they pressed hard. As we talked, one cameraman from WWOR/Channel 9 tried to sidle around Michael to get a zoom shot of Adam's picture. Michael scowled at him and shielded Adam's face from view. And when we thought we'd concluded and got up to go, Denny Lee whispered to us that more reporters wanted to do interviews, including Ronald Smothers from the *New York Times*. And CBS local news had arrived late from Manhattan after being trapped in a bus accident on Route 3—could we reread our statement for their cameras? We did—and then fell into the arms of our friends the priests. I began crying as Mother Elizabeth held me—and I looked up to see the cameras taping even this.

At last we thanked everyone, hurriedly agreed that some could come interview us at home, and escaped—or so we thought. The cameras followed us out, trailing us to the parking garage the way we'd seen happen to other people on the news, but had never imagined happening to us. "Don't jaywalk in front of them!" I hissed half-jokingly at Michael. "That's all we need is for the state to see and take away Adam!"

Once we got back into the van I called Nancy at home from the mobile phone. She was rattled; the phone at the house hadn't stopped ringing. I looked at Michael, awed and alarmed. As we rolled up Route 21, who should be cruising along in the van next to us but the same Channel 7 news crew that had accompanied us out of the ACLU offices. Then we realized that they weren't going back to New York; they were heading to our house.

Our home on Lincoln Avenue was surrounded by media trucks. Nancy looked as if she wished she had a bazooka to fend them all off. She was busy cleaning Adam's fingerprints off the windows so they wouldn't show up on television. My birth mother had gotten in far deeper than she could ever have imagined that day seven months before when she had driven down to Kearny to meet me for the first time.

Ann Mary was waiting for us, with Danny my godson, making her way through the media people, as Danny, age ten, scurried to get himself in the background on the television cameras filming the family. Although I knew she was proud of how she had taught me to fight for my rights, I could tell by her face that she was unnerved by what her doctor had told her the day before. I let her know I felt guilty that I was so preoccupied with our fight for Adam and with all these media people when she was in the midst of a crisis. I hugged her extratight. "Oh, phooey," she said. "You're doing the right thing." She hugged me back even tighter. "Now go talk to those reporters and give 'em hell for Adam."

Michael and I managed the press more firmly now, tripping over their cables only once each, as we went out to insist firmly that, if they wanted footage for their story, they could feature only "Mark" from an unrecognizable distance or from the back. They couldn't even go near Madison. People obeyed. NBC would show us walking down the street, but from the back only, so that Adam was visible only as Anytoddler. Adam was intrigued by all the activity. He bounded around the cameras as if he'd been given a whole new toy box to explore. The tech people and the news reporters were charmed. Active, delighted, he was his own best witness for his health and happiness in our house. Even from a distance.

That evening, after what seemed like an endless stream of media phone calls and in-person interviews, Michael finally got to return a call from his mother. "We saw the *Bergen Record,* and the news. You guys did a wonderful job!" she exclaimed. "And everyone we know has been calling!" Their pinochle-playing friends, Adolph's law-office colleagues and professional acquaintances, long-lost cousins, even a nun they had known years before at Blessed Sacrament Church in Paterson—all were calling in to offer their support. These were the people Michael's parents were worried about finding out Michael was gay, and now they were congratulating Adolph and Dorothy for raising a son who would stand up for his rights and his children. The nun friend had gone so far as to tell Dorothy, "You truly are a blessed mother." "They're all so proud," Michael's mother said. She lowered her voice, and it quavered a little. "And Mike—your father and I—do you know how proud we are of you?"

Michael had been waiting fifteen years to hear those words from his mother—for any reason. He could not have been happier. Today would be a major turning point for both him and his parents. Still, I had to wonder—why weren't Dorothy and Adolph here with us, supporting us? Why did they just phone in their support? I would tell my mother-in-law my feelings later on, and Michael would back me up. They had to learn to be supportive on the scene, and we were getting more confident and insistent about telling them what we needed.

Every single story that appeared that night on the news and in the papers the next morning was positive. Every single one. With the story of our family featured as the evening's lead television story, we were perceived not only as two gay men but as parents standing up to the state bureaucracy. Both of our parish priests, Father Kevin and the Reverend Linda Strohmier, were interviewed on the air praising our parenting skills. *The Record* ran an editorial headlined "Let Them Adopt"; the *New York Times* printed a sympathetic story, as did all the state newspapers. "See, there is a God," Ann Mary told me—this from a woman who had just found out she had breast cancer.

The response was a huge boost for our cause because it meant that the political environment was right to allow DYFS to reverse its policy and that a judicial decision in our favor would not buck the views of New Jerseyans. And it was a big lift to our own feelings of legitimacy as a family out in the world. My only complaint was that when the cameras filmed me walking back to the parking garage from the ACLU, I had so much stuff jammed in my back pockets—my wallet, my speech—I looked like Adam with a full diaper.

Our silver lining had only a few nasty clouds. That weekend, Michael's father called Granddaddy to ask him if he'd been following the story of our lawsuit. "Yeah, I saw it," he grumbled. "He's ruining the family name." This hurt Adolph's feelings a lot, because, just like Michael, he's sensitive to the opinions of his father. Michael was sure that Angela had not only made her antigay opinions known to Granddaddy but had sent news clippings on our lawsuit to her son Bob Enyart out in Denver.

Dorothy called to report that Bob's mother had announced her own Jon-and-Michael rescue mission. "Aunt Angela told your father she really, really needs to 'save' you and Jon," Dorothy reported to Michael. It seems Angela and Ralph—her other, local fundamentalist Christian son—had been commanded by the pastor at their church to try to save us, if they themselves ever wanted to get into heaven. This did not sit well with me. I had a few suggestions about how Angela, Bob, and Ralph could improve their souls, but my notions didn't have a damn thing to do with converting ours. Yet Michael didn't want to disrespect his aunt. He'd grown up loving her dearly and caring about her, and no matter how much he disagreed with her, Michael said that if Angela persisted, we should hear her out. No way, I said—I didn't want that woman and her condescending hatefulness in our house. "Let's not look for trouble," Michael said. "She just doesn't understand yet."

Matt Coles, the head of the ACLU Lesbian and Gay Rights Project, had invited Michael, Adam, and me to join their contingent in the New York lesbian and gay pride march. For nearly thirty years, upwards of a million gay people have either paraded down Fifth Avenue on the last Sunday in June or watched other gay people do it, taking over the city for a day and showing the world their complex colors. Various lesbian and gay rights groups marched; Michael Adams agreed that it would be good for the folks at their organization to be joined by actual plaintiffs—and it would be good for the visibility of gay parental rights as well.

Michael and I had gone to the march when we lived in New York City—but only to watch. We didn't think of ourselves as marchers. Because we were "tolerated" by our employers and by Michael's family and accepted by mine, we never felt compelled to do it for political reasons, and for us as a couple it had never been a social event. The sidelines used to be where we belonged—standing on the curb, waving a little rainbow flag, as our fellow gay people surged down the avenue: people with AIDS and HIV, dykes on bikes, drag queens, gay folk in recovery, gay Jews and Episcopalians, even a small contingent of lesbian moms and gay dads.

Michael balked at going; the event didn't seem like us. Besides, we were still recovering from the media uproar around the press conference and worrying about Ann Mary—not to mention getting used to our new diet: on June 23, exactly a year after we had given up red meat, we stopped eating poultry and, like Madison and Adam, became total vegetarians except for a once-a-month slip with tuna steak or scallops. Adam's triglycerides level was inching downward, so the no-meat diet was working for him and was more healthy for all of us. The parade was one more little transition in a life that wasn't unfolding quite as we expected. "They're our lawyers," I told Michael. "How can we not do it? Besides, if it's too weird, we can just duck out and take Adam to a movie."

That sunny and steamy Sunday morning, Nancy arrived to baby-sit Madison, and we packed up Adam in the minivan together with his stroller, a cooler, and that by now well-worn denim diaper bag and drove over the George Washington Bridge into New York City. Still, driving in, negotiating the preparade traffic and parking at the Ziegfeld Theater parking lot, we found it strange to think we'd be in the street, marching. We were sidewalk people.

This day turned out to be one of the most heartening, thrilling, wonderful days of our lives. It transformed how we saw our family in the world.

We were wearing the three T-shirts I'd gotten made that read DADDY, FATHER, and SON respectively, which gave everyone a pretty big reminder about where he or she might have seen our faces before. I felt the statement was important to make. Just as we rolled up to the ACLU parade contingent, a 1010 WINS radio interviewer descended to do a quick interview, and then a photographer dove in front of us, snapping our picture as Michael grimly protected Adam's face.

"We're at a parade. We're allowed to be in public with our son," I told Michael.

"Yeah, but we chose to march in this parade," he grumbled, adjusting the sun hat to shade Adam from the sun and the cameras.

"Aren't you those guys from New Jersey?" asked a woman who couldn't have been more than twenty, with a bunch of girls who looked as if they'd wandered in from a Mary J. Blige concert.

"Yes, we're from New Jersey," Michael answered cautiously.

"And this is your son?" They peered at Adam, who peered happily back. "He's beautiful. Listen"—they met our eyes—"thanks so much."

"No," Michael said. "Thank you."

As we set off down Fifth Avenue, the bands blaring, the banners flapping, with Matt Coles and Michael Adams striding beside us, more and more people leaned over the police barricades to yell hello and good luck. We waved back happily, feeling a little unsteady with the heat and the attention, as if we were on an ocean liner just setting sail. By the time we marched past the shuttered doors of St. Patrick's Cathedral, with its pathetic little group of antigay protesters across the street waving their tattered placards telling us we were going to hell, I felt as if our family were being swept along less by our own feet than by the cries of the crowd. Every fifteen seconds someone would cry out, "Hey, gay daddies, you rock!" "Hey, good luck!" "We love you! Thank you!" People would wriggle past the barricades or come from other parade contingents to shake our hands and say hello to our son. At one point we had to leave the parade and dash down Thirty-eighth Street to change a nasty diaper. In the midst of it I looked up to see that a bunch of onlookers had glimpsed us and started striding our way to say hello. I've never changed a diaper so fast in my life.

As we moved down the avenue into the more residential neighborhoods, the crowds thickened. "There's those guys!" we kept hearing. "That's them!"

"Go, Daddy!"

"You go, guys!"

"God bless you!"

The women yelled more than the men, but the men screamed and applauded too—especially the very young men and men older than we. The thirtyish, Chelsea-style men seemed startled by us, taken aback that here were two gay men doing something that seemed so different from the customs in their urban enclaves. That attitude would change, though, in the months to come, as gay men of all ages began to realize they could become fathers—and came to like the idea.

For a while Matt Coles himself pushed the stroller, until Adam wriggled out and began running to the sidelines, one of us close behind, exchanging high fives with the onlookers on lower Fifth Avenue, laughing, as charismatic as a rock star. Matt grinned at him. "He works the crowd better than any politician," he said to us as he dashed to scoop him up and lead him down the street.

"So what do you think?" I yelled to Michael as I picked up Adam to carry him the next few blocks.

Michael grinned, kissed Adam, kissed me. "Amazing."

The last half hour of the march became surreal. I felt the three of us were surging down the avenue on the sea of excitement. When we turned the corner at Washington Square, the crowd was twelve deep on either side, with people massed on the stoops of the buildings, hanging off fire escapes—"Go, Daddy! Go, Father! Go, Son!" we kept hearing, over and over. The chant was *deafening*, bouncing off the brownstones: *"Go, Daddy! Go, Father! Go, Son!"* Our bodies literally vibrated. Over the next few blocks, between Washington Square and Christopher Street, the cheers grew even louder. The sound went right through us. The parade paused as we stood in the middle of Christopher Street separated by twenty yards from anyone else before or behind us in the march. We were in a canyon of people. They were cheering and waving. Adam was on Michael's shoulders, laughing in full delight. Crying, grateful, we looked at each other, in awe at the power of our child.

Less than a week later, on July 3, over Fourth of July weekend, Ann Mary entered Hackensack University Medical Center to undergo breast-cancer surgery. I was home taking care of the children, waiting by the phone, jumpy and anxious. All my life I'd taken care of my mother, through three marriages and two widowhoods. I didn't know how to take care of her now.

Herb called me before the surgery, again while he was waiting, and as soon as he got a postoperative report from the surgeon. Nervous, edgy, Herb told me she had lost her left breast and much of her right; the doctors removed many of her lymph nodes as a precaution, which was unexpected and extra-scary.

That night I went to the hospital, leaving the children with Michael. Mom looked drawn and pale, but she put on a good, strong front. Her main goal seemed to be to keep us from worrying about her. Herb stood by the head of her bed, big, quiet, steady, and I felt a wave of affection for him. Here was a man who loved my mother, without a doubt, and would be there to take care of her. I didn't have to do it all by myself.

She reached over to the windowsill. "Look what I got." She pointed to a beautiful bouquet of gerbera daisies with "Love, Dot and Adolph" scrawled on the card. "And can you guess who those are from?" She gestured to another arrangement. "Those are from Nancy." She grinned up at me. "You have terrific mothers, don't you?"

That summer, as Michael Adams and Lenora prepared their briefs in our lawsuit and filed our adoption papers, we tried to live like a regular family. But our lives had changed and everyone knew it, from our fellow parishioners at church, where people gathered around us at coffee hour after the service to clap us on the back and tell us they were starting a letter-writing campaign on our behalf to newspapers and state officials, to strangers who intercepted us on the street, in shopping malls, at the grocery store. It was invigorating and affirming; we encountered not a single bad reaction, which reinforced our judgment that to make our case in public was, in fact, in the best interests of our Adam and Madison.

The people at Michael's job were wonderful. A daily parade of people came through his office, and several of the well-wishers ended up in tears—surprisingly, it was all men doing the crying. At Paparazzi restaurant at Garden State Plaza, a woman came up to us, her two elementary-school-age children in tow. After admiring Adam, she told us she had written a letter to Governor Whitman urging her to let us adopt our son. "Being gay shouldn't make any difference," she told us indignantly. "Is there anything else I can do?" I was especially impressed that she could talk to two gay men about their parenting so comfortably in front of her own children, and I wished more parents would be like that. She wouldn't be the first person to say she'd appealed to the governor on our behalf. One person, Sue Garahan, surprised us the most as she took to us and our fight with letter writing and phone calls to all branches of the New Jersey government. Sue also enlisted others to do the same. Or maybe it wasn't that she was the most surprising to us—she might just have been the most heartwarming: Sue was the girlfriend Michael had left behind fifteen years before, for me.

People would cross the aisle in the mall to tell us they were praying for us. Aunt Angela would have felt pretty lonely outside Nordstrom's that summer.

Even closer to home, the shop owners on Pleasant Avenue in Maywood were incredibly friendly. I grew up with Billy Loschiavo, whose parents owned the ice cream store, and I frequently stopped there with the kids on our daily stroll into town. His entire clan would fawn all over the kids as they reassured me that we were in their prayers. Mrs. Barber, my brother Stephen's third-grade teacher, now in her seventies, came up to me in the vegetable aisle of the Maywood Market. "It's just ridiculous that there's all this conflict about homosexuality," she announced. "As if all heterosexuals have sex in the same way! You go ask a roomful of married people how many of them have sex in just the missionary position, and you'd be surprised! We all do it differently! You are doing a beautiful thing, and this child should be yours!" Right on, Mrs. Barber.

We were elated by all this positive response, but we had to be careful how we managed it, for our own psychic health and the well-being of two very impressionable children. First, no matter how many people shook our hands or wrote the governor, the real power lay with the courts hearing our lawsuit. The support from New Jersey citizens helped, but the courts would decide the fate of our adoption petition. Second, we had to make sure that the attention didn't unbalance our family in some way. We had to live normal lives, as much as we could. If we can make a larger difference, great, but we were Jon and Michael, Adam and Madison's parents, first of all. We were receiving uncommonly good press for gay people, and that would help to create an environment that would be more positive for Adam and Madison someday.

With everybody peering into our windows and over our shoulders, we sensed a new pressure—to be perfect parents. I felt I had to be showered and combed and dressed up before I left the house in the morning to drop off an absolutely presentable and well-behaved little boy to his summer program. Having people come up to us at Paparazzi to express their support was terrific but exhausting, especially when Adam was acting like the two-year-old he was about to become. Michael and I imagined people peering over their menus saying to each other, "There are those gay parents. Let's see what they do with that screaming kid." After a while, we had to let go and just relax. We might be poster parents, but we were private parents first of all. Our goal was always just to be really good parents; perfect parents simply don't exist.

The children thrived under the extra attention they received. Adam was at the developmental stage when everything in the world revolved around him anyway. In every way, both Adam and Madison were flourishing. Madison watched it all go by, serene as Athena. She was progressing to solid food, the same low-fat items that Adam, Michael, and I were eating. It seemed like a good idea for all of our hearts, even our youngest and our healthiest, to eat right from the start. Adam's triglycerides were still high, at 700, but slowly coming down. Michael's parents remained confused by our food habits. "I don't know what to make for you! What do you eat?" asked Dorothy in frustration. She would offer cheese tortellini Alfredo to Adam. "Well, it doesn't have meat! Can't he just have a little?" she would ask us, missing the point of fat-free entirely.

Nancy had taken a fat-free cooking class so that she could prepare food for us. She was concerned about all of us getting enough protein, and whenever she visited, we waved our beans in front of her to persuade her that we knew what we were doing. Certainly, we all looked great. Michael and I had put on weight when Adam first arrived, but with our new diets we were the leanest we'd been since college, and probably the healthiest we had ever been.

Nancy had also taken a course in pediatric CPR, which allowed her to be approved by DYFS as an alternative caregiver for our medically fragile daughter. Ann Mary had taken the course earlier, which now meant the children were allowed to stay overnight at their houses. Nancy would play with Madison gently, coddling her as if she were a fragile piece of crystal. She was a baby girl, delicate and "precious," as Nancy always put it. She was alarmed when Madison would take a tumble and I'd just sit there. "Mom, she's okay—this is what little kids do." Having a baby girl in her life was unfamiliar to Nancy. Gradually I persuaded her that I was capable, a good stay-at-home parent as competent as a woman to raise children—even a little girl.

Nancy constantly fretted that we were going to lose Adam, as a couple of the media people had sensationally written—not to mention the risk she saw looming for Madison. We worried less. We were taking Loretta McCormick at her word—that DYFS would not do anything to challenge the presence of either Madison or Adam in our house. The media scrutiny the case had gotten also insured us against overt retribution from the state. Nancy and Dorothy were the two who most worried that some nutcase out there would attack our family. Ann Mary kept her worries veiled beneath her bravado. I was able to comfort Nancy a little, and that brought us closer together.

I'd met Nancy's husband, Roger, on Valentine's Day, when I'd driven over to Chappaqua for lunch at the Hensons' house, bearing flowers and a carefully selected, not-too-emotional Valentine's card for my mother. Roger had been instantly genial, caught up with the idea of having grandchildren. Over the next months he would hit it off with Michael and also with Michael's father, as the two patriarchs vigorously debated the business of the world. From the start I'd never thought of him as just my birth mother's husband. As I grew closer to him, I even began to think of him as a father. Calling any man *Dad* was a tricky proposition for me, because I'd had so many fathers disappear on me like Cheshire cats, from Danny and Joe to Richard Hartman, but I started getting used to the idea. First, however, I had to figure out what to call Nancy. And before *that,* I had to make the acquaintance of my brother Don.

Nancy remained worried about how Don would react, finding out at age twenty-seven that he had a brother he'd never heard about. She put off telling him because Don was away on business trips, but her husband urged her to do it soon, before Don began questioning his mother's newly emotional behavior. Roger brought up the subject spontaneously at dinner one night that May. Don was shocked, thrown, confused. When he was a little boy, he'd had an imaginary older brother who lived in the spare room. That used to break Nancy's heart. But now this older brother was flesh and blood, and gay. When Don told his new girlfriend, Megan, that he had a brother, she was excited and intrigued. "You have to meet him right away," she told Don. "And you have to bring me along when you meet his babies!"

I followed up with a letter to Don introducing myself, saying that I really wanted to meet him, but that he should take all the time he needed to get used to the idea—and wasn't it all really weird? Don called the day he got the letter and invited me to lunch.

"Sure," I said.

"How about tomorrow?"

"Uh, sure. Okay."

Michael came home early the next day to stay with Adam and Madison, and I drove to meet Don at Houston's at Riverside Square in Hackensack—he'd mentioned it was his favorite restaurant. The moment I entered and saw his face, I knew what he was thinking: *He looks just like my mother.* At that moment I became real for him, and he was overwhelmed.

And I thought, *He looks nothing like his mother.* Actually, he looked just like Donny Osmond.

After we agreed that we were both scared out of our minds, we got along pretty well, trading stories about Nancy, starting to exchange several decades' worth of information about our lives. I told him I worried he wasn't going to be able to handle the gay thing, and he looked at me as if I were speaking Latin, and perhaps I was—maybe straight young men today don't have so much fear and prejudice ground into them from birth. And maybe also Nancy raised an openhearted son.

"I hear that Adam's a ball of fire," he said as we picked at our spinach and artichoke dip. "And Madison's precious."

"*Precious.* That's a real Nancy word."

He looked confused for a second that I'd mentioned his—our— mother by her first name. When I showed him pictures of the kids, he examined them carefully and asked about Michael and about our lawsuit and agreed it was the right thing to do. "Congratulations," I said, "you're an uncle."

It was the start of a very nice brotherhood. He and his girlfriend would become a young couple central to our lives—Uncle Don and Aunt Megan. Our elastic family extended once again.

What was I supposed to call this new mother in my life? Should I call her Mom? Did she want me to? The more I got to know and love her, the more I didn't know how to address her.

I tested out calling her Mom in a conversation with Don as he romped with Adam and Madison one summer afternoon in the back- yard, rolling around the lawn as Megan and Michael were preparing lunch in the kitchen. "I think Mom really likes having grandchildren," I commented, oh so casual. Don didn't blink an eye. That emboldened me to say *Mom* more to him until I was truly saying it naturally. Now I had to try it out on Mom—er, Nancy.

I'd called Dorothy Mom for years, and Ann Mary, of course—whose feelings I didn't want to hurt. And every time I said *Nancy* I heard

Mom in my head. Once, I snuck in a *Ma* on the telephone—and she snapped at me.

"I hate *Ma*," she said. "Don has never called me Ma." Then, in a gentle voice she added, "If anything, it's *Mom, not Ma.*"

Now I was more confused than ever—shot down, I thought. Nancy brought it up the next day when we met. She had been caught off guard to hear that word from me. And wasn't this going to be difficult for Ann Mary if I called Nancy Mom?

"It was difficult for me to say it," I said. "I just don't know what to call you."

"You have to decide what you want to call me."

"I want to call you Mom."

Seriousness and sadness left her and her face lightened. "Then Mom it is!" she said with great finality. And so it was.

My next hard task was to tell my mother Ann Mary what I had agreed to call my mother Nancy. "You just have to talk to her," Michael told me. "You're not doing anything wrong. You love your mother. And besides, you call *my* mother Mom. You're projecting that Ann Mary will be hurt."

Ann Mary was totally fine with it. "I know who I am," she said.

Nowadays I call my mother Mom and my mother Mom. It's a happy solution.

Our nice new minivan was packed to the windows and sported a clam-shell on top, a while plastic storage bin courtesy of Mike and Maria next door, now lovingly referred to as Uncle Mike and Aunt Mia. For our second vacation to Provincetown as a family, we came prepared, complete with two booster seats to make restaurant dining for toddlers easier, no matter how gay the place.

We didn't really need the booster seats. Most restaurants had them this year, and that was an indication of how Provincetown—and the gay world nationwide—was changing its attitude toward children. Gay men and lesbians were getting used to seeing children in their midst. Gay and Lesbian Family Week in Provincetown had drawn over two hundred families—more than twice as many as the year before. Commercial Street suffered from stroller gridlock.

Our Provincetown friends Kelly and Marguerite and their son, Sam, had visited us in December for dinner and a play date, and now they lent us a Portacrib to show off Madison. This year we were joined by our friend Keith, Madison's godfather, and his partner, Artie, whom we'd met back in our California days. Juliette, a friend of mine from AT&T Wireless, served as our nanny in return for free accommodations. We had rented a house big enough for all of us, including acrobatic Adam. Many of the couples we met had heard of our lawsuit, and a lot of people came up to us to offer their support, their experiences, and their strategies for dealing with adoption services agencies.

Also coming up to us were not just the more mature folks who had admired Adam the year before but younger gay men—and they weren't sneering, like the man who'd muttered the year before, "Oh, isn't that *cute*. They think they're a *family*." This year, gay men in their twenties would grin at our family, squat to say hello to Adam, stroke Madison's round, regal face, and then barrage us with questions: They really gave you a baby? How do you do this? You're lovers? You didn't have to hide that you were gay and they gave you a baby? I could see their sunburned minds working as they pondered the new possibility of maybe becoming parents someday.

One night when Michael and I put a tuckered-out Adam and Madison to bed and left them with Juliette to go out dancing, three vacationers came up to us on the dance floor of the Atlantic House. "Where are your kids?" one of them asked.

"You ever heard of baby-sitters?" I replied.

"*Oh*," the guy said wonderingly. It seemed to be occurring to him that you could be a gay father and still go out dancing. A lot of gay men who are twenty-five now will decide in five years to become fathers. The expectant-father looks on their faces—along with Madison's first imperious encounter with the ocean—were the best parts of our vacation.

"She was there right after Madison was born. She wants to see her sister again," Gary, Madison's social worker, told us during a foster-child home visit right before Labor Day. "Her name is Rosa, and she's fourteen, and she lives in the Woodley group home for adolescents with family problems, just over in Ridgewood."

I looked at Michael, whose face was tight. "Now you don't have to agree to it," Gary went on. "As a sibling she has no legal rights in this situation. But she asked me, as her caseworker, to ask you."

Rosa came from a family that had been completely dispersed by the state, and she had survived a painful family life. She had lived with her adored grandmother for a while, but now the old woman was too sick to take care of her. She'd run away from home and had tried to kill herself when she was twelve. DYFS had rescued her from a psych ward at St. Mary's Hospital. She had been placed in group homes. Trying hard to make the group home work, she was attending Ridgewood High, one of the best and richest schools in New Jersey. But she had been badly hurt by her childhood, Gary said; she was rebellious, physical, volatile. If we agreed to let her see Madison, she would receive therapy about what it meant to her to meet her sister and us; she'd be told how important it was to protect the confidentiality of her sister's foster parents.

I knew what Michael was thinking because I was thinking it too. We didn't know this girl at all. If we gave in to her plea to see Madison, we could open ourselves up to a lot of trouble.

We were told that Rosa didn't know who we were or where her sister was, which was the way the system is supposed to work. The identity of foster parents is withheld from their foster children's blood relatives, to protect everyone involved. If we chose to reunite Rosa and Madison, we would be giving up the last little bit of anonymity and immunity we had. Madison wasn't ours legally yet, and we were in the midst of a very public battle to adopt Adam into our publicly gay family. In fact, we were hoping any day to get a final court date to hear a judge's decision on our petition to adopt Adam. What if Rosa didn't like us and reported us back to her mother or other relatives, or the state? If we reached out to this girl, would we put Madison at risk?

Michael and I talked about it and talked about it. Every one of our relatives was alarmed we were even considering visiting this girl. Loretta McCormick, generous as she had been to Adam's mother, Diane, and women like her, warned us that we had no idea what we were getting into, although she did say that Woodley, Rosa's group home, was the best in the state, and that the girl might well be up to the challenge of the place.

Michael and I talked about it some more. We prayed about it. Finally, we decided God had to be telling us something. This girl had gone out of her way to seek out her little sister. We had to honor that. And besides, I'd sought out my own blood relative the year before. Couldn't I allow this girl the chance for the same kind of family reunion I had had?

One visit, we told Gary. We'd go up there to the home and introduce Madison to her sister for one hour only, and see what happened.

Michael took the afternoon off from work and we drove over to Ridgewood after school let out, with both Madison and Adam in the backseat. We'd dressed Madison in a new, pale blue dress and new shoes—we wanted her to look well taken care of. The home itself was a big old Victorian mansion donated to the state and transformed into a ten-bed center for girls without other stable homes. Madison or Adam could have ended up in a place like this, I thought. In a town that is wealthy and mostly white, Woodley's largely black and Latina tenants would stand out like gems in the snow.

The girls were tough and loud, as if they were all competing to prove how fierce they were—we noticed that right off. The residential social worker led us into the dining room, and there sat a girl who looked just like Madison, only older and scarred.

Rosa sat on the edge of her chair, looking cocky and anxious. Her hair was in a high, flouncy ponytail, and she was wearing white shorts, a white T-shirt, and little white socks with the Puerto Rican flag on them. "Yeah, pleased to meet you," she mumbled, shaking our hands, avoiding our eyes.

When we handed her Madison to hold, her face blossomed. Madison looked up into her sister's eyes, studying her gravely. Our little budding diva has never taken to new people easily the way Adam

Rosa and Madison, sisters reunited.

does—and right then he was his charming self, dashing around and greeting everyone, making himself the leading man in the lives of the girls in the residence. Madison had attitude. She looked at Rosa. Smiling, Rosa looked at Madison. It was scary and lovely to see.

Kim, Rosa's staff counselor, knew who we were from the newspapers and was surprised we'd agreed to the visit. We told her how cautious we were and that we weren't committing to anything. "So what's Rosa like?" Michael asked.

Kim, smart and savvy, grinned at us. "She's a total princess."

Michael looked at me and laughed. I saw Madison out of the corner of my eye, waving her fat little hand at Rosa like Queen Elizabeth reviewing the royal guard. "Then she would fit in fine at *our* house," I said.

Rosa invited us to a party at Woodley the following week. We came, gave her some more time with Madison, and sat her down to ask if she had any problem with our being gay. "No, not anymore," she told us. Before long she was referring to Michael and me as her sister's parents, which relieved us a whole lot. When one kid from a boys' group home visited Woodley and said something snide about how Rosa's sister had fags for parents, Rosa read him until he was a quivering pile of debris. She finished him off by saying, angry and wistful, "At least she *has* parents!"

Michael could tell by his father's uneasy voice on the phone that Adolph hated what he had to say, and sure enough, Aunt Angela and Cousin Ralph wanted to come convert us.

Michael was caught in the middle by his family once again. I left it up to him, secretly praying that he would tell Aunt Angela to take a leap. But he decided he would see her. He called her and set it up for two nights later at 8:30 P.M., purposely at an hour when Adam and Madison would be asleep. That way, if Angela and her son tied us down and exorcised us, our children wouldn't have to witness it. Or hear any screaming or yelling. "Honey, it's my family. All we have to do is listen," Michael told me. "Let them say what they feel they need to. At least we can say that we heard them out. Besides, maybe they'll understand." I promised to turn over a new leaf and keep my mouth shut.

On a hot and humid evening, Aunt Angela arrived, tall and edgy, carrying a Bible and a sheaf of pamphlets from her church, with Cousin Ralph behind her, a nondescript, slightly overweight man who looked like a door salesman. We said hello and gathered around the dining room table. Michael served them coffee and cake ("Let them drink water," I'd muttered).

"I'd really like to congratulate you on your children and see them," Angela began, sounding grief-stricken. "But I can't do that. It's *just so wrong.*"

How was I ever going to keep my mouth shut?

"I've talked to my pastor"—she held out the pamphlet with her pastor's picture on it—"and he told me I was called to come here, because we have the knowledge of heaven and hell, and since we know that homosexuals don't get into heaven, and we have the knowledge that can save you, *we*"—she gestured at her son, mute beside her— "could not get into heaven unless we enlightened you about how you can change your lifestyle so you won't be forbidden entrance into heaven."

Ralph piped up. "My mother was very nervous about coming here, and I'm here to support her. But she's right—and if I didn't come here with her, it would be held in front of me when I'm judged."

God, are they screwed up. I sat on my hands. I literally sat on my hands.

"Everyone's entitled to their beliefs," Michael said carefully. "You've been my favorite aunt. I'm sorry that there has to be this kind of contention in our family."

Angela leaned toward him, waving her pamphlet. "Right here, my pastor says . . ." She went on to deliver a pretty standard-issue you're-going-to-hell-for-your-sin-of-homosexuality speech, and how through Jesus Christ we could mend our ways.

"I really don't agree with that philosophy, because being gay is the way Jesus Christ made me," Michael countered.

"Well, we're really here to make sure that we give you the message and save ourselves as well as save you from the sin of homosexual behavior," Angela said. From what I could tell, trying to rescue Jon Holden and Michael Galluccio was some kind of fundamentalist merit badge Ralph and Angela were determined to win.

"I don't think there's anything to save me from," Michael said evenly.

"But we're all sinners," Ralph said. "For example, I've repeatedly sinned and it's hard for me not to, but I pray each and every day not to sin that way anymore."

After more back and forth I couldn't stand it anymore. "Can I just say one thing?" Michael glared at me, as if to say, *And you were doing so well.* "Aunt Angela, Michael and I could break up right now and go meet women and marry them. And we could have sex with them. But there is no doubt that while we were having sex with them, we'd still be thinking of men. Of each other. It's not about our behavior, it's about who we are, deep down—it's part of our essence. Can't you get that?"

Angela sat back and stared at me, looking appalled. "And then to bring children into it, to show it to children. That makes it even worse. Can't you save yourself for the sake of your children?"

"My children are very lucky," Michael replied. "Because of us, they know what it is to see two parents who deeply love each other." He glowered at them. "I think we've spoken enough."

Angela sighed quietly, looked at Ralph, and they rose to go, having saved their souls if not ours. Just as they opened our front door and left our house to march to their car across the street, the sky thundered violently, the heavens opened, and rain came pounding down in torrents. They ran to their car, drenched.

Michael turned to me. "Well, I guess that's what God thinks of what they had to say tonight."

One Saturday afternoon early that September, Michael was working at the dining room table while I went up to retrieve Adam from his nap. What I discovered made me laugh uncontrollably. "Michael! Come up here right away!" I called downstairs.

Michael thumped up the stairs, an anxious look on his face, until he saw that I wasn't upset but laughing—and why. Standing in the doorway to the nursery was Adam, dusted completely white, a cloud around him.

Adam had woken from his nap and somehow managed to lean over the gate to his room and grab a container of baby powder, which he had dumped over his head. His blond hair was caked to his scalp. The only visible parts of his face were his brown eyes and the inside of his laughing mouth. His clothes, the floor, and the walls looked as if a snowstorm had passed through. Michael looked at Adam, then at me, then burst out in guffaws.

I grabbed a camera and snapped the picture we would use on our son's birthday invitation, captioned, *Adam's 2!*

The invitation also said, *Come Celebrate.* No matter what the courts decided, we had reason to rejoice. Over the last year, Adam's health had normalized almost totally. He was no longer classified as having HIV antibodies. Thanks to Roger and Nancy, he had a new set of grandparents, Gramps and Nana. He'd become a public baby and flourished with the attention. Because he had spent so much effort getting over his physical maladies, we had worked to spur his developing brain

ADAM'S 2!
COME CELEBRATE

circuitry in every way we could, getting him to talk, reading books with him, asking him questions—"Where's the remote control? Can you go get Father's shoe?"—and then helping him answer them. Teaching him to follow a line of direction, we had happily become those anal-retentive parents that people make fun of, the kind that use every opportunity as a chance to educate their children—but we didn't want to lose any occasion to stimulate Adam into being the best and bright-est boy he could be. Only now would we start relaxing, when he went to nursery school and started getting an official education.

We had a big birthday party for him in the backyard, complete with a clown and a slide for the kids to play on. A magician did tricks and the children from his preschool class at Maywood Co-op, where I was class father, sat rapt. Nancy and Roger came, and so did Don and Megan. Herb and Ann Mary had come, even though she was queasy and gray from chemotherapy. Adolph and Dorothy came with friends. We'd wanted Rosa to attend the party but she couldn't, since we weren't her foster family. DYFS didn't know how to handle it, and Rosa's birth mother wasn't around to sign off on a visit. Three other couples attended from Lambda Families—Jill and Vicky with their son,

Richard; Frank and Arnold, who had two African-American boys; and Stan and Hal, with a son adopted from Mexico. Adam, Madison, and those children all contrasted with my cousin's kids, Alexander and Victoria, blue-eyed, white-blond children, a rainbow of skin colors as all the children took their turns down the slide. It was cool to watch.

A year had elapsed since Elizabeth McGovern at ARC had informed me I couldn't adopt my son. We'd come a long way and had further to go. Michael Adams and Lenora had told us that we would soon be receiving a court date when we would hear the decision from Judge Sybil Moses, who had assigned the case to herself. I didn't know anything about Judge Moses, and that was the way it was supposed to be. All she would know about us was what she had heard and what she read about in the ACLU briefs and in whatever report Loretta had written, and what she had seen in the media. But as Michael and I watched Adam go laughing down the slide again like a normal kid, smearing low-fat birthday cake all over his new jeans, I wished she were here to see our son in action, among his family, happy, flourishing, at home. There was so much I wanted her—and all the world—to know.

NINE

BEST INTERESTS OF THE CHILD

Michael Galluccio

Around six-thirty on the morning of October 22, Adam clambered into bed and pulled at my face, tugging at both my cheeks until I opened my eyes to see his smile. He did this nearly every morning that I slept past my 4 A.M. wake-up time and was home when he woke up. "Get up!" he demanded. "Get up, Fadder! I want panpakes!"

This morning we were scheduled to appear in court to hear Judge Moses's decision on our petition to adopt Adam. After getting our coffee and giving Madison her bottle and some baby cereal, we were still moving in zombie mode, doing by rote the morning child care that was second nature by now. Jon was making us pancakes. "Today's the day you're going to become a Galluccio!" I told Adam. "Don't forget to smile and be cute for the judge!"

"Adam, you're going to meet a lot of new people today, and they're going to like you a lot!" Jon said. He and I were incredibly nervous, but we weren't about to let on to Adam and Madison that today was a culmination of all we'd been fighting for—and that we had no idea if we would win or lose the right to adopt them together.

I was in the shower when a newspaper reporter from the *Star Ledger* called and got Jon. "I'm glad I caught you," he said, "because I know you've got to leave for the courthouse any minute, and I want to ask you what your feelings are. After all, in an hour you'll be in the judge's chambers and—"

"What you do mean, *in an hour?*" Jon asked. "The court appointment isn't until one-thirty."

"No, no, no—it's at ten-thirty. I just spoke to the court clerk. You better get a move on."

Jon hung up, called the court, found out our court time was ten-thirty, and dashed upstairs to the bathroom. The door burst open and the shower curtain was ripped aside. Fortunately I wasn't reliving the pivotal scene in *Psycho,* although from Jon's wild face I couldn't be sure. "Michael! The reporter called! The time got mixed up! We have to leave in *twenty minutes!"*

It was as if the house itself had flipped a switch into overdrive. I finished my shower in ten seconds, donned my bathrobe, then grabbed the kids, one under each arm, and gave them baths at fast-forward speed, while Jon called all our lawyers to make sure that they knew the correct time. Michael Adams and Denny Lee were shocked and would try to make it as soon as they could. Fortunately, Lenora Lapidus and Barbara Fox, the adoption specialist handling our case in partnership with the ACLU, were local; they could make it. Jon then made strategically placed calls to friends and relatives— my parents, Grandma Grace and Papa Nooch, his two sets of parents and his cousins, Father Kevin, Loretta, Juliette our friend and Provincetown nanny, and Lou Maack, the president of the New Jersey Foster Parents Association, to tell them to drop everything and get there pronto.

Next Jon leaped into the shower, shaved, picked out clothes for the children, and got himself dressed. Adam took this opportunity to audition for the U.S. Olympics gymnastics team; Madison regarded our frenzy as the perfect opportunity to practice walking. This time we knew we were wearing suits—not more U.S. Open Golf Tournament for the media—and we dressed Adam in comfortable clothes, in blue cords and blue sweater, because he'd have to sit still for a long time today. Still, we wanted him to look good, a 100 percent all-American boy, because there would be media people there, and for the first time they would be able to film and photograph Adam face-to-face. Although he was seen by the media before his adoption, our wishes were respected and his face was never captured on camera.

No matter the outcome, would the battle continue after today? As we careened into the minivan and drove up Passaic Street into Hackensack, Jon and I had the deciding episode in a discussion that had continued between us for weeks. "What if we lose?" Jon muttered. "What if she says, 'Jon, you're a nice guy but the law is clear and, Mr. Galluccio, you're the one with the job so you're the father here'? Then what?"

"I've always said we have options," I told Jon. We had heard from Michael Adams that the state had said it would not appeal any decision by the judge to grant us the joint adoption. If we lost, the battle could continue. If we won, we won for good.

"But Judge Moses has got both cases. If she says no today, there's not much hope that she's going to turn around and say yes to the class action suit."

"That's right," I said gingerly. If we won, the suit might still fail, but if we lost—with all our good arguments so far, and with editorial and public opinion sympathetic to us—then the suit didn't have much chance.

"So then you'll be Adam's father all by yourself," Jon said tartly.

"Jon, we've done about everything we can do. Adam would be protected, at least somewhat, and then you'd come in later. And we would know we had done all we could do."

Jon was quiet at that. He glared out the window, lips pursed. I knew he was reliving all the struggle and challenge we'd endured over the last thirteen months. He kept staring straight ahead as urban Hackensack flicked by. "One way or another," he said finally, "Adam is getting adopted today."

"So we don't contest if we lose."

Jon looked grim. "We'd just better not lose."

We found a spot, parked the car, and sprinted into the courthouse with the children in tow, bearing our briefcase of paperwork and the conspicuous denim diaper bag. My mother was already there with two of her friends, halted at the courthouse metal detector and begging the guard to let her in with their video camera. We all managed to get in, because Judge Moses had cleared the way for us to bring in cameras, and dashed down the hall to the elevator. We were all too breathless and anxious to maintain our nervous chatter, because looming in all our minds was one question—what would Judge Moses say?

By the time we made it to the judge's outer offices, we were actually early, two minutes to be exact. Cooling our heels, we sat and watched Lenora and our lawyer Barbara Fox arrive. Loretta slipped in too and gave us a shy smile; she was there as a DYFS representative, her official role limited to formally declaring that the state would not contest our victory. Michael Adams and Denny Lee were still on a bus somewhere between New York City and Hackensack. Adam was bouncing from lap to lap and scaling the benches in the anteroom. "I cannot believe this is finally happening," Jon whispered to me. "I never thought we'd make it here."

At precisely ten-thirty a woman emerged from behind a pair of glass doors. "Judge Moses will see you now," she intoned. Jon handed Madison over to Juliette, who had just arrived, and one by one all the main interested parties filed down the hall and into the judge's private chambers—the lawyers, my parents, Loretta, and the two of us, with Jon holding Adam tight against his chest. Jon's parents had yet to arrive—the time change for the hearing had made it all but impossible. Nancy arrived as the glass doors closed. She saw us head into the chambers, said a prayer, and searched the hallways for her precious Madison.

Beyond a pair of high oak doors, the judge's chambers looked straight out of the set of an expensive movie—perfectly appointed furniture, a massive conference table, sleek and sturdy law volumes lining one wall ceiling to floor, and totally intimidating, with the exception of some photos of smiling little ones framed on her credenza. I felt as if I'd been completely enveloped in the mahogany precincts of the law.

Judge Moses was sitting in her judicial robes behind her broad desk, framed by the wall of windows overlooking the courthouse lawns. She was an athletic and serious-looking woman in her fifties, with thick, bobbed, silvering hair and dark, large eyes that stared straight at you, promising justice and, maybe, a little mercy. Firmly, briskly she said, "You're the parents? And this is the baby? Please sit there," indicating the wooden armchairs directly in front of her desk. She looked up as my father slipped in the door, and her face registered recognition and surprise. "Hello, Counselor. I didn't realize you were involved in this case." Apparently Judge Moses knew my father as a member of the northern New Jersey community of lawyers and judges.

"No, Your Honor, I'm the grandfather."

"Oh." Judge Moses gave him a small, brief smile. Her eyes swept the room to make sure we were all seated, that Barbara Fox was here, and that Adam was calm, which he was, in Jon's lap, as Jon took off his blue-plaid coat with the wooden buttons and hood. If he started to act up at all, Jon was ready to hand him off to my mother, seated next to him; he and I were both absurdly nervous that if Adam didn't behave, Judge Moses would take him away from us on the spot. I tried to read from her expression an indication of what she might be about to tell us—or even who she was as a person—but her face was impassive. She looked like the law. This judge could have a second career as a poker player.

I glanced behind me and caught Loretta among the people seated in concentric semicircles in the back of the room. She was wearing a sharp-looking, mint green go-to-court blazer and looked very official. She'd been with Jon and Adam and me from the start, and it was good to see her here. Because her department was on the other side of the law from us, we'd treated her like an independent party and respected her role as Adam's caseworker, not our advocate with DYFS. It was enough that we knew she wanted the best for Adam.

Judge Moses began the session as the stenographer took notes. In this closed-court session she fired us a lot of basic adoption questions, from our names and ages to our financial situation, all of which were covered in court papers but which she wanted to put in for the record of this session. Barbara Fox had been pretty businesslike in all her dealings with us, but now her tone was softening as she conveyed our basic adoption qualifications to the judge. We were sweating just on general principle. Adam cried out; this was boring compared to Barney, or compared to just about anything else he could be doing on a sunny October morning.

Then the judge took a breath, put on her reading glasses, opened up a folder, and began reading. "In the matter of adoption . . ."

She was citing cases, precedents, facts, sociological studies on gay parenting, on one parent as compared to two parents having custody of a child, and other instances of adoption cases that had come before courts all over the country. Clearly, like any good judge, she had done her homework. But as she was reading in that steady voice of hers, neutrally presenting the research, Jon and I sat there with absolutely no clue what direction she was going. Our suspense mounted, and being legal civilians we soon got lost in all the precedents and claims and counterclaims, especially with Adam somersaulting in our laps.

The more she read, the less Adam could sit still, and Jon and I kept passing him back and forth between us, trying to soothe and distract him. Judge Moses's eyes flashed. She glared at us above her glasses. "Grandma," she said to my mother, "would you please take the baby." Then the judge handed him a yellow Hi-Liter, a red marker, and a legal pad so that he could draw. I felt flushed with embarrassment. That's it, part of me thought—no way will she let us adopt him now; I haven't been the perfect parent. I knew Jon was also feeling scared. Please, Adam, I tried to beam into his little head—stay quiet until the judge decides this!

As Judge Moses went on reading the background material on adoption, I imagined the family and friends who had to be gathering on the other side of that oak door behind us in the hall outside the judge's offices and chambers—from Grandma Grace and Papa Nooch to Nancy and Roger, my sisters, and all our friends. Among my biggest fears was walking out of this chamber having lost. I dreaded that. So many people had opened a vein for us—and I, good considerate Michael, could let them down. If we were denied a joint adoption now, I'd feel responsible not just for Adam's lack of two-parent security in the eyes of the law—and Jon's grief—but the disappointment felt by other people, from Lou Maack and the New Jersey Foster Parents Association to all those Go-Daddy supporters—not to mention Lambda

Families, whose class action suit would have no precedent to boost its chances.

Jon and I were sitting, taut in our business suits, looking attentive, our terror probably visible on our faces, ready to cry just from the tension alone. At least my parents were here—knowing that my mother was beside me and my father two rows back made me feel as if Jon and I weren't alone. Now at last, I had my parents literally backing me up. They might be hurt if we lost, but at least they would feel the pain too and comfort me.

I looked at Adam. He was quiet by now, sitting at my mother's feet, her hands on his shoulders. I realized in horror that he wasn't drawing on the pad. Instead, he was drawing *on his face*—all around his lips and eyes: he was trying to put the marker in his mouth! My mother batted it away from him, which only smeared it more. How could he ever show his face now? And if the judge saw him . . .

Judge Moses kept talking and I tried to pay attention like a good boy. I kept watching for any sign, any detail, of how she might decide, from the flicker in her eyes to the timbre of her voice. I glanced at Jon and he was doing the same thing.

Then something changed—first in her tone, her voice rising, and then in something opinion-making and conclusive that she said. In the midst of all her legal words it took me a minute to realize what was tipping the balance in our favor: a recommendation submitted by Loretta McCormick.

We hadn't known Loretta was going to say anything at all. But from what we were hearing, Loretta had gone against her employers—saying that Jon Holden and Michael Galluccio were absolutely fit parents, and that the best interests of the child would be served if the joint adoption was granted without the consent of DYFS. It was a beautiful recommendation. And it was brave. And it seemed to be making all the difference.

I met Jon's eyes and knew that he too had realized what Loretta was doing for us; his face had cleared, as if a warm front had just blown in. I resisted the urge to look over my shoulder toward Loretta in the back of the room, but I wanted to vault my chair and hug the breath out of her in gratitude.

Making it clear that the class action suit remained an open issue, one that she would rule on separately, Judge Moses concluded that Adam, ward of the state, should be pronounced the legal son of both Jon Holden and Michael Galluccio.

Through our tears Jon and I smiled at each other and *we knew*: our spirits rose out of our chairs in joy. In the room behind us people let out their breath, and we heard gasps and sobs of joy, which may have belonged to my mother or my father or Lenora or Barbara or Loretta— or maybe us.

After that, people may have clapped and laughed and cheered and maybe even Judge Moses smiled—I don't know, and Jon doesn't either, because all that existed in the world were Adam and his two fathers and their happy tears. We scooped him up, smeared as he was with red and yellow marker like an ancient warrior, and we hugged our son.

Adam was passed from grandparent to parent and to Judge Moses, as my mother wielded her video camera. "This is my favorite part of being a judge—doing the adoptions," Judge Moses said as she bounced Adam in her arms. When she tried to hand him back to my father, Adam wouldn't go—he held on to her necklace. It was as if he too knew that Judge Moses was his personal deliverer.

I glimpsed Loretta's green blazer through the crowd. She was standing all by herself, watching her handiwork, the late-morning light from the judge's huge windows streaming down onto her and haloing her, appropriately enough. I caught her eye. She was beaming at me. I grabbed Jon's hand and we wriggled our way through the people and we embraced her. "You're our fairy godmother," Jon exclaimed. "Thank you!"

"Awwww," she said. "You deserved it. You earned it. You're great parents. Congratulations."

There *are* people out there who will put themselves on the line for the best interests of a child.

I opened the oak door to the hallway leading to the judge's antechambers, and my mother rushed ahead of me and rounded the bend to the outer office. I heard a cheer rise up, like a huge wave, and then saw my mother through the glass doors in front of me. She had her hand in a thumbs-up. Massed just beyond the doors were my grandparents, people from Lambda Families, both sets of Jon's parents, my mother and father's pinochle-playing brigade, Juliette holding a smiling Madison, Don and Megan, reporters, and people we didn't even know—thronging toward us.

Everyone crowded around us, hugging us, clapping us on the back, kissing us, and doing the same to Adam, held aloft by Jon and laughing in delight at the love billowing over him. For Jon, perhaps the richest moment was when Ann Mary rushed over sobbing. "I'm so happy for you!" she cried. "I wanted you to have this moment, so that you would know how much you can love an adopted child."

I saw my son through the crowd's eyes—his face smeared with red and yellow marker, especially around the mouth. For somebody who hadn't seen what Adam was up to in the judge's office, it looked as if somebody had scratched him and bruised him. Needless to say, this was not what we wanted anyone's first impression of our newly adopted son to be. I hissed at Jon, "We have to clean his face!" and we huddled against the wall for a moment and went at Adam's mouth and jaw with our handkerchiefs. That only smeared the markers worse; now our son's round face looked like a badly dyed Easter egg. We would have a lot of explaining to do. But somehow, as we would find out, every newspaper and television story about Adam's adoption decided his mouth was red with lipstick—from his grandmothers' kisses.

A court official came up to us. "Listen, there's a lot of media out there—reporters, television cameras, radio. Would you like to go out the back?"

"No," I said firmly. "We want everyone in the world to know how happy we are." We made one more feverish attempt to get the marker off Adam's face. "Well," I said, shrugging, "he's two." We straightened our ties, tugged on Adam's blue-plaid coat, kissed each other, and stepped into the elevators.

As we exited the courthouse, the reporters swarmed around us, barraging us with hand microphones, boom mikes, camera flashes and clicks, and questions. Compared to this, the ACLU press conference was an intimate dinner for two. We couldn't stop smiling. "He's been our son the whole time, and now it's official," Jon declared, and that was our basic proclamation for the day.

All of the family would appear on television outside the courthouse the day of Adam's adoption, and some of them would talk to reporters. My father was still reserved and clipped when talking in public about his gay son and his grandson. "I love my son, and I'm very happy for him. People do what they have to do, fighting for things like this," he said, his words joyful but still tinged with tolerance. My mother was nervously grandmotherly, happy, and supportive. Papa Nooch and Grandma Grace were interviewed and both were jubilant. Protective of their privacy, Nancy and Roger chose not to speak to the press. Herb and Ann Mary were so happy as well, and Ann Mary found the energy to stand and do a short interview, even though her chemotherapy treatments had by now deeply drained her energy.

Adam held each of our hands and walked between us, pleased by the lights, the cameras, the action. I picked Adam up, Jon put his arm around us, and we stepped up in front of a bouquet of microphones. Jon announced to the world, "From the bottom of our hearts, we are truly grateful to stand before you today with our son, Adam, as a family." The name *Adam* was pronounced loud and clear; he would no longer be the pseudonymous baby Mark. It was a huge relief just to be able to say his name out loud in public. We answered everything the reporters threw our way—What are you going to do today? Does Adam know what's happening? What about the girl? We let them photograph Adam's face, as long as they didn't spook him. Adam wasn't scared. Marked with red and yellow pen that looked like lipstick, he looked them square in the eye, and he grinned.

We would no longer shield Adam's face from the camera. Jon and I had thought through it hard, and as we awaited the fateful day of Judge Moses's decision, we asked ourselves how much we should allow Adam to be seen by the outside world. It was definitely scary to decide to give up the protection we had gained because no strangers knew exactly what Adam looked like. (Madison, still a foster child, would retain her anonymity.) We would now live with the extra fear someone would recognize him and grab him from our backyard to rescue him from his homosexual parents. Yet the benefits outweighed the risks, we

Lenora, Jon, Michael, Vicki, and Michael Adams, at the press conference following New Jersey's agreement to revise its adoption policy.

decided. Any carping we might receive for "using" our child would be criticisms we could answer. Here outside the courthouse, and later at our Maywood house, we would consent to the cameras photographing our son—for at least a little while, until we sent the press away so that our family could celebrate. To present Adam's face to the world, we decided, was, first of all, good for Adam—as well as good for our cause. The world needed to see the thriving toddler who had been a frail, sick infant and know the difference a foster or adoptive family could make for other sick infants.

Ever since the press had pounced on the fact that two gay men were parenting a baby, we had realized that the public interest in our child was key to making our case for joint parenthood of Adam. As we were awaiting the decision from Sybil Moses, friends of ours recommended that we talk to Jim Robinson, a former speechwriter for California governor George Deukmejian and head of public relations for the trucking industry in Washington, D.C., who told us that he agreed we would be accused of exploiting Adam. But being honest and public was im-

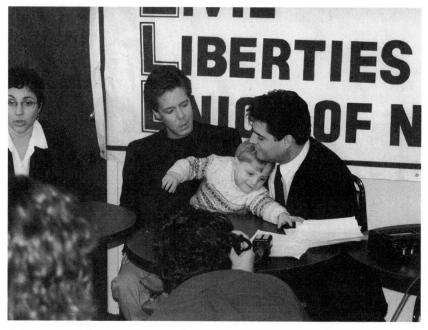

Adam appeared at the press conference too.

portant. "If a couple in Kansas is sitting eating breakfast and watching *Good Morning America* and see just the two of you, they're only going to notice two faggots from New Jersey," Robinson told us. "But if they see Adam sitting on your lap, they're going to focus on Adam and see a child with his parents. They'll still see faggots—but they will see a family first." Being forthright and public as a family was important not only to our pride and inner honesty; it was important for the cause of other foster children and of course lesbian and gay people and their families.

Wouldn't we sacrifice our children's privacy by going public? When people asked me that, I would respond by saying that my children will be taught what I learned from my parents—giving back. Adam and Madison have been given so much by so many people—starting with their mothers, who had the grace to give them up; to the people at the O'Neill Center, who took great care of them; their fathers, who centered their lives around them; and all the other people who poured out their affection and care. Now the children had an opportunity to do something individually and as part of a family, for the other Adams and Madisons. They could do for other people as had been done for them.

Thanks to Adam and Madison, Jon and I had been taught this lesson ourselves; we had been given so much in our lives, and now through Adam and Madison—and our fight for them—we could do some good not just for our family but for the larger world.

We retain our privacy and integrity as a family. Most important, we have no secrets to hide. With the nature of our family open to the world, we have nothing to be ashamed of, no dark, resistant places of guilt and fear that can warp and consume so many supposedly all-American families. In the best sense of the phrase, we have no shame. That kind of authenticity is good for our children's sense of balance and honesty as they grow up. And if our family can make enough of a change in the world now, then our children will not have to be bullied or intimidated for who they are; they will have helped to make a world that will not condemn them but honor them.

One warm late-fall Sunday several weeks after the adoption, we visited my parents' house for a barbecue, sitting out on the deck and enjoying the Indian summer. Adam was toddling from person to person, putting his hands on their knees, waiting to be picked up, talked to, praised, and adored. Aunt Angela was not there. Adam went up to Granddaddy and said, "Hello!" and put his hand on the old man's leg, expecting to be hugged and held. Granddaddy looked down at him, through him, and looked away. Adam's expectant face collapsed.

Although he was only two and couldn't put it into words, he knew he was rejected. I could see it on his face. My heart broke in anger. You can dis me and I can take it, I thought. But what that kind of action does to the ego of a two-year-old child is unacceptable. I told my father and he grimaced as if in pain. "I'm really sad," I said to my mother. "I feel like I've lost my grandfather. He's alive and sitting here, but he's gone." I told her we had to pack up and leave; the day had soured too much to stay. I could see her slide into dismay and anxiety.

From October through December, we tried to maintain a regular family life even as the media controversy over the decision and the pending class action lawsuit kept bringing network news trucks to our house on Lincoln Avenue. From *USA Today* and CNN to a special Thanksgiving report on the local CBS network affiliate, WCBS, it still seemed that our family was everywhere, at the very time we were busy trying to get Adam acclimated to half days at nursery school and celebrating Madison's first birthday.

Thanksgiving was a surreal family event, thanks to the WCBS camera crew who wanted to see what the holiday looked like at a two-child, two-father household—a family that was truly thankful this holiday. Jon and I hosted the event at our house, complete with my parents and my brother and sister and their kids, Papa Nooch and Grandma Grace, Nancy and Roger and Don and Megan, as well as a woman who had worked with me at Sprint, along with her best friend. Herb had whisked Ann Mary off to Boston for the holiday weekend; she was still shaky from her cancer treatment and Herb wanted to give her a respite.

It was a real coup to be the family members hosting Thanksgiving. It made us feel that we belonged. And by the time Jon carved the turkey, we could all forget that the cameras were taping over our shoulders and that a lot of other families in the New York metropolitan area would get a glimpse of our holiday. I bet they realized our holiday looked almost exactly like their own. But hardly any other family could have been as thankful as we were that November.

We kept Madison's birthday celebration small and intimate. Adam's had been a big, morale-boosting bash in the middle of the adoption trauma. Now we had the chance to get back to the core of our family. It was an especially important event for Nancy, I think—not only did it mark the first-year anniversary since Jon had been reunited with his birth mother, but the special bond that she had developed with her granddaughter was very moving. She doted on Madison and was still convinced she needed special protection from cold and to safeguard her daintiness. "I want to throw a big party for Madison when she's adopted," Nancy told me in the midst of putting the candles on Madison's cake.

Our daughter was still technically HIV-positive, but was blooming so much that it was clearly only a matter of time before she would officially be classified as HIV-negative. She was still small for her age, but that was to be expected for a baby born weighing only three pounds and a few ounces, her fetal development sapped by heroin. In every other way she was excelling, and it was beautiful to watch.

Dressed in a little white dress with pastel roses on it that Nancy had picked out for her, Madison was firmly in command of her birthday party. Already walking at twelve months, she was blabbing a lot and making her demands known through the few words she had already learned. Her big, lovely head was still nearly bald, and she wore a ribbon in her hair to remind the world she was the diva she promised to be. Contrary to Adam, always a happy-go-lucky kid, she was always *intense,* retaining that calm, scrutinizing gaze we'd first seen nine months before at the O'Neill Center, as if she looked not at you but into you, to see if you'd meet her standards and expectations.

The night of her birthday, after the presents had been opened and the low-fat cake smeared on the carpet and all the relatives had gone home, I crept into Madison's darkened room and watched her sleep, exhausted from the celebration. Ever since she'd arrived in our house that warm March day, it had lain heavy on my mind that she was only a foster child. Because she was not yet ours, we could lose her, the way we had lost Andrew. Or the state could contrive to take her away because of the uproar we'd caused trying to adopt Adam. But now the specter of our loss of Andrew had receded, Judge Moses had permitted us to adopt Adam, and Madison was well on the way to being adopted. As I looked at her, the light from the hallway streaming over her peaceful face, I knew, without fear or reservation holding me back, that Madison absolutely inhabited my heart.

Michael Adams called Jon one early December afternoon. I watched Jon's smile widen as he listened to what Michael was telling him. "I have really good news for you guys," he said. "The state's decided to settle." The state attorney general's office had agreed to amend the DYFS adoption policy to treat unmarried couples, gay and straight, on equal terms with married couples. "It's a complete victory," Michael said. "Congratulations."

This meant that Judge Moses would not have to issue a ruling on the class action suit; instead the judge would merely sign off on an agreement to insure that the new policy would be enforced. As part of the agreement to settle the suit, the state would send a letter to every foster parent in New Jersey announcing the change in policy and inviting unmarried people in committed relationships to apply jointly to be foster or adoptive parents if they chose. I was really glad about this part of the decision. Not only had we changed the policy, but official word from the State of New Jersey would disseminate it. That would encourage other potential parents to step forward, able to provide more love and security for other Adams and Madisons—and Andrews and Rosas.

"So as soon as this thing is official, at the drop of a dime we're going to have a press conference," Michael Adams said. "Will you be available?"

"Will we be available?" Jon repeated. He looked at me and I didn't even have to say anything. "Absolutely."

Three days later, back in the same drab ACLU conference room where we had begun our battle six months earlier, Jon and I gathered with Michael, Lenora, and Daphne of Lambda Families—along with so many reporters that it seemed the walls would pop from the pressure of people. This time we looked like winners, not golf dads. I wore a suit and Jon wore a sweater and sport coat: Business Father and Casual Sporty Daddy. Our hair was freshly cut and neatly combed, and our back pockets had no unsightly bulges. And we were much better prepared this time to respond to a roomful of reporters—many of whom by now were familiar faces.

In the last months both Jon and I had developed a new confidence—not only as plaintiffs and fathers but as people. If I could handle news reporters, remain composed in the face of the Aunt Angelas and Bob Enyarts of the world, and take on a state bureaucracy, then I could handle just about any encounter my life demanded of me—including, as it later turned out, enduring Jerry Falwell and his friends.

"The state of New Jersey has agreed to repeal its policy which bars— I mean, *barred*—unmarried parents from adopting a child jointly," Michael Adams announced. He made it clear that the new policy set a national precedent about how government and society should define families. Then Daphne Riggs spoke on behalf of Lambda Families, and it was our turn. Adam sat on my knees, front and center, toying with a little white plastic bottle of water as Jon began speaking. Adam dropped the bottle on the table and it bounced into my lap, spilling on me, on him—right on national television I had a lapful of cold water—and then tumbling onto the floor to douse the microphone wires. Fortunately, it was just a momentary disaster that stirred laughter among everyone in the room—a human moment in an official event, and a new adventure in parenting. I delivered my statement sitting down.

The ensuing media stories were different from what they'd been back in June or even in October after Judge Moses's decision. The case was no longer just a New York and New Jersey story, with an occasional *USA Today* article thrown in the mix. No more was it just local dads make good. Now it was national and international, with stories in *Time* magazine and on the front pages of the *Washington Post, USA Today,* the *Los Angeles Times,* even the *Wall Street Journal,* and coverage from Argentina to Singapore. More than we'd expected, the new policy became a major news story, and we were in the middle of it.

Policy had been changed; America itself was changing. Our case had renewed debate on the place of gay people in America's families, and not just about adoption but lesbian and gay marriage—questions we sidestepped, to keep the focus on adoption rights. "Today, this is about Adam and adoption and how lucky the kids are in the state of New Jersey that there are so many more families for them now," I told the reporters in Newark that day.

All this meant that the controversy level ratcheted up hugely, and that Jon and I would come face-to-face with our critics for the first time. Up to now we hadn't been hammered with the moral and ethical questions our case raised for many people, and that had been just fine with us. We had been seen as an exception to the rule; now we were setting a precedent for how families should be recognized in America today. We were changing the rules.

Back in Maywood after the press conference, a Fox News TV van with a satellite dish appeared outside our door, for a live television hookup with the gay fathers and their dynamo of a toddler, and soon television cables snaked everywhere in our house as reporters interviewed us and cameras turned their hard white lights on us. Fox wanted us to face off, live, against Steve Schwalm from the Family Research Council, the main engine of antigay right-wing conservatism. We agreed and tried to stay measured as he expressed consternation that Adam now had a stable and secure home headed by two gay men. Schwalm also showed up the next morning on *Good Morning America*, to which we were whisked, exhausted, via ABC limo—complete with a car seat for Adam—from Lincoln Avenue in Maywood to the ABC studios on West Sixty-sixth Street in Manhattan at five-thirty in the morning. "This is a really happy day, I guess, for Jon and for Michael," Schwalm said with elaborate reasonableness, "but it remains to be seen whether it's a going to be a happy day for Adam in the long run." He went on to slur all gay men in the universe by citing a long-discredited study that declared that 29 percent of all children in gay homes are sexually abused. I wanted to throttle him. Jon actually laughed at him. How dare you use those shoddy and homophobic findings to defame my family? But instead Jon and I sat a placid Adam in our laps. "Steve, this is what it's about," I said. "This is a family, an American family. I know there're people who aren't going to see it that way, and change is never easy, but we're a family. A family like any other."

When *Larry King Live* called, we agreed to appear—and only later did the producers call back to tell us that the Reverend Jerry Falwell would go on in opposition to us. Should we tangle with the leading antigay religious leader in America? We consulted our parents and our priests asking if we should do it—after all, it could be painfully contentious, and it would give Falwell and his Christian-right views a forum. Everyone we talked to said we should do it—because we had nothing to prove. "Don't think you need to argue with him," said a friend of my father's who happens to be a U.S. congressman. "Just be yourselves, just be parents," Mother Elizabeth Kaeton said to us. We didn't have to "win" on religious points and debate the Bible—we had the truth of Adam, the truth of our parenthood, and that would carry us through.

We told King's producers we would do the show with Falwell as long as Michael Adams appeared with us and we didn't have to confront Jerry Falwell directly. Michael Adams would respond to Falwell first, and our answers could be addressed to Larry. In the New York studio as we began the broadcast, all of us hooked up by satellite, with Michael Adams and Jon and me in New York, King in Washington, and Falwell in Virginia, I felt burdened by the notion that I was not speaking for myself but was a poster homo, a sales rep for gay people's rights everywhere. So many people gay and straight would see us tonight.

Falwell's litany of hateful, condescending ignorance got me more and more incensed. He said thousands of heterosexual married men and women were waiting for children like Adam—which didn't exactly jibe with the fact that abandoned children at the O'Neill Center were going begging for families. Did Falwell's parishioners want to adopt any of them?

"Michael," Falwell said soothingly, his wide chins quivering, "I believe you. I really do sense sincerity and love in your voice and heart. I would say to you that if you ever change your mind about Adam and would be willing to place him in a heterosexual family, I will take [him] the first day and place him in a family that I know you'll approve of."

Jon put his hand on my leg and dug his nails into my thigh, to keep me from opening my mouth and lashing out at the prospect of Jerry Falwell taking my son from me. Instead I took a deep breath. Fatherhood would carry me through.

After a week of positive news stories of our victory—just at the time our lives were falling back into a regular rhythm, with me being able to get through a day of work without having either coworkers duck into my office to congratulate me or someone phone and want to talk to us—I got a call from a newspaper reporter who had written about Adam's adoption and the DYFS policy reversal. "I just think you should know," he said, "that somebody sent us this really weird and nasty opinion piece about you. A guy named Bob Enyart. He claims to be your cousin."

"He is my cousin," I said unhappily. "What's he saying?"

"Really mean stuff—all about gays and pedophilia. It's a real rant. We're not going to print it, of course, but I thought you should know."

"Thanks," I said grimly.

Cousin Bob had finally surfaced. Over the next couple of days we would find out that other newspaper people in the area had also received Bob's submission. Apparently he'd been following our story in the papers—and probably hearing the details from Aunt Angela. A gay father and his antigay, born-again cable-TV host of a cousin—would that be exactly the kind of story that the tabloids would pounce on? Fortunately, as we realized when we got a copy of his piece, his diatribe was so wild that no one wanted to touch it. "He won this battle but I will not give up," Bob wrote in his op-ed screed. "Michael's homosexuality has brought much heartache to our family. Now, we will grieve anew because we know this ruling will further the destructive influence that homosexuals have on children."

Enyart went on basically to pronounce us guilty by association with the ACLU, which defended child pornographers, which most homosexuals were anyway. The bulk of the article went on to repeat the slur on gay men that Schwalm had flung our way—namely, that gay men are more likely to abuse children than straight men are and are also more likely to tolerate child sex abuse from their fellow homosexuals. Then, getting more personal, he wrote, "Families have tried to hide their shame when one of their own gives in to vile passions. Many homosexuals claim to have their parent's [sic] complete acceptance, but almost without exception gays show no physical affection, not even a peck on the cheek, in front of parents and grand-parents." Well, Cousin Bob, maybe it's just that gay couples are too sensible to show affection when they're in the same pizza parlor as you.

The article ended with a sentence that echoed in my head and sent ice down my spine: "Out of concern for children, and for my nation, and out of a desire that my cousin experience justice, I will continue to fight to recriminalize homosexuality."

A desire that my cousin experience justice. Jon went ashen with anger when he read those words. My father's face filled with anger and grief. My mother began shaking, and she cried.

America was changing. Now that our victory had ignited the debate, more challenging questions would come to us that spoke to the big fears our society has about sexuality, children, and alternative families. Some responses to the new policy were outlandish, Enyartish, while other reactions, such as Falwell's, were slightly more subtle and therefore more dangerous. More mainstream queries arose from a more vulnerable, if ignorant, place, and those were worth answering: Do you think your kids are going to grow up to be gay? Do your children have mother models? How will poor Madison learn what it means to be a woman if she's surrounded by males? How can you raise children knowing they will be picked on in school? For the first time we were going up against people who vehemently opposed us and who thought we were warping our children's souls and headed to hell. But we were also talking to thoughtful people who had been moved by our family and were revamping their values and widening their hearts. Those people were the majority.

Many interviewers were preoccupied with Adam's masculinity and eventual sexuality. We live in a society that is confused and nervous about how you become a man and what it means to be a man in the first place. Often, people would ask us what "role models" Adam would have—in other words, would he have any men around him showing him how to be straight? Would Madison have straight women to teach her how to be a female? In response, we would say we want to make sure Adam spends time with his uncles, cousins, and grandfathers because they love him and he loves them. It's not that we aim to expose him to straight males to toughen him up or somehow armor him with heterosexual maleness. Nor should Madison have women around her just so she can learn the rules of womanhood. When it comes to seeing how the two genders interact, certainly we want both Adam and Madison to learn by watching how husbands and wives communicate and love each other. We want our children to witness *all* healthy relationships—between two men, two women, and a man and a woman. "After all, we don't live in a vacuum—we live in America," Jon would often exclaim. All of God's varieties are important for them to behold, and they will learn by relating to all sorts of people.

I don't think either of my children will be confused about their sexuality as they grow older. Our children's sexuality exists in them already. Growing up in a home headed by two gay men won't make them gay. As Jon likes to point out, nearly all gay men and lesbians grew up in homes with straight moms and dads, so if having hetero-sexual parents is supposed to make you straight, it doesn't seem to be working very well. And besides, what would be so wrong with having children grow up to be gay? Interviewers would constantly ask us if having two gay dads meant Adam and Madison had a higher "risk" of turning out gay. Is becoming gay really something you risk, like getting lung cancer from a parent who smokes? I don't think so. I know it's a wonderful way to be.

Having grown up in an environment of honesty and open discussion, Adam and Madison will have to *think* more about who they are and what they want regarding their sexuality. No matter how much the world evolves over the next decade or two, our culture will still instruct them that heterosexuality should be their default sexual choice, but Adam and Madison will have the facts and experience to be able to ponder these questions for themselves, as everyone should. As they grow into openhearted adults, their innate spirits will tell them how they want to relate to other people romantically and sexually, and they will find their own authentic paths. That seems to be true of most children of lesbian or gay parents.

Will our kids get bullied and threatened because they have gay fa-thers? Sure. When people asked me if Adam and Madison would suffer in school as a result of having two fathers, I said yes, they would— until the parents of those bullies insist to their children that intolerance is wrong. Kids pick on kids—I was terrorized in fifth grade because I was fat, and my other schoolmates were abused for being short or ugly or poor. Jon and I can do two things to help our children. First, we can try to change people's minds, so that being harassed for having a gay parent (or for "acting gay") has about as much force as being kidded for having freckles. Second, we can insure Adam and Madison will grow up having the strength and self-esteem to be who they are. My children will be raised to be confident and secure enough that they'll be able to respond to intolerance and taunting with fierce pride. "Your dad's a faggot!" some boy will inevitably inform Adam. "Yup," Adam will say. "What about it?"

According to one study, the only psychological characteristics distinguishing children of gay mothers and fathers are greater confidence, tolerance, and open-mindedness than the norm. Aren't those wonderful strengths to engender in a child?

Adam seemed to relish the attention he was receiving and have a knack for it. He would hug strangers, smile at them, want to sit on their laps. When someone from the press interviewed us, he would be his usual rambunctious self, pulling down tripods, nosing into camera cases, and smearing his fingers over the lenses. Then I would say, "Adam, the nice man wants to make a movie of you coloring at your table. Will you?" Adam would stop what he was doing, go to his little yellow table and sit down at his little orange chair, and intently color for as long as the video camera ran. Happy, gregarious, openhearted, Adam was the reason that the attention we received was so positive. He was an incontestable reflection on his parents' skills and love. No matter what their opinions about gay adoption when they entered our house, people would leave persuaded by Adam.

As the news of the state's new policy spread, letters, faxes, and phone calls came in, from everywhere, people congratulating us, from heterosexual mothers in Minnesota to gay men and lesbians in Asbury Park. On the night of the adoption, a man who would not identify himself called, speaking quietly with what sounded like a Middle Eastern accent. "I just wanted to tell you that some of us can't be as brave as you have been. I want to thank you for what you have done." Click.

A lot of men and women called us wanting to know how they could adopt, and that made us feel terrific. Teenagers called wanting our advice, and that was trickier. Many times, Jon or I would pick up the phone and a young, shaky voice would whisper, "Hello?" and plunge into scared, urgent questions that made it clear this person had never talked to anybody else about his or her sexual feelings. I'm gay and my parents don't accept it; I might be a lesbian but I'm not sure; I am definitely gay and the other eighth-graders beat me up all the time—Jon and I would handle these phone calls with sympathy and extreme caution. It was not our job to play therapist, nor could we assume that all our callers, however honest, just needed a little helpful nudge to emerge from the closet trumpeting their gayness. That wasn't fair to the complexities of human nature, giving such prescriptions to people we didn't know. Nor did we want to walk into a trap set by some right-wingers who could proclaim we were recruiting children to our banner. Be true to yourself, we said to everyone who called. Talk about your concerns to people you can trust. Be brave. And if you work to discover your truth honestly and openly, you may well find out that people will admire you and love you for living an authentic life. That's what Jon and I had found out in our lives—and with our parents.

One December night in Detroit, a man named Raymond was sitting in front of his television surfing the cable channels when something caught his attention. He hit RECORD on his VCR. "My first cousin Michael Galluccio is a homosexual," declared a mustached, bespectacled, sputtery man sitting behind a talk-show host's desk, "and he adopted a baby boy, which is *an utter tragedy.*"

Raymond, a gay man, had been following the story of the two fathers in New Jersey who had won the right to adopt their foster son. He leaned forward and listened more carefully. The man on the screen seemed indignant, wild. He went on to say that he had written "a long letter" that "was too well-written and thoroughly documented" to be printed by any newspaper. "They forwarded it to my cousin," the man announced. "My mom and my brother went to talk with him recently and laid it on the line, which was very good."

What Raymond heard next scared him so much he had to do something.

Christmas was coming, which meant shopping with the children—visiting Santa Claus, negotiating the crowds. One afternoon, Jon and

I were at the Garden State Plaza and decided to watch a performance of the *Nutcracker* that was about to begin on a stage in the midst of the mall. It seemed like something Adam and Madison would enjoy. We wedged ourselves into a corner of the upper atrium, along a waist-high glass wall, next to a pillar, which would give us a good view of the show on the level below us. Madison sat in her stroller and Adam stood next to her, peering down at the colorful stage below.

A crowd formed around us, people pressing in on all sides. As the ballet began, I lifted my eyes from the children to the dancers. Then I looked down again. Adam was gone.

My heart plunged to my feet. "Jon, *where's Adam?*" I hissed. My first thought was that someone had seen him and snatched him.

Jon looked at the empty space where Adam had been and stared at me in horror. He was thinking what I was thinking.

We spun around and looked frantically everywhere and could see nothing. Then a second later, Adam appeared, zipping around from the other side of the pillar. He was just being Adam, just running around. I gasped and grabbed him and held him until he squirmed to breathe.

It was a scary moment that all parents experience, when an active child vanishes in public. But for us the fear was compounded because we knew we had enemies out there. Even counting every medical fear we'd faced when Adam was a baby, this was the single most horrifying moment we'd ever faced with our child.

Jon picked up the phone and told the unfamiliar, nervous-sounding voice that, yes, this was Jon Holden speaking. He assumed it was another call from a media person or a stranger who had heard about our case.

"You don't know me, but my name is Raymond, and I was flipping through the channels the other night and I came across this lunatic from Denver named—"

"Bob Enyart."

"Yeah, and he claims to be your cousin—"

"He's my husband's cousin."

"Well, I don't know if you're aware of it, but he comes pretty close to saying you guys should be killed."

Jon felt cold in his bones. He asked Raymond to send us his tape, then begged him to call Adolph. Raymond did call and got my mother. We all got together to see a copy of the tape.

On his cable TV show, which Bob has claimed is carried on cable systems in fifty U.S. television markets, he did indeed say that our adoption of Adam was a tragedy—the same term Jerry Falwell had used. Moments later, he broadcast a fake commercial. Backed by thumping music, these words appeared on a blank screen, one after the other: DEPRESSION—ALCOHOLISM—DRUG ADDICTION—SUICIDE—DISEASE—HEPATITIS—HIV—AIDS—DEATH. Then comes the tag line: FRIENDS DON'T LET FRIENDS BE HOMO. And then on a separate screen: "Presented by the Partnership for a Homo-Free America."

It was so absurd that I would have laughed if I hadn't been so alarmed and angry. On the tape from Raymond, Bob was next seen taking some calls from viewers. Mike from Kenosha, Wisconsin, asked, "What do you think about gay-bashing?"

"It's cool," Bob said quickly, and nodded.

"Like, what do you think it does to—"

"Hopefully it irritates them," Bob said brightly.

Rounding off the tape was Bob's announcement of his 100-Day Plan to rescue America. Included in his rescue mission was the closing of all "homosexual establishments" and the immediate termination of employment of homosexuals in the government. "Managers knowingly retaining homosexual, bisexual, et cetera employees must pay restitution of double the amount of salary and benefits paid to the illicit employees, and two, they will be flogged."

Bob also included this proclamation: "Anyone performing, attempting to perform, or encouraging homosexual behavior from this day forward, upon conviction, will be executed."

Bob didn't exactly command people to go out and kill his cousin Michael Galluccio in Maywood, New Jersey. Did he have to be explicit? He had ranted on about his gay cousin Michael Galluccio, and he had also told the world that all gay people should be killed. Anyone could do the math. It was death by association.

Jon's anger rose to a level I had not seen in years and years. "Screw your family—this guy has to be stopped! If someone kills you . . ." Jon was protecting Adam and his family. It hadn't even occurred to him that he too was now a target. I was pulsating with fury. I was afraid. I was sad. I had to concentrate on remembering all the people who loved us, from our children, to my parents, sitting here with us in our family room watching this tape, purple with indignation and rage. All that love would be my family's armor. But I was still filled with wrath and fear.

Adam's adoption and the successful resolution of the class action suit—those were Jon's and my Christmas gifts that year. Adam got a fire truck and a car-carrier truck that he loved. Ann Mary gave Madison a little pink stroller with a baby doll in it. On Christmas afternoon, I heard a happy shriek and turned around to see Madison in the toy stroller, with Adam pushing her around the living room. He was mirroring what he was seeing his Daddy and Father do every day.

That holiday was so much easier than the previous Christmas, when Andrew was crying so hopelessly and was about to leave our home, when the state would not let us both be legal fathers to Adam, and we were so worn and tired. Now Adam belonged to us, Madison and Nancy had brought fresh life into our lives, my parents had stood tall beside us, and we had a stronger sense of who we could be in the world. Certain things still shadowed our family, from Ann Mary's uncertain prognosis to the dangerous hatefulness exemplified by the Bob Enyarts of the world and the Jerry Falwells, who agreed our parenting was a tragedy that should be stopped. Over the past year we'd been even more sobered by the hard path so many gay people have to take, and we'd developed an increased awareness of a world that needed a lot more parents for all the Adams, Madisons, and Andrews, all the children left behind. Still, even here there was reason to hope. Just before Christmas we received a card from Andrew's grandmother. Mrs. Alvarez had written how well Andrew was doing and included photos

Madison would grow more ladylike with age.

of the boy. Dressed up in his Sunday best, Andrew looked wonderful—like a boy version of Madison, a healthy, round child smiling into the camera, as one of his brothers held him in his lap. Andrew looked happy, clean, and loved. However, Mrs. Alvarez never did mention whether Anna, her daughter, had lived or died in the intensive care unit that day we returned Andrew to her.

On Christmas Eve we held our traditional family open house. Twelve to fourteen of my parents' friends showed up. It was the first time the pinochle brigade—the same ones who had shown up at our adoption hearing—had ever visited our home on Lincoln Avenue. Cousins, sisters, in-laws, kids, old friends, were there, along with priests and new friends from church, friends from my office and their children. Hal and Stan from Lambda Families came with their son.

Everyone brought gifts for the kids; Santa had tough competition this year. Gifts had come in from strangers—and not just for Adam. Even though we had shielded Madison's face and identity from the public, people knew we had a little foster daughter, and presents poured in for her as well. They both received a McDonald's commem-

A much happier Christmas this year.

orative play set from a man in Philadelphia. An older lesbian couple in western New Jersey who had seen our family on the street in Provincetown sent each of the children a beautiful outfit from Lands' End. We got dolls and singing *Sesame Street* characters and Beanie Babies—my God, did we get Beanie Babies.

Hovering over all this was a national *CBS Evening News* crew, filming for a segment to air three days after Christmas. One uncomfortable moment ended in a sweet exchange between Jon and my mother. "I can't believe I had to discipline Adam in front of the TV cameras because he smacked me in the face," Jon told her.

"You have nothing to worry about," my mother said firmly. "I watched you. You're a better mother than any mother I've ever seen." That comment warmed the heart of a father who had learned over the past two years to relish being Mr. Mom.

The holiday season also marked our first Christmas with Rosa. Now fifteen, Madison's sister was moving out of her thug phase and into young womanhood. She was now allowed to come for day visits to our house, and slowly we were building a trusting relationship. Christmas was the first time Rosa was allowed an overnight visit, taking her place in the guest room next to the nursery so she would be near her sister. She soon developed a bond with Adam and with us as well. By the time New Year's Day arrived, she was a regular visitor to our household and on her way to becoming an unofficial but deeply loved member of our family.

Ann Mary celebrated that New Year's Eve with Herb, a plate of herring in wine sauce in front of her and a glass of champagne in her hand. It had been a hard year for her. The surgery had been bad enough, but the five months of chemotherapy had been a long and debilitating siege. New Year's Eve was her last chemotherapy treatment. Ahead of her lay six weeks of radiation and a lot of uncertainty. But the worst seemed to have passed, and now she could start to enjoy her life again—including the two grandchildren Jon and I had given her.

"Father's home!" I announced as I came in the front door one evening two weeks into the New Year. My delighted toddlers tackled my knees, yelling, "Father, Father!" Their greeting was the high point of my day, as it is most days.

Jon was smiling triumphantly and waving a letter. He kissed me hello, then said, "We got something real nice in the mail today."

It wasn't much to look at—just a one-page form letter from the DYFS administrator, photocopied on letterhead. "State of New Jersey," it read in Gothic letters, below the state seal, and then, "Department of Human Services, Division of Youth and Family Services." "Dear Current or Prospective Adoptive Parent," it began. "I would also like to make you aware of a recent change in our policy. This change states that in the case of an unmarried couple co-habiting, both or either person can be named in the consent for adoption based on the case plan for the child. In other words, unmarried co-habiting couples seeking to adopt shall not be prohibited, by the Division of Youth and Family Services, from jointly adopting due to their marital status or sexual orientation." The next line was a huge understatement, at least

Granny (Ann Mary), Big Poppy (Herb), and the kids on Easter.

for our family: "This should simplify the adoption process for some applicants."

I gazed at Jon and grinned, the letter still in my hands. All over the state, on this same evening, other foster parents were holding this same letter and reading it. Married or single or in committed nonmarital relationships, they would know that they would be judged not by their status but by the depth and care they could provide to their children. I looked from my husband to my two children, tugging at my jacket, trying to get me to play. I felt chills going down my spine—the good kind of chills. Our family was helping to change the world.

TEN

AN AMERICAN FAMILY

Jon Galluccio

On April 16, 1998, I went with Michael to the same courthouse in Hackensack where we had adopted Adam—this time to have my last name changed to match my husband's. Sixteen years *to the day* that we first became a couple, I would now be Jon Holden Galluccio.

I also had a surprise planned for Michael that morning.

For a long time I had pondered changing my name, and adopting a son had spurred me even more. Once when Adam was very young I was waiting in an impossibly long line in a department store and plucked up an American Express charge-card application. Idly, I imagined Adam Holden-Galluccio filling out the form—and realized that there weren't enough spaces for his name. How could we do that to him? This hyphenated-last-name business has always struck me as silly—what if Adam falls in love with a hyphenated person? What would his children's names be? At some point, the madness had to stop.

Holden had been the name of my second adoptive father, which I'd taken on at age ten, legally changing my name to match my mother's, less than two years before he died on me. Holden was part of my identity, but I had only a brother with that name, not a mother who was Mrs. Holden or dozens of cousins dubbed Holden. It was only my name, and if a more significant name came along, one that simplified life for my son and daughter, well, that would be fine, I'd decided.

Michael and I talked about creating our own family name, like *Golden,* even silly things like *Holluccio,* but the more we discussed it, the more *Galluccio* seemed the right choice for the entire family. Michael, the oldest son, had been raised to honor the family name and carry it on, and I respected that. Still, I resisted. Partly, I was tripped up by the idea of changing my surname to an *Italian* one, because it echoed the name I'd been given by my first adopted father, Danny Dell'Olio, who'd so rudely deserted me by dying. Yet as Adam's presence and my own fatherhood helped me heal around that issue, I felt ready to enjoy having an Italian last name again; it would pay tribute to Danny. It was a way of coming home. I wouldn't be losing an identity but gaining one. Having one surname would cement us even further and simplify our children's lives. Adam, Madison, and their spouses will thank me someday.

My mother Ann Mary, whose last name hadn't been Holden in ten years, was furious with me when I told her my plan to change my name. "I will never, ever, refer to you as Jon Galluccio," she told me. "It's like saying *they won.* You would actually take Michael's grandfather's name, after all the horrible things he's done to you?"

"No. I'm taking my husband's name. They just happen to be the same." That ended the issue.

The legal procedure that April day could not have been more mundane—totally different from winning joint adoption for Adam, six months earlier, and just two floors away in the same building. In the company of Adolph's law partner, Harvey Browne, who was handling the name change for me, I answered some standard questions from the judge and got lots of papers bearing an official seal from the court clerk to fill out and send to credit-card people, the state motor-vehicle office, and the like. (I have a lot of sympathy for the many women who go through the same procedure when they get married and change their surname.)

But I had a surprise for Michael—and a plan. On our way to get extra copies of my name-change forms from a different office, I more or less forced Michael out into the courtyard. I was aiming for the front steps of the courthouse, where I could get down on one knee in front of him and ask him a question. In my pocket was an art deco antique ring I'd given Michael for his birthday ten years before, with a sapphire in the middle and a diamond on either side. He'd lost the sapphire and the ring had ended up in a drawer. I'd retrieved it, replaced the gem, and had it reconditioned.

It was raining. So much for the courthouse steps. What other stairs could I find? The steps part seemed extremely important somehow. I pushed Michael back inside. "What are you *doing?*" he asked me.

In the lobby, I spied a marble staircase next to a newsstand. "Come over here."

"But, Jon, we have to go downstairs to get the copies—"

"Just come over here!"

Michael obeyed. I maneuvered him onto the staircase. I managed to get down on one knee. I dug into my pocket for the ring. Michael saw the ring in my hand and smiled. "Michael, will you marry me? On Father's Day?"

Michael beamed. "Yes! Of course I will."

After sixteen years together, as the parents of two children, it was time we celebrated our relationship and "made it legal"—in the eyes of God, anyhow—and had it solemnized in the presence of our family, our friends, our children, and our church.

Michael and I had gone through so much together, over so many years, and I knew I loved him more than I ever had. Sixteen years ago, I'd first seen Michael in the student center of Glassboro State College, which is now Rowan University. Going up the stairs on the far side of the Student Center were a band of Teke brothers wearing their red fraternity shirts. One guy with long, wavy brown hair, wearing cutoff jeans, sockless sneakers, and a short-sleeved football jersey that revealed his abs, was helping carry a big silver chest. I'd find out later that the chest contained all the Teke meeting ritual paraphernalia. That

Future Father and Daddy, 1983.

didn't interest me at all, but the man carrying it sure did. Those legs. I'd seen Adonis. I had to meet him. I'd even join his frat, if that's what it took.

Now, more than a decade and a half later, with a houseful of children, two cars, and dogs, we were very different from those innocent boys. But Michael delighted me more than ever. In September 1981 I had to meet him; now I had to marry him.

Before I asked Michael to marry me, I'd talked it over with Father Kevin. He asked if we wanted to do the wedding as a public event, one that would make a statement not only to our family and friends but our fellow parishioners at the Episcopal Church of the Atonement in Fairlawn, and to the world at large. As much as I knew the value of getting the word out about the truth of our gay lives, I did not want to have our man-to-man ceremony turn into a circus. "You were reluctant to go public with Adam's adoption effort," Father Kevin told me, "and look at all the good that happened when you did. By making your union with Michael a public ceremony, you could do a lot of good again." We could crystallize our relationship not only for the sake of our partnership and our family but also as a symbol of the truth of gay couples' lives that would show what they deserved from our society.

Michael agreed that we should have our service be not just a family event, but a church event, one that would include the parishioners who had supported us in our fight for Adam and given us a spiritual home. We could do the ceremony as part of a Sunday church service— on Father's Day! Adam, Madison, and Rosa would be present; our family would be part of the larger church family. And we could do a private wedding the night before, for just ourselves, our immediate family, and God. That was a tradition many couples had observed over the years when they wanted something spiritual and intimate, and we could follow it too.

We faced a number of obstacles. First, we had to obtain permission from the vestry—the church's governing board—to combine our ceremony with the Sunday worship service. Second, we had to ensure that the event remained sacred, without cameras and klieg lights everywhere, even if the media were invited to attend. Third, we had to obtain permission from Bishop Spong to hold the service in an Episcopal church. Our diocese has embraced gay people as part of its flock, but having a same-sex holy union was still controversial and required the okay of the bishop, at least for a service that would be this public.

Father Kevin, Mother Linda Strohmier, and Mother Kaeton of Oasis, the diocese's gay ministry, had no problem getting an endorsement from the bishop, who would issue a public statement approving of our holy union. When we agreed that only a few photographers and just one video camera would tape the actual holy union, the vestry consented to our plan. I was touched by this. The people in our church were salt-of-the-earth Christians, heterosexual family men and women; from the beginning they'd welcomed our family without any qualms. They'd supported us during our battle for Adam—several church members had started a letter-writing campaign to the governor and a prayer chain—and now they were willing to open their hearts and their doors to bless our union. We'd been exiled from the Roman Catholic Church because it would not accept our love as valid; now we were able to come home.

Once our plans went public, threats started coming in. The diocesan office and several local churches received phone calls, saying nothing specific about us or our church, but the diocese was concerned nonetheless. In the midst of organizing the service, inviting our friends, figuring out what the children would wear, ordering flowers and buying suits and picking the right tie and shirt, I had to meet with the Fairlawn chief of police to help ensure nobody would get blown up or shot by snipers. The police agreed to send bomb-sniffing dogs into the sanctuary before the service. They would guard the premises during the service, after cordoning off several blocks around the church early that Sunday morning. If Bob Enyart wanted to broadcast hate or kick off his campaign to execute homosexuals, he'd have to do it a block away.

At the same time, Michael and I were encountering resistance from Adolph and Dorothy. They didn't have a problem with our having a holy union, but did protest against having the press in attendance. "Why do you have to have media people at your wedding?" Adolph grumbled to Michael and me in our family room one evening. "Can't this just be a family thing?"

Michael had gotten good at giving speeches by now. He confronted them head-on. "Dad, can you imagine if you and Mom couldn't marry legally? If you could get arrested in half of the states in the country just for making love with her? If you could never, *ever*, hold hands in public, or kiss, without watching your back? That's why Jon and I do the things that we do. We deserve recognition for being good parents, good husbands, good men. People out there need to see people like us. This is important. I won't sit still until I know for sure that my children won't have to live the life that I led, if they should turn out to be gay."

Adolph hugged Michael and said, "I hate it when you're right." Never again would he question what Michael and I have said in public.

Two days before Father's Day, I was home talking on the phone with Ronald Smothers, a reporter for the *New York Times* who was doing a story about our holy union. The doorbell rang. The postman handed me a large box, surprisingly light for its size, delivered by express mail. The Hawaii return address included no name.

Right away I got scared. "I just got an unmarked package here," I told Ronald Smothers. "You want to stay on the line while we open it? If I blow up, you have a headline."

Michael sent Adam and Madison to the family room, at the other side of the house, just in case, and carefully slit open the tape sealing the top of the cardboard box. I watched, my heart thumping, as Michael took a deep breath and opened it.

Wafting up from the open box was the most wonderful fragrance I'd ever inhaled. Across the top were wet paper towels, and below that, wide leaves, like palm leaves. Inside were seven beautiful handmade, natural-flower Hawaiian leis. Each one was an interlocking strand of gorgeous yellow-orange, bell-shaped flowers; six were full-size and one was smaller. Nestled among them was a card from Ron Melillo and Jon Lagon, the male couple in Hawaii who were among those suing the state for the right to civil marriage. They had read about our wedding and sent us these wedding gifts—traditional celebratory leis they had woven themselves from the flowers in their yard.

We decided immediately to wear them at our ceremony. We would give one to each other and one to each of the four priests who would be performing our holy union. The little lei was for Adam, but he would have trashed his in about ten seconds, so we reserved that one for Rosa, who would sit with us.

I ran next door to Mike, our neighbor, who is a florist. "Mike, do you or Maria know what I should do to protect these?" I cried. "I want these to last!"

"Just put them in the refrigerator," he said soothingly, looking very impressed with our gift. We gay people really know how to have a wedding.

Even after the sun had gone down, it was blisteringly hot that Saturday night before Father's Day, as we dressed in our second-best suits (reserving our new ones for tomorrow's ceremony) and packed up the children in the minivan to drive the few blocks to St. Martin's, a small church associated with our own Church of the Atonement. Father Kevin had wanted to have the private service at St. Martin's so we wouldn't be distracted by any reporters lurking around. And sure enough, just before we left the house, Rosa turned on the news to see an ABC reporter standing in the parking lot of the Church of the Atonement, priming the viewing audience for the story about our wedding the following morning. "Kevin was sure right to have us go to St. Martin's," Michael said. The last thing we needed was to bump into cameras on a night meant to be just about us and our families.

In the high-beamed, Old English sanctuary of St. Martin's, we were unbothered by anything except intense heat as we gathered with Father Kevin, his wife, Cathy, and our family in choir pews around the brilliant blue altar. Witnessing our private union were just our closest family members: my mother Nancy and Roger, my mother Ann Mary and Herb, Adolph and Dot, Grandma Grace, Papa Nooch, Adam and Madison and their baby-sitter Samantha, and Rosa.

As the spirit of God's love enveloped Michael and me, Adam charged around the chancel, his cheeks rosy in the heat, trying to climb out the window. We said our private vows at the prompting of Father Kevin and then exchanged rings. The world disappeared. Surrounded and filled with the Holy Spirit, Michael and I stared into each other's soul. It was magical. The dream I had given up on when I accepted my homosexuality had come true, and once again I would be a changed man forever.

All of us hugged, kissed, and then went out to dinner at a restaurant in Hawthorne that Adolph had picked out—he knew the owner—and had a delicious dinner that Michael and I were far too wired to eat. It felt like a rehearsal dinner for a traditional wedding, except that maybe the gifts were better.

Father's Day.

Sunday morning dawned hot and bright. Full of nerves and awe, we bounded out of bed and ran around getting the kids ready, dressing Madison in her white, flowered dress with a lace collar, and Adam in knickers, white shirt, bow tie, and blue jacket. Michael wore a black suit and a gold shirt with an orange and yellow tie, and I put on a navy blue suit with a blue shirt and a vibrant yellow-gold and blue tie. Don and Megan took pictures as we pinned on our boutonnieres, purple-tipped orchids that Mike, our neighbor the florist, had provided us.

Do most married-couples-to-be drive to their wedding in a minivan? We piled in with Adam, and Don and Megan, who would be in charge of wrangling Adam and Madison, with Samantha following behind to help them out. We were determined that Madison be shielded from the press because she was still a foster child and we needed to safeguard her privacy, so she and Rosa went separately, with Nancy and Roger.

The street to the church was barricaded by the police; no traffic or parking was allowed in the couple of blocks around the church. A lone protester stood with a sign: "Gays don't go to heaven. Repent."

A big, tough policeman held up his hand to halt us from coming through. Michael rolled down the window and said with a smile, "I think we're okay. It's our wedding."

The cop peered in, saw us, saw Adam, and broke into a big smile, then stepped away to pull aside the police barricade. "Congratulations!" he shouted after us. We drove through, but before we could even get out of the car, we were swamped by reporters, fifteen or twenty with camera crews and microphones. We made nice with them as they asked us mostly the softball questions you'd ask any marrying couple: Are you excited? (Yes.) Will you say where you are going on your honeymoon? (No.) Have you received any backlash? (No.) Squiggling in my arms, Adam pulled at the microphones—which by now was a family tradition. Then we waded through the cameras to get to the church, already full of family and friends, and sweltering. "Now I have some idea what Princess Diana felt like at her wedding," I joked to Michael. It was even hotter than St. Martin's had been the night before. Don and Megan shepherded Adam and Madison downstairs to Sunday school; they would come back up to join us for the last part of the service with the rest of the children.

Despite the fans in the front of the church, I was sweating and feeling faint already as we floated into place at the back for the standard Sunday-morning processional to the altar, which would today include us. Michael gave me a loving look that told me I would be the most important man in his life for eternity. "Hold on to me," I whispered back to him as the sanctuary did a pirouette. "I think I might pass out."

When our friend Julie Sabitier sang, I felt myself rising into a place of feeling I'd not inhabited before—some combination of joy and light-headedness, accomplishment and hope. We proceeded down the aisle, glimpsing on every side our friends old and new, church members who had cheered us on in our crusade to be parents, and—closer to the front—the family members with whom we'd established a hard-won realm of understanding. I kept telling myself not to pass out. It would be so embarrassing. Look at your feet, concentrate, listen to Father Kevin, I said to myself. Rosa was standing next to Michael, holding on to his arm and putting her head on his shoulder—when she wasn't fanning him. "Are you okay, Father?" she whispered as Michael dabbed sweat from his neck.

"I'd like to ask everyone here who has a father to raise their hand," declared Mother Linda Strohmier as she began her sermon, standing just inches from the first row of pews. That got a laugh. Rosa raised both her hands. "I have two!" she said loudly. Linda went on to talk about the covenant that we make with our sons and daughters, just as God has made a covenant with us. "It happens not just between blood fathers and their children—as we know. For a year and a half we have been watching the progress of this life with Jon and Michael and Adam, to see that a covenant made between fathers and a child is a powerful, powerful thing. It can transform governments. It can change the image of all sorts and kinds of folks in the world. It *can not* be broken. It is a bond so intense and so profound and so filled with love there is no force greater in the universe."

Father Kevin brought us before him to deliver our vows—a tiny variant on the words that marrying men and women have said for generations. Michael took my right hand and began, breathing out phrase after phrase. "In the name of God, I, Michael, take you, Jon, to be my spouse, to have and to hold, from this day forward, for better or worse, for richer, for poorer, in sickness and in health, to love and to cherish, until we are parted by death."

I took Michael's right hand. "In the name of God, I, Jon, take you, Michael, to be my spouse, to have and to hold, from this day for-

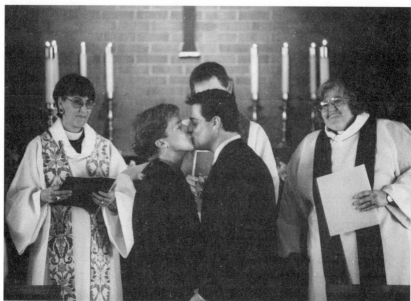

The wedding kiss.

ward, for better or worse, for richer, for poorer, in sickness and in health, to love and to cherish, until we are parted by death."

Then Father Kevin turned us around to face our family and our friends. "Congregation," he proclaimed, "you have just heard these two men make promises and vows. It is your turn to do the same."

His eyes swept the sanctuary. "Will you who have witnessed these promises do all in your power to support these two persons in their union?"

Adolph Galluccio had never expected that he would be sitting in the front pew of an Episcopal church watching his son marry another man. But as a lawyer, he had long ago learned that the world was complex and unpredictable, and that its truths could reveal themselves to you from unexpected quarters—truths that would alter the nature of the evidence and make you change your verdict.

He had learned that lesson in his home as well. For years, it had seemed to him that his older son had not lived by the laws that Adolph had believed were unchangeable and right. His son was gay, and that had taken a lot of getting used to. Not getting married, not producing grandchildren, having a man for a partner—his son seemed as contrary to him as another Italian man could be.

Over the last several years he had grown to know his son differently. His son was a father, and his son was—in his own way—the marrying kind. Adolph had to acknowledge they were not that different after all. Michael his son had realized it too. Both men were gregarious, but both held some of their most basic emotions close to their chest. Both men had built their lives around their family. Adolph could take the shape of his family for granted; Michael could not. But both men would fight for their children like Roman centurions. Along with their Italian blood and their strong, fine features, they had each learned they had family in common.

The priest was asking the perspiring congregation to acknowledge the vows: "Will you who have witnessed these promises do all in your power to support these two persons in their union?"

Adolph looked at his son Michael. In a voice meant to be heard across a church or a courtroom, he uttered *"I will."* It wasn't the "We will" that the congregation recited back to the uniting couple a moment later. It was *I will*, and it was loud, and it was meant for his son Michael to hear. One family man to another.

Adolph's voice rang in my ears. I looked at Michael and saw his eyes lock on his father's. Michael was hearing a million words in that one *I will*. He had his father back. I was so happy—for Michael, for us, for Adolph.

We exchanged the sign of the peace. I put a lei from Ron Melillo and Jon Lagon around Michael's neck; he put one around mine, and we kissed and embraced. Michael draped one over Rosa's hair; she pressed it to her face and smiled. We slipped leis over the heads of Kevin and Linda and Elizabeth Kaeton and our fourth priest, Ellen Barrett, and exchanged with family and friends the traditional hugs and kisses. Hugging Michael hard, Adolph told his son he loved him.

Right as the Communion part of the service began, a *Herald News* photographer stepped back into a table at the back of the church and sent the carafe of Communion wine crashing to the floor. The altar guild members had to scramble to clean up the mess and get more wine for the offering from the people. It was a minor disaster, but we were used to those. We had a two-year-old.

Adam and Madison came up the aisle helping to bear the offerings; then Madison nestled far from the cameras in Nancy's lap. As the Communion service progressed, Adam sat between us—until he climbed over the pew and sat with Ann Mary and Herb, until he mounted another pew and tumbled into Don and Megan's arms. We all came up to receive Communion—Michael and me, the newly united couple, and then our family and friends. Adam joined us then, and as we steadied his shoulders, Mother Linda laid her hands on his blond head and blessed him.

Afterward, gulping down coffee and cake, hugging and kissing family and strangers, we gathered with press people in a church-school classroom. Adolph's vow was still ringing in Michael's ears as we sat there, holding hands so that our rings would proudly gleam. The priests were all forthcoming about why they had participated: we were good people and good parents, and it was important to unite a couple in God's eyes and to show the world that lesbian and gay people deserved to have their love honored by the community. Meanwhile, Adam was tearing at his bow tie and pulling off his jacket just to get cool, and just because he was Adam.

Why was marriage so important to us? one reporter wanted to know. When we came out sixteen years before, I said, a holy union wasn't even an option. "We thought we had to give that up because we were gay," I replied. "And as we're together longer and longer, we're finding out we don't have to give up anything because we're gay. Sometimes we just have to ask for it a little bit louder." Michael grinned and squeezed my hand.

We grabbed Adam and Madison and made our way to the minivan. Heading out, we saw that a second protester had arrived, his sign claiming, "This is not God's house," which meant he'd not ventured into our church that day, because God was definitely in residence. We headed to Adolph and Dorothy's for a family barbecue, complete with Adolph's famous sausage and peppers.

On the third Sunday afternoon in June, the gay and lesbian community of New York sponsors a rally that features speeches from gay politicos and regular citizens as well as music and comedy. This year the rally would include us, fresh from our wedding ceremony—and Cyndi Lauper.

Inhaling the smell of sausage and peppers, we'd eaten our pasta salad and vegetables at Adolph and Dorothy's, interrupted by back-slapping and hearty handshakes from family and friends and pinochle players, including church people and colleagues from Michael's job—all of them packed into our parents' backyard and exclaiming over the food, the children, and the ceremony. We'd changed out of our suits into shorts and T-shirts, which gave Michael's brother, Mark, the excuse to throw Michael into the pool. That was fun to watch and gave Michael something new to fret about—how his chlorinated hair would look in front of ten thousand gay people at the rally in Manhattan's Bryant Park.

Don and Megan accompanied us into the city to serve as Adam wranglers. Madison and Rosa stayed at the party to play in the pool. A spot was reserved for our minivan on Forty-second Street so that we could grab Adam, the denim diaper bag, and our speeches and dash into a holding area. We were going to be the last speakers before Cyndi Lauper's finale. Amid the congratulations from assorted rally participants, we kept eyeing Cyndi Lauper, over in a corner singing to herself, getting warmed up. Atop her scarlet hair was a purple Dr. Seuss–style hat. I had to meet her and I was shameless. "Adam," I whispered, "there's Cyndi Lauper. You want to meet Cyndi, right?" Adam, who wants to meet everybody, said yes. So we trotted over. "Hi, Cyndi," I said. "We're Jon and Michael, and this is our son, Adam. He wanted to meet you. Didn't you, Adam?"

Cyndi just blinked and nodded.

The crowd learns that Adam knows his ABC's.

"Adam, this is Cyndi," I prodded. "Say hi to Cyndi."

Adam looked at her. He cocked his chin. He pointed to her head. "Clown hair!" he exclaimed.

Before we got a chance to become Cyndi's best pals, the rally em-cee called our names and brought us forward, introducing us beau-tifully, talking about our adoption fight and our *very* recent wedding, as we strode to the podium to the strains of the classic rock 'n' roll song "Chapel of Love." Don and Megan kept a hold on Adam back-stage. The crowd stood and cheered us and applauded. It was awe-inspiring. I cried, of course; I really let loose and I couldn't even talk. My nerves had combined with the joy of this day to put me over the edge. Finally we began speaking, telling the crowd about our mar-riage and about our wonderful son, Adam. "Adam, come here!" Mi-chael called out.

Adam came bounding out and scooted right to us. A huge cheer rose from the crowd. I picked him up and he grabbed the microphone,

Madison at her adoption party.

stand and all, put it against his mouth, and started singing at the top of his lungs: *"A, B, C, D, E, F, G . . ."*

In the months since our wedding, our lives have centered around our children and our continuing effort to ensure the rights of foster children and alternative families. We could never have gone back to the life we had before we had to fight for Adam, because we're no longer the same people.

On May 17, 1999, Michael and I jointly adopted Madison. Billy DeMarco, Adolph's pal who had initially represented us with Adam, handled the legalities for Madison's incorporation into the family. When we left the courthouse with Adam in tow and Madison dressed in a frilly white dress covered with an abundant rose print, with our family around us snapping pictures, a court official came up to us and made us the same offer we'd heard the day we adopted Adam: There were reporters here, following up the story of the Galluccio family. Did we want to leave by the back door? "No," I said. "We want the whole world to know how happy we are."

Our Madison has grown into quite a little girl. Her three-year-old personae range from the perfect lady, demanding that her shoes be changed because they don't match her headband, to a full-out tomboy—tackling her brother in a race to be first playing with Big Bird. She almost always says "please" and "thank you," she covers her mouth when she sneezes, and she holds her napkin on her lap at dinner. She is quick to tattle and set anyone straight who breaks the rules—including her daddy and father. "Daddy, say 'skooze me when you fart!"

We've watched intrigued and pleased as she has taken on the complex feminine characteristics of her grandmothers. Like Nana, she is protective and coddling and has exquisite manners. From Dot she gets a sense of herself as a woman—for their Christmas present last year my mother-in-law took Rosa and Madison to a spa for manicures and pedicures. From Ann Mary, Madison has learned that no one will tread on her and that she has every right to be a spitfire.

Madison, who is so good at playing Mommy in her games with Adam—he plays Daddy or the baby—has started asking us vague questions about her mother. I sat her aside one night and told her that, yes, everybody in the world has a mommy. Some children have a mommy who can be there all the time. Other children have a mommy they came out of, but that mommy can't be there. Instead, they have other people who love them, just the way Madison herself has a daddy and a father who love her more than any other little girl in the universe.

At age three, Madison won't understand three-quarters of what I've told her about the complications that mark the lives of mommies and daddies. We'll have this conversation again and again over the years as Madison asks more sophisticated questions. But Michael and I will reiterate the truths of her life to her—and to Adam—so that it will be easy and commonplace to ask questions. These conversations will grow more complex as eventually our children come to know the facts about their parents. However hard those facts will be to hear, they will know that their birth mothers loved them enough to set them free and give them parents who loved them. There will be gentleness and care among us, but no secrets.

Rosa is getting almost all A's and B's in high school and wants to become a bilingual special-education teacher. She has softened dramatically in the last two years. Many of the clouds behind her eyes have dissipated. She has become, in many ways, a typical teenage girl. She goes to the mall and to school dances, and she talks on the phone incessantly, and she has boyfriends we disapprove of. Michael and I have been classified by the state as foster parents for Rosa. She has become, all but legally, our daughter. Here is one child who had a choice about her parents—she had to decide whether to stay in a group home the state offered her, or to join a family headed by two gay men. Rosa didn't hesitate.

One October night a week before Rosa's sixteenth birthday, we dropped her off at Woodley after hosting her at our house for the weekend. We spent the next week remodeling the guest room she used when she stayed overnight. There was nothing pretty about the room; its furnishings were all mismatched, cast-off stuff. Rosa had confessed to us she'd never once had her own bedroom. We painted the room rose for Rosa, bought her lace drapes, blinds, a comforter with roses on it, bed linens, and a rug, hung pictures and mirrors and little angels. This was our birthday present for her—transforming the guest room into her own pink, girly space. In décor and accessories, it would be the teenage girl's room she had never had.

When she arrived that Friday evening from an event with the Woodley group home, we were falling all over ourselves to give her her gift. But Rosa was taut-faced, anxious.

"Come on upstairs—we want to give you your present," I said.

"No—no. I can't. I have to talk to you first," she said.

"Honey, we've got something to show you," Michael cajoled her.

"Please, just let me talk to you for a second!" she insisted. She sat us down in the living room and perched on a hassock in front of us. "I saw my therapist at Woodley today and she said I had to talk to you about something."

Now I was confused and concerned. What was going on with Rosa?

She scrunched up her face and her words seemed to catch in her throat. "You are the only family I've ever really had. I want you to adopt me."

Warmth flooded through me. I looked from Rosa to Michael and saw his face break into a smile. "Awwww," I said, oh gosh, oh gee, sure.

"Come upstairs!" Michael urged her, and we hustled her up the steps.

There was a big ribbon on the door. She opened it. Candles were burning all over the room. Sitting on the dresser was a vase of long-stemmed roses. Roses and a rose-colored room for Rosa. She started crying and we joined in, and we all hugged each other.

As the candles burned down, the three of us sat on her bed talking. Immediately we said we would seek to adopt her, and that we wanted her to move into our house full-time, if she would accept not only the security and love we provided but our authority as her parents. She agreed. It hasn't always been easy since that day—we are in charge of one battle-scarred and very headstrong teenager—but Rosa counts as Madison and Adam's sister and our oldest child.

Last spring she told us about what had happened to her one day at Ridgewood High School, as she sat in health class just before the period began. "You're moving?" asked a guy Rosa barely knew.

"Yeah, this summer." Rosa would be leaving Woodley and coming to her rose-colored bedroom for good

"Is it true you're gonna have two fathers?" the guy demanded. "And a brother and sister?"

Rosa could tell where this was heading. And now the whole class was listening.

"But they're, uh, *gay,* right?" the guy asked sarcastically.

Rosa took a deep breath and looked the kid in the eye. She flipped her long black hair over her shoulder. "Yeah. My fathers are gay. So?"

The boy shrugged. "Just asking," he retreated. And then class began.

Madison and Adam are strengthening their own self-esteem from Rosa's tough sense. She tells her friends that her parents are "the bomb." When her friends visit, she waves in our direction and says, "These are my dads."

Last year, Granddaddy's sister-in-law died, the wife of one of his brothers. We attended the funeral in Paterson, and amid all the relatives and family friends of all ages, we went over to express our sympathy to Michael's grandfather.

"Granddaddy, I'm really sorry," I said. I'd been calling him Granddaddy for fifteen years.

Granddaddy looked at me, his old eyes cold. "You can either call me Otto or Mr. Galluccio. I'm not your grandfather."

Moments like that still happen in our family, and they still hurt. Granddaddy is strained and tense when he is in the same room with us and our son and daughters. It seems he believes at age eighty-seven that he's on his way to hell if he is nice to our children. We know who has introduced that notion into his head. Holidays are hard. When Michael and I hosted Thanksgiving dinner again last year, Granddaddy ended up dining in a restaurant with a lady friend, apart from his family.

Shortly after we won the right to adopt Adam, Loretta McCormick left DYFS and moved to upstate New York, where she works with children. We keep her up-to-date on our children's progress and make sure Adam and Madison pray for her regularly. We're forever grateful for someone who lived her principles and was brave enough to help us do the right thing for our son.

Every day we grow closer to our many mothers and fathers, who give us great support—and who are great baby-sitters! Among them is Ann Mary, better known as Granny, who lives less than a mile from our home in Maywood, in the home I grew up in. The kids bring her their favorite book, *The Little Red Hen,* which she always reads to them for the umpteenth time. After nearly a year of chemotherapy and radiation her body was declared clear of cancer—which leaves her free to spend a lot of time with Madison and Adam.

Nancy talks to our children every day, baby-sits frequently, and often serves as our "on-site" caregiver when we take the children along with us to a speaking event. Madison calls her Nana, and Adam calls her Manna. Both names are music to her. Sometimes when Michael and I come home in the evening when she's baby-sitting, we'll find her asleep in Madison's bed, her granddaughter nestled against her. It's a precious moment to behold, especially for me, as the pain of my long-time separation from my birth mother is healed by our love for our children.

Dorothy Galluccio has always been a diplomat in her family, negotiating, smoothing over conflict, worrying. When people don't get along, she gets so anxious she can't sleep. After Granddaddy went out on his own for Thanksgiving, she felt pushed to her limits. Her nephew Bob's attacks on her family were still haunting her, still pulling at the fabric of the family. She wrote her sister-in-law Angela a letter. Why can't you let us be happy? she asked.

Angela came by for coffee, and the two women, who have known each other for nearly forty years, sat in Dorothy's kitchen. They didn't talk about old times or about their children growing up together, playing in this very yard, and they didn't gossip about who was getting married or having a new baby, the way mothers can do. Aunt Angela had some pamphlets she said Dorothy just had to read. Dorothy said no, she would not read them. Angela said that Michael would have to leave his homosexual boyfriend before the family could be reunited. Jesus would not be ignored, Angela said. Dorothy said Jesus *wasn't* being ignored.

They talked carefully for a while, disagreeing. Angela left the pamphlets on the kitchen table and got up to go. At the door Dorothy said good-bye. "Just remember," she noted. "Family doesn't treat family badly."

We'd won our own family's battle, but a war was still going on, nationwide. Ever since 1998, the backlash against alternative families has infected congressmen and state legislators everywhere, even as we make progress, state by state, family by family. We've been told adoptions in our home state have gone up 30 percent, thanks in part to adoptions by unmarried couples. Yet families like ours have increasingly been under siege by "pro-family" religious conservatives and their allies. The Galluccio family might be safe, but we still had work to do on behalf of everybody else.

More and more we have been going out on the road, using our own experience to drive home the value of families like ours and to urge that all of America's doors be opened to children in need of homes. The widespread public support Michael and I have gotten has spurred us to appear on college campuses, from Princeton to Indiana Universities. We are advocating more and more for the rights and safety of lesbian and gay youth and the right to same-sex marriage, both of which are central to our own story and to the truth of the changing American family.

And all that means we've become the object of a lot of fear and anger. The Family Research Council has used us as whipping boys in their antigay mailings—and what's worse is that they have mentioned Adam's and Madison's names, which makes us nervous, and which inspired an op-ed piece by *New York Times* columnist Frank Rich entitled "Family Research Stalkers" about their vicious attacks on our family. We never forget we have enemies out there.

Second only to parenting, our work as advocates is the most rewarding thing we've ever done. It can also be incredibly frustrating. But we know we are making a difference when we travel to speak about our quest to make a family. After we spoke at Penn State's Abington campus, as the students came up to congratulate us, a black girl sidled up—a little, scared shadow of a person. She thrust a note in Michael's hand and hurried away. The note said, "You guys are great. You made such a difference. I love you. Thank you so much."

Every time we tell our story in public, somebody's hovering on the perimeter with a sad story that needs to be heard and understood and transcended. Michael and I have gotten pretty savvy at making sure that in the after-speech hubbub we connect with that person out there: The nineteen-year-old who has told no one he's gay. The girl who was beaten by her father five years before, when he found her kissing another girl. The young man who just found out his *father* is gay. The mother whose gay son is so angry he won't speak to her and who needs advice on how to break the ice between them—and the dad too grief-stricken for words. The woman who was forced by her family to give her infant son to his father's family when she fell in love with a woman, and who could tell nobody about it because she'd lose her job.

We want to bring these into the family circle. We want to make sure that they know we gay people deserve to be free to choose our own lives. We can find a mate to marry, someone to love, someone our relatives can and should accept and honor. We can each parent a child. It's our calling—to remind people gay and straight that every one of us deserves a family.

Adam and Madison, and our quest to adopt them, have changed the two of us completely. Once we were men who were a little lost in the world. Now we belong in so many places—from the family dinner table to the bedsides of our children, to gay pride marches, to the piano bars where we sometimes belt out old show tunes, and to the broader table set by our extended families. We have the full array of human possibilities available to us.

Yet by no means is our story finished. Adam is nearly ready for kindergarten, full of curiosity we need to encourage and energy we need to channel. Madison is growing into a real person of substance, headstrong and full of smarts and promise. We know that ahead of us are not only lots of joys but trials and heartache. Most of those difficult moments, we hope, will involve the ordinary uproars of childhood and young adulthood that all parents must confront. We know that Adam and Madison will ask us a lot of questions about who they are and why we made the choices we did. We will tell them the truth, which at its most basic level is this: They should be happy with the family they have and happy with themselves. That regardless of what anyone might say to the contrary, we are a happy, healthy, loving, stable American family.

———

The most satisfying part of our lives happens at home, around our children, in the family room, at the dinner table, or in the backyard, as we experience the little trials and triumphs that come with watching children grow. Adam burps and thinks it is hysterical. Madison paints her bedroom walls with red nail polish stolen from Rosa's room. Rosa has taken the telephone hostage.

At eight-thirty, Adam and Madison are finally in their beds, their teeth brushed, their faces scrubbed. Adam is in his Batman pajamas, Madison in her Winnie-the-Pooh nightgown. They are sleepy but don't want the day to end.

It's Michael's turn to put Adam to bed tonight. It's my turn with Madison. After saying our prayers I sing Madison some lullabies: "Hush, Little Baby," "Rock-a-bye Baby." She's still awake, so we start talking. "Guess who's going to pick you up from school tomorrow," I say to her on this particular night.

"Nana? Why?"

"We're working on our book tomorrow afternoon."

"You are? Am I in your book?"

"Yes, you are, when you were a little baby."

"What's it about?"

"It's about you, and it's about Adam, and how we got you, and how much we love you. We tell the stories of all our lives in this book."

"Why?"

"Because we're changing the world."

"Oh," Madison says wonderingly, like a three-year-old. She reaches out her arms, hugs me so tight, and says, "We're the *best* family."

This brings me to tears. I tuck her in, kiss her good-night, and close the door behind me. Michael is across the hall, in Adam's room, finishing the "La La Lu" lullaby from *Peter Pan*. It's the same song Michael crooned to him the night we brought him home from the O'Neill Center a couple lifetimes ago, the one Michael's mother sang to him when he was Adam's age.

Adam kneels beside his bed. He goes through his little litany of family. "God bless Adam, God bless Madison and Rosa. God bless Daddy and Father, and God bless Nana and Gramps, and Uncle Don and Aunt Megan, Grandma and Little Poppy, and Granny and Big

Poppy, and Grandma Grace and Papa Nooch. Thank you for my family. And please help me be a good boy."

Michael sees me in the doorway. He smiles. Everyone who lives in this house will fall asleep tonight knowing this one truth: A family is made of love.

A FAMILY ALBUM

Our co-author, David Groff, plays circus elephants with Adam and Madison.